SEX IN GEORGIAN
ENGLAND

A.D. Harvey was educated at St. John's College, Oxford and University College (now Wolfson College), Cambridge. He has taught at the Universities of Cambridge, Salerno, La Réunion and Leipzig.

Also by A.D. Harvey

Britain in the Early Nineteenth Century

English Poetry in a Changing Society, 1780–1825

Literature Into History

Collision of Empires: Britain in Three World Wars, 1793–1945 (Phoenix Press)

A Muse of Fire: Literature, Art and War

Warriors of the Rainbow

SEX IN GEORGIAN ENGLAND

*Attitudes and Prejudices from
the 1720s to the 1820s*

A.D. Harvey

REVISED EDITION

PHOENIX
PRESS

5 UPPER SAINT MARTIN'S LANE
LONDON
WC2H 9EA

A PHOENIX PRESS PAPERBACK

First published in Great Britain
by Gerald Duckworth & Co. Ltd in 1994
This paperback edition published in 2001
by Phoenix Press,
a division of The Orion Publishing Group Ltd,
Orion House, 5 Upper St Martin's Lane,
London WC2H 9EA

A CIP catalogue record for this book is available
from the British Library.

Printed and bound in Great Britain by
Butler & Tanner Ltd, Frome and London

ISBN 1 84212 273 8

Contents

List of Plates   vii

Introduction   1

1. Women's Bodies – and How Men Looked at Them   11

2. The Waning of Female Lust   38

3. Seduction   54

4. Rape   75

5. The Desperate   89

6. The Deviant   111

7. Separating the Spheres   154

Notes   170

Index   197

Plates

(between pages 88 and 89)

1. Quality control in a condom warehouse, 1744 (British Library).
2 & 3. From Govard Bidloo's *Anatomia Humani Corporis*, 1685 (British Library).
4. Nell Gwyn and her son the Duke of St Albans, by Sir Peter Lely, *c.* 1667 (by permission of the Trustees of the Denys Eyre Bower Bequest, from the collection at Chiddingstone Castle, Kent).
5. Hans Baldung Grien's 'The Seven Ages of Woman', 1544 (Museum der bildenden Künste, Leipzig).
6. Lady Henrietta and Lady Elizabeth Finch by Charles Jervas, *c.* 1730 (English Heritage Photo Library).
7. Nude by William Etty (Tate Gallery).
8. 'Nude Woman with a Crucifix and Skull', by William Etty (Board of the Trustees of the Victoria & Albert Museum).
9. 'A Nude Reclining and a Woman Playing the Piano', by Henry Fuseli, *c.* 1799-1800 (Oeffentliche Kunstsammlung Basel, Kunstmuseum; photo: Martin Buhler, Basel).
10. Mary Paterson, an eighteen-year-old Edinburgh prostitute murdered by Burke and Hare in 1828 (British Library).
11. 'Meditations among the Tombs' by Thomas Rowlandson (British Museum).
12. From the *Les épices de Vénus* section of the 1803 edition of *L'Aretin Francais*, probably by Tommaso Piroli (British Library).
13. Illustration, probably by Hubert François Gravelot, from the 1766 edition of *Fanny Hill* (British Library).
14. 'Cunnyseurs', by Thomas Rowlandson (British Museum).

15. Keeking by candlelight, probably by Tommaso Piroli (British Library).
16. *La Carriola*, the wheel-barrow, from the 1803 edition of *L'Aretin Francais*, probably by Tommaso Piroli (British Library).
17. Another position from *L'Aretin Francais* (British Library).
18. The woman on top again, by Rowlandson (British Museum).
19. 'Mr. B———s and the Magdalen': Andrew Stoney Bowes raping Elizabeth Waite (British Library).
20. From Alexander Gill's *A New and Complete Collection of the Most Remarkable Trials for Adultery, &c.* (British Library).
21. John Motherhill, a tailor, raping Catharine Wade in the churchyard at Brighton in September 1785 (British Library).
22. 'A Corner, near the Bank; – or – An Example for Fathers', by James Gillray, 1797 (British Library).
23. Young debauchees admiring their friends' sexual technique. From the 1766 edition of *Fanny Hill* (British Library).
24. Fanny Hill being touched up by Phoebe Ayres, her 'tutoress' (British Library).
25. Three women enjoying the company of a man disguised as a nun. From the *Les épices de Vénus* section of the 1803 edition of *L'Aretin Francais* (British Library).
26. Contemporary print, probably by Isaac Robert Cruikshank, showing the arrest of the Right Rev. Percy Jocelyn, Bishop of Clogher in July 1822 (British Museum).
27. The most explicit of the 'divers wicked lewd impious impure bawdy and obscene Prints' in Alexander Hogg's *A New and Complete Collection of the Most Remarkable Trials for Adultery, &c.* (British Library).
28. A woman being burnt at the stake during the reign of George II (British Library).

Introduction

This book is about attitudes and assumptions. It is not a history of sexual behaviour in the sense of normal, every-day sexual behaviour. Normal every-day sexual behaviour, in the eighteenth century as in the twentieth, was not very dramatic or distinctive, and generally took place in private. Since the 'Kinsey Report' in the 1940s there has been no shortage of statistical surveys purporting to show what goes on between the sheets, but the reliability of such enquiries is a moot point, and it is not necessarily a total catastrophe that no comparable material exists for the period covered by this book. In the absence of statistics, however, much of the available source material for the history of sex relates to the non-average. It is no accident that one of the most revealing accounts of a marriage ever produced, Nigel Nicolson's *Portrait of a Marriage* (1973), deals with a couple who were both homosexual and that the richest source for love letters between supposedly 'ordinary' people – not artists or intellectuals – is the evidence submitted in murder trials that take place after one of the happy couple has knifed or poisoned the other. One of the abnormal features of abnormality is that it shows up more: but we cannot altogether deduce the normal from the abnormal.

The eighteenth century was the century of Fanny Hill and Casanova. How many Casanovas were there? My guess is that, both today and 200 or 250 years ago, only a small minority, mostly belonging to fairly specific social groups – but in most cases a minority within these groups – ever had more than thirty sexual partners during their entire lives. Unfortunately Casanova's memoirs break off when he was forty-nine and are not exactly reliable anyway, and the intriguingly-titled pamphlet *The Case of Seduction: being an Account of the late Proceedings at Paris, as well Ecclesiastical as Civil, against the Reverend Abbée, Claudius Nicholas des Rues, for Committing Rapes upon 133 Virgins* (London 1726) is for the most part a dry-as-dust legal discussion, the Abbé's alleged victims being in any case (as far as one can tell) professional tarts rather than what one would usually understand by 'virgins'. And only legendary status can be accorded the statistical exploits of Mozart's Don Giovanni:

> *In Italia seicento e quaranta;*
> *In Almagna duecento e trent'una;*
> *Cento in Francia, in Turchia novant'una*
> *Ma in Ispagna son già mille e tre*
> *Mille e tre, mille e tre.*

(640 in Italy, 231 in Germany, 100 in France, 91 in Turkey, 1003 in Spain: that's a total of 2,065.) On the other hand there is something depressingly plausible in Leporello's explanation:

> *Delle vecchie fa conquista*
> *Pel piacer di porle in lista,*
> *Sua passion predominante*
> *E la giovin principiante.*
> *Non si picca se sia ricca,*
> *Se sia brutta, se sia bella*
> *Porchè porti la gonella*

(He knocks off the old ones for the pleasure of adding them to his score. His chief passion is the young beginner. He doesn't care whether she's rich, or ugly, or beautiful, so long as she wears a skirt.) Another of the more notorious lovers of the eighteenth century was Friedrich August I of Saxony — Augustus the Strong, King Augustus II of Poland — but the figure attributed to him of 364 illegitimate children seems apocryphal, though he did achieve a record in that no fewer than three of his illegitimate offspring became field marshals. Perhaps the best documented sexual career of the eighteenth century is that of our own James Boswell. Between the ages of twenty and twenty-nine Boswell slept with three married gentlewomen, four actresses and Rousseau's mistress Thérèse Le Vasseur, kept three lower-class women as regular mistresses, and had commerce with sixty streetwalkers. During his career as a whole he had gonorrhoea seventeen times. The frequency with which he contracted the disease was something of a joke among his friends, some of whom may have been inclined to regard his sexual activity as slightly exceptional.[1]

Lawrence Stone of Princeton University has linked a *possible* increase in prostitution with a fall in the average age of marriage and a related increase in prenuptial pregnancies in order to make a case for 'the growth of sexual activity in the eighteenth century'. The fact that people were marrying younger and increasingly finding means to evade the supervision of the older generation in order to anticipate the physical pleasures of marriage does indeed indicate a probable increase in overall sexual activity, but only to the extent that people were embarking on monogamy a year or two earlier in life, though in most cases still not until well into their twenties. That would hardly represent the modern idea of a sexual revolution. As for the incidence of prostitution, which Stone cites as part of the evidence for his argument, there are simply no reliable figures. Prostitution and seduction feature to a remarkable extent in almost all eighteenth-century discussion relating to sex, but this reflects the importance of these topics in the minds of the individuals who produced the discussion, not their absolute objective importance. It is quite likely that prostitution provided economic support for about the same number of adults in the eighteenth century as organised religion – though usually at a less comfortable level – but it was discussed, in sermons and pamphlets and poems, in quite different and more dramatic terms, with the result that the annals of prostitution seem in retrospect to loom much larger than the annals of organised religion: but the size of a shadow always depends on the angle of the light.[2]

Despite Boswell, and despite the barrage of comment on the subject of prostitution, it seems likely that for the majority of people in the eighteenth century – certainly for the overwhelming majority of women – premarital chastity was not merely the ideological norm, it was the actual practice. One reason for this was the fact that dominated the sexual activity of women until well into twentieth century: the natural physiological connection between sexual intercourse and pregnancy. Condoms had been known among the *cognoscenti* since the seventeenth century: though the first recorded mention in modern times is in Gabriello Falloppio's *De Morbo Gallico*, posthumously published in 1564, it was a persistent belief throughout the eighteenth century that they were an English invention. Condoms (usually made from sheep's intestines) were regarded as a means of preventing venereal infection by the better-off males who consorted with streetwalkers in London and other large cities – a treatise of 1717 described them as 'the best if not the only preservative our libertines have found out at present' – but they were not widely available, and were not perceived as a practical means of avoiding pregnancy. Other contraceptive techniques, such as the rhythm method, coitus interruptus or saline douches, were known but were disapproved of: they may have been the kind of thing married couples rather than unmarried people knew about, and there is little evidence of recourse to such methods in premarital sex.[3]

The mean age of marriage fell slightly during this period: it is calculated to have been 26.4 years for men, 24.9 years for women in the second half of the eighteenth century and 25.3 years for men, 23.4 for women in the first half of the nineteenth. The age of menarche – the onset of menstruation and fertility in females – seems to have been falling since the 1830s and is now on average nearly three years younger than in the eighteenth century: but even then menstruation occasionally happened at ten and in perhaps a fifth of cases by the age of thirteen. On average women were fertile for about eight years before they married. The legal age of consent was twelve: the fictional Fanny Hill began her sex life at fourteen, the real-life Harriette Wilson at fifteen. George III's sister Caroline Matilda was married off to the feeble-minded King Christian VII of Denmark when she was fifteen and was eighteen when she began her affair with the German-born doctor Johann Friedrich Struensee, which led to an extraordinary dictatorship, a *coup d'état*, Struensee's death on the scaffold, and Caroline Matilda's death in exile, allegedly from poison, ten weeks short of her twenty-fourth birthday. The future Countess of Strathmore fell in love with the brother of the Duke of Buccleuch when she was thirteen: he had to leave for Germany to take part in the Seven Years' War and died there of smallpox, but it was a serious relationship, involving a secret exchange of rings, and was recalled as such by the Countess nearly thirty years later. Less romantically, a colonel who dallied with a girl placed in his wife's care while her parents were in India and 'who should have been the guardian of her virtue and her morals' but instead 'became the plunderer of both, and RUINED her, when NOT FOURTEEN YEARS OF AGE', claimed in his defence, 'she was, in point of chastity, the very lewdest of her own lewd breed, the Parya; a race to be compared only with the inhabitants of Otaheite.' But teenage sex shows up much more strongly in anecdotal material than in the demographic statistics reconstructed by the Cambridge Group for the study of Population and Social Structure. Modern research into the incidence of illegitimacy in rural parishes shows that it rose from 1.5 per cent of births in the early seventeenth century to 3 per cent around 1750 and 6 per cent around 1810, while births within seven months of marriage were 10.2 per cent of first births 1650-99, 25.5 per cent a hundred years later and over 30 per cent in the early nineteenth century. This suggests that most premarital sex was between people intending to marry – just as, today, it is mostly between couples planning to stay together. It will be noted that the figures for illegitimacy and prenuptial pregnancy rise as the age at marriage falls; so there was definitely a trend towards young people assuming sexual maturity at an earlier age, but this earlier age still remained several years subsequent to the commencement of fertility. Much of what follows in this book will be incomprehensible if it is not accepted that sexual restraint remained normal practice throughout this period.[4]

Of course sexual life is subject not merely to myth-making but to deep-rooted reticence. Abortion is not exactly a popular dinner-party topic even today: in the eighteenth century it was regarded as more or less criminal, though it did not actually become a prosecut-able offence till 1803. The Countess of Strathmore confessed to having induced two abortions with a 'black inky kind of medicine', and, in a third attempt, when this medicine failed to have the desired effect, by 'eating much pepper and drinking a wine-glass of brandy', but few of her contemporaries were so frank, and the extent of the practice is simply unknown. Another topic that was – and is – rarely discussed is menstruation. This is not precisely a sexual matter of course, but we can hardly pretend surprise that we know so little about women's sex lives two centuries ago when we don't even know for sure how they handled their monthly periods. The poet-physician John Armstrong noted how

> ... from Love's Grotto ...
> Oozes the sanguine Stream thro' many a rill,
> Startling the simple Lass

but not what the simple lass did to keep clean. One leading historian of sex has suggested that before the late nineteenth century most women – or at least poorer women – simply menstruated into their clothes, i.e. let it soak into their shifts. Towels were certainly used in the seventeenth century: 'I protest, Child, to have heard the Menstruous Cloath painted to the Congregation in plain colours, more obscene and filthy than the thing itself', says a fictional madam of 1683. Towels continued to be used well into the twentieth century. Perhaps I can introduce a note of personal reminiscence. My landlady in Aberystwyth (where they are proverbially less mealy-mouthed on such topics than in English coastal resorts) told me that when she was a girl every household with young adult women used to have the towels – well-boiled but still betraying a characteristic discoloration – hanging out in rows on the washing line in the back garden whenever someone was having their period. If this was still the case when I was a child in the 1950s, my mother omitted to draw it to my attention. We lived, however, close to the older part of the barracks area in Colchester, the end of our garden being separated from various military workshops only by a narrow alley named Artillery Folly. On Monday mornings the 'Folly', as we called it, used to be festooned with gauze bandages and blood-stained cotton-wool pads, this being the mode of sanitary protection favoured by the women who provided the soldiery with goodnight embraces in the last half hour before they reported back to the main gate round the corner. I suppose there would never have been more than five or six of these bandages, but they would be uncoiled to maximum extent as if this was part of the nocturnal festivities. I don't recall ever seeing this aspect of 1950s popular culture analysed in print. Even the word we schoolboys – and probably the soldiers – used for the stained cotton-wool pads does not appear in the revised *Oxford English Dictionary*: they were called 'jam rags', 'jam' being nineteenth-century slang for the female pudenda, without necessarily referring to bloodstains; 'rag' in this context seems to be a more recent American usage. It is probable that most of us know such minor details about the history of sex in our own lifetime: details that are unknown to historians of sex who only get their information from books. Unfortunately the following pages relate to sexual activity previous to my own lifetime, so I am basically just one more historian of sex who only gets his information from books.[5]

Among my predecessors in the book-recycling game there are two I should particularly mention. The first two volumes of Peter Gay's multi-volume *The Bourgeois Experience*, published in 1984 and 1986, deal with sex in the nineteenth century – mainly the later nineteenth century – in the leisurely and expansive manner that characterises a certain brand of American scholarship. My own book leaves off where his begins but in any case has been written under completely different intellectual, social and financial conditions, which have led me to conclude that the subject could be handled better in a short book than in a long one. I have obtained considerable assistance from Peter Gay's work but have sometimes felt that his motive for allowing himself so much space was to make it easier to skirt round important issues. On this side of the Atlantic, the late Michel Foucault published the first three volumes of a never to be completed *Histoire de la sexualité* of which the first volume, the general introduction, appeared in English translation in 1981. His complex and obscure paradoxes have enjoyed a considerable vogue, suggesting that he was one of those ideologues, like F.R. Leavis before him, who was percipient enough to recognise that academe provided him with his most effective political platform. As a scholar he was an outstanding specimen of a type that seems to flourish in today's universities more than at any earlier period, enthralling large audiences by the effrontery with which he misread half the available documentary sources and the nonchalance with which he ignored the rest. According to Foucault it was the seventeenth century that gave rise to 'the great prohibitions, the exclusive promotion of adult marital sexuality, the imperatives of decency, the obligatory concealment of the body, the reduction to silence and mandatory reticences of language'. I should have thought most of this occurred centuries earlier, though 'the onanistic child who was of such concern to doctors and educators from the end of the eighteenth century to the end of the nineteenth' probably dates from around 1710. Basically I don't agree with Foucault's view that ideological repression is a modern invention, though I do believe its style and idiom is constantly developing and transforming itself.[6]

This book is not a history of a transformation, merely a close look at one phase – or at least, a hundred-year stretch – of a continuous and still continuing transformation. I deal with certain attitudes that come in and establish themselves during the period covered; but as I write this introduction I find myself wondering whether I have really done justice to how different the situation was in the 1820s as compared to the 1720s. In the latter part of the period the self-assured, self-righteous tones of a middle-class, Victorian ethic become recognisable, albeit within the matrix of a still aristocratic, lord-loving system. Yet on reflection many of the attitudes, and the earnestness, were already in evidence in the 1720s. Perhaps it is merely the idiom that has changed. It is difficult to imagine an early-nineteenth-century poet writing about the unattractiveness of an oversized vagina in the terms used in a popular work published in 1736:

> But hapless he,
> In nuptial Night, on whom a horrid Chasm
> Yawns dreadful, waste and wild; like that thro' which
> The wand'ring *Greek*, and *Cytherea's Son*,
> Diving, explor'd Hell's adamantine Gates ...
> ... the dire Effects
> Of Use too frequent, or for Love or Gold.

The same author also thought it reasonable to suggest that premarital sexual relationships were proper and normal and that when the liaison became known, the man should either marry the woman, if at all suitable, or else

> at least secure
> From Penury her humble state, by thee
> Else humbled more, and to Necessity,
> Stern foe to Virtue, Fame, and Life, betray'd.

Both passages are from Armstrong's *The Oeconomy of Love*, one of the eighteenth century's better-selling books: there were at least twenty-three British editions between 1736 and 1791. After 1791, however, Armstrong's poem went out of fashion. There is a London edition *circa* 1800 with a false 1768 imprint, and a Bristol edition of 1813, but otherwise *The Oeconomy of Love* disappeared from circulation. In 1819 Thomas Campbell described it as a 'disgraceful poem' and as a 'nefarious production'; much later in the century the *Dictionary of National Biography* claimed, 'A more nauseous piece of work could not easily be found.' Contemporaries were themselves acutely aware of changing values. In 1811 the poet Coleridge asked,

> who now will venture to read a number of the *Spectator* or of the *Tatler*, to his wife and daughters, without first examining it to make sure that it contains no word which might, in our day, offend the delicacy of female ears, and shock feminine susceptibility?

And yet, while the Duke of Grafton's open association with Nancy Parsons, 'a Nymph, who is almost as chaste as she's fair', in 1768-9, during the first months of his premiership, and the Earl of Sandwich's cohabitation at the Admiralty, when First Lord of the Admiralty, with the singer Martha Reay, previous to her being shot dead by a rival lover in 1779, seem to epitomise the loose morality that went out after 1800, the Marquess Wellesley was still allegedly living openly with tarts while Foreign Secretary between 1809 and

1812, and Lord Melbourne was prosecuted for criminal conversation (i.e. adultery) while Prime Minister in 1836. Macaulay's claim, in 1831, that 'We know no spectacle so ridiculous as the British public in one of its periodical fits of morality ... once in six or seven years our virtue becomes outrageous', is often quoted as typifying a new primness, but Macaulay's point was how selective and sporadic this primness was, and continued to be. Similarly Mrs Grundy, the standard of genteel propriety so often referred to in Thomas Morton's play *Speed the Plough* of 1798, turns out on closer examination to have more to do with good old-fashioned social emulation than with any new standard of sexual morality. But in any case we have no scale by which to measure the dimensions or extent of changes in ideology or ethical norms, especially for periods when we have few reliable statistics regarding individual human behaviour. All we can do is look at what people said and wrote, and try to discover the meanings behind the raised voices.[7]

1

Women's Bodies – and How Men Looked at Them

Examination of the pages of *Playboy* or *Mayfair* (or of one's own chest in a mirror) reveals that the human nipple is surrounded by an area, perhaps an inch in diameter, of slightly darker pigmentation, which is called the areola or areole. Examination of paintings of the female nude in any art gallery reveals that, before 1830, European artists almost never took account of this phenomenon.

Occasionally the nipple was depicted as a minute pink blob. Where the subject of the painting required the nipple's projecting quality to be emphasised, as in Bronzino's 'Venus, Cupid, Folly and Time' in the National Gallery, London, where Cupid squeezes Venus' left nipple between two fingers, or in Sebastiano del Piombo's 'Martyrdom of St Agatha' in the Pitti, Florence, where Agatha's nipples are being ripped off with pincers, the artist would show the nipple as protruding but of the palest rose colour. Very occasionally, as in Guido Cagnacci's 'Death of Lucretia' in the Musée des Beaux Arts at Lyons, or Sir Peter Lely's portrait of Nell Gwyn reclining between a marble urn and a landscape, at Chiddingstone Castle in Kent – one of the first formal nudes ever to be painted in England – the areoles are shown, but are of distinctly juvenile size: but what was most usual was the depiction of the breast simply as a round, white, nippleless, featureless swelling.

Even the plates in Govard Bidloo's *Anatomia Humani Corporis* (Amsterdam 1685) show the nipple as unpigmented, except in one drawing of a dissected breast. Bidloo's work was a standard treatise on anatomy for nearly a hundred years: William Cowper's *The Anatomy of Humane Bodies* (Oxford 1698), which was the authoritative text in England throughout the eighteenth century, was little other than a bare-faced piracy of Bidloo's book, and some of its plates were reproduced in Andrew Bell's *Anatomia Britannica: a System of Anatomy*, as late as 1798.[1]

Given the preoccupations of today's *Playboy* culture, it is perhaps ironical that the one case where painters were disposed to show the human areole accurately was in the depiction of the male body; especially that of Christ on the Cross. The traditional iconography of Christ emphasised his mortal fleshly status: the New Testament story, as interpreted by the Roman Catholic church, was meaningless without the recognition that, in taking on human form, God had taken on fleshly weakness and fleshly corruption. Occasionally in German drawings of witches, or paintings of the Damned suffering the torments of Hell, pigmented nipples are shown on females but this is because, as with Christ on the Cross, the emphasis is on the imperfections of the flesh; but even Hans Baldung Grien's 'The Seven Ages of Woman' at the Museum der Bildenden Künste, Leipzig, which has the growth and decay of the flesh as its subject, shows the four adult women, each older than the one next to her, with faintly coloured bobbles on their breasts, but no areoles.[2]

Artists of the sixteenth and seventeenth centuries were disposed to edit out the human nipple because they believed in presenting ideal images of beauty. The influence of classical sculpture was important here. It seems probable that the sculptures of the classic Athenian period were painted in flesh colour, but two thousand years of exposure to sun and rain, or burial in the earth, had removed all traces of colouring. When artists began to study ancient sculpture in the Renaissance, one of the first lessons they learnt was that ideal beauty in the human body did not include pigmentation or body hair.

The process of idealisation extended even to the shape of the breasts. Only the oldest of the living women in Hans Baldung Grien's 'The Seven Ages of Woman' has breasts that droop, and even though drooping they are still plump and high. This is in marked contrast to the very oldest depictions of the female nude, from prehistoric times, which show either mountainous breasts sagging onto a fat stomach, as in the so-called Venus of Willendorf, or scrawny hanging breasts as in some of the 12,000-year-old La Madeleine reliefs: the technique of the latter is generally too crude to be seen as depicting realistic detail, but one of the reliefs clearly shows the woman turning on her side, with her breasts drooping flaccidly with the force of gravity downwards across her chest. It is possible that these stone-age sculptures are intended to represent *middle-aged* women, embodying a combination of motherhood, sexuality and perhaps even political authority. Greek art focused by preference on youthful beauty, but the Greeks, too, attached no value to very high bosoms: most of the best-known classical nudes show women with breasts set relatively low on the chest. Renaissance artists, for some reason, broke with their classical models in this respect: their preference was for small high cantilever breasts. Botticelli's 'The Birth of Venus', though in most respects the prototypical western European pin-up, is unusual among Renaissance paintings for the relative droopiness of Venus' breasts.[3]

Small high breasts, as depicted by Titian and Giorgone, remained the ideal throughout the eighteenth century. John Hall-Stevenson was probably referring to size as well as shape when he wrote:

> Lucy was not like other lasses,
>   From twelve her breasts swell'd in a trice,
> First they were like cupping-glasses,
>   Then like two peaches made of ice.

The precocious Lucy seems to have added only a few millimetres by the time she was thirteen, when she is described as having

>   ... breasts as round
> And springy as a tennis ball

We are not told what happened to her later; but in *Venus in the Cloister* (1725) we learn that fifteen-year-old Sister Eugenia 'is neither Fat nor Lean; her Breasts regularly divided, round, and not too prominent; she is, however, full-chested, and very slender in the Waste'. Polly in *Fanny Hill* (1749) has 'two ripe enchanting breasts, finely plump'd out in flesh, but withal so round, so firm, that they sustain'd themselves in scorn of any stay'. Fanny's own breasts, 'now in no more than a graceful plenitude, maintained a firmness and steady independence of any stay or support'. Not that it was to be taken for granted that breasts needed no support: we read in *The Genuine and Remarkable Amours of the Celebrated Author Peter Aretin* (1776), 'her breasts were small and hard, and though unsupported, did not hang in the least'. Even if in origin aesthetic, this preference was supported by medical folklore: according to Sinibaldi, 'Little breasts in women are a greater sign of lust, than great ones'.[4]

Though preferred small, breasts were considered an important feature of feminine attractiveness. A work by the French cleric Jacques Boileau which appeared in an English translation in 1678

under the title *A Just and Seasonable Reprehension of Naked
Breasts and Shoulders* claimed that women 'know as well as men,
that the beauty of the bosome hath this property, that it almost
continually inspires dishonest sentiments'. Indeed Lovelace, in
Samuel Richardson's novel *Clarissa*, evinces especial glee in re-
counting how

> Encouraged by so gentle a repulse, the tenderest things I said; and
> then, with my other hand, drew aside the handkerchief that con-
> cealed the beauty of beauties, and pressed with my burning lips the
> charmingest breast that ever my ravished lips beheld,

and a treatise of 1745 entitled *The Pleasures and Felicity of Marriage* mentioned among the pleasures that 'Those panting,
snow-white Breasts, which before you hardly could presume to look
upon, much less touch with one Finger, you may survey all o'er with
eager Eyes, and imprint with burning Kisses'. Even the moralising
Dr Johnson had to confess that he dared not venture behind the
scenes at the theatre because 'the silk stockings and white bosoms
of your actresses excite my amorous propensities'.[5]
   The Fruit-Shop, an anonymous work of 1765, devoted five and a
half pages to passages in French, Italian, Latin and Greek compar-
ing breasts to apples, *The Pleasures and Felicity of Marriage* alluded
to 'those *Hills of Nectar* and Banquet of the *Gods*', and a lewd poem
of 1707 contains the line

> O! stroke my Breasts, those Mountains of Delight.

Lucy's 'two peaches made of ice', in John Hall-Stevenson's poem
'Antony's Tale', have already been mentioned. Such flights of imagery – which of course had no counterpart in descriptions of the
male body – were satirised by William Woty:

> What know your country Loobies!
> The Orbs of Bliss to them are Greek,
> But well they know, whene'er you speak,
> Of pretty pouting Bubbies.

The rhyme, incidentally, suggests that the then current slang for
breasts, *bubbies*, was already in some parts of England pronounced
more like the modern *boobs*.[6]
   Although Samuel Croxall wrote of how

> Like Velvet Buds the crimson Nipples rise,
> Firm to the Touch and grateful to the Eyes.

and John Cleland, in *Fanny Hill*, when describing breasts, noted how 'their nipples, pointing different ways, mark'd their pleasing separation', the focus of interest seems not to have been the extremities of the breasts or the cleavage as such, or the degree to which the breasts projected, but the (hopefully) smooth and snowy expanse of flesh between collar-bone and cleavage. In polite discourse this was referred to as the *neck*:

Niece: I never knew that one's Neck was an obscene part.
Aunt: What you call your Neck is ... this is your Chest, your Bosom, this is the Pit of your Stomach, these are your Breasts; you make a strange long Neck of it; and are like the Sign-painters, who only call it a Head, tho' they Paint a Man or a Woman as far as the Waste; you may as well call it your Chin as your Neck.
Niece: Well, let it be called Bosom or what Part you will.

In the *Spectator* Richard Steele, in the persona of a female correspondent, complains of 'an old Batcheler ... [who] snatches Kisses by surprise, put[s] his Hand in our Necks, tears our Fans'; *in* our Necks, not *on* them. Similarly, when Lovelace bursts in on Clarissa when she is in her night attire he finds her with 'Her spread hands crossed over her charming neck; yet not half concealing its glossy beauties'. Sixty years later, when the same conception of the 'neck' still prevailed, one could purchase an object called a *divorce*, 'designed, most unnaturally, to separate what the hand of the Creator had brought into the most graceful union ... a piece of steel or iron, of a triangular form, gently curved on either side ... covered with soft material ... placed in the centre of the chest to divide the breasts'. The idea was to increase the area of flat succulent flesh at the top of the chest and to prevent the appearance of a cleavage. A round-shouldered posture would also contribute to the desired effect and accordingly shoulders were admired in proportion to their not being square: at least one fictional heroine had shoulders with 'so fine a fall, that one would imagine it impossible to hang a gown on them', and another, aged fourteen, boasted 'an easy fall of the shoulders [which] took off, in some degree, from that plumpness before, which is uncommon at my age'.[7]

*

Such was the force of artistic convention that even artists who wished to make a point of depicting the female body as it really was tended to edit out obvious details. In 1776 the sculptor Jean-Antoine Houdon found himself in trouble at the Paris Salon because of his life-sized 'Diana the Huntress'. This plaster model showed neither nipple nor pubic hair, but scandalised objections were raised to Houdon's attempt to indicate the vulva. The plaster model was barred from the Salon, and in the marble and two bronze versions which Houdon produced subsequently there was no indication of female sexual organs at all.[8]

The establishment of the areole as a fit subject for art seems largely to have been due to William Etty. Before the 1820s English painters had rarely depicted unclothed women. Sir Joshua Reynolds had produced an incredibly awkward pubescent Venus lying half-naked on her side, entitled 'Venus Chiding Cupid for learning to cast Accounts', and both William Hamilton and Henry Fuseli had painted Eve in various Miltonic situations as originals for the engraved illustrations in editions of *Paradise Lost*: the Swiss-born Fuseli had also painted Eve for a commercial project called the Milton gallery, and one or two smaller format nudes for his own amusement; but Etty was the first painter of the English school to make a speciality of the female nude. Etty seems to have looked up to Fuseli as one of his masters: in letters from the continent written to Sir Thomas Lawrence in 1823 he asks to be remembered to him, but his own nudes have nothing in common with Fuseli's toneless flesh and the strip-cartoon-like simplification of his body contours, and it is possible that he was unfamiliar with this part of the Swiss-born artist's work. In one respect at least, Etty owed more to his female models than to his male artistic precursors: by the 1830s his nudes were regularly shown as possessing pointy, pigment-ringed nipples, though it is questionable how far this was mere literalism, since the women in his pictures tend to have impossibly compacted bodies with bosoms that seem to sprout directly from their collar-bones, so that one often feels that the colouring is the only thing really life-like about his painting. He was to some extent ahead of his time: the famous 'Liberty at the Barricades' by his younger French contemporary Eugène Delacroix shows no more than a vague rosiness at the tips of Liberty's breasts: the distinct areoles shown on the version used in the modern French 100 Franc note have been supplied by the Banque de France. In 1857 Delacroix produced a small odalisque based on a photograph which has survived and which shows large, darkly-pigmented areoles: these do not appear in the painting. Yet, curiously enough, early photographs of naked women have often been retouched to remove the pubic hair and to accentuate – *not* eliminate – the nipples, which frequently lacked adequate definition because of the primitive quality of early cameras. After the death of Etty in 1849 nipples and areoles began to be established in French art but dropped out in the works of English artists such as Burne-Jones and Alma-Tadema, though the existence of these physiological phenomena was now an officially acknowledged fact: Sir Astley Cooper, who had twice been President of the College of Surgeons, announced in 1840, 'The breasts, from their prominence, their roundness, the white colour of their skin, and the red colour of the nipples, by which they are surmounted, add great beauty to the female form.'[9]

It seems very doubtful whether Etty regarded himself as a pioneer. He made a slow start as a painter (most of his surviving work dates from after his fortieth birthday) and was assiduous, even when an established artist, in his attendance at the life classes at the Royal Academy: despite this, it is doubtful whether he ever learnt to draw very well, or even to observe human anatomy very closely. He never commented on the fact that he was the first English painter to specialise in female nudes, and since he never married, kept a mistress or, as far as is recorded, went with loose women, it seems possible that, apart from the sentimental excitement of one or two immature 'crushes', his interest in women was devoid of sexuality. He wrote a brief autobiography, printed in *The Art-Journal* at the time of his death. It communicates his prototypical Victorian high-mindedness and conscientiousness:

Like many other men, my character has been much misunderstood by some – not a few – because I have preferred painting the unsophisticated human form divine, male and female, in preference to the production of the loom; or, in plainer terms, preferred painting from the glorious works of God, to draperies, the works of man. I have been accused of being a shocking and immoral man! I have even heard my bodily infirmities – brought on, in a great measure, by my ardent devotion to my Art, and studying in hot rooms in Life Academies – turned against me; and, unacquainted with my temperate habits, been accused of *drinking*. I confess my sin, I am fond of drinking, but only an harmless beverage, *tea*; and I certainly venerate the memory of the man, be he who he may, who invented tea, and to any who thus calumniate me I forgive, and only ask them to examine my life. That I have had errors and failings too many, I know, and trust to the goodness of God to forgive; but it is a duty I owe to myself to state, what I do with sincerity, that in whatever station I found myself thrown, whether printer's devil or Royal Academician, my honest endeavour has been to do my duty in it to the best of my power; a principle I can with confidence recommend to all who may come after me, and one to which they will never regret to look back upon.

... suffice it for me to feel I have *endeavoured* in this life to earnestly and seriously do my duty; a principle I can with confidence recommend in the language of the immortal Nelson: 'England expects thus every man this day will do his duty.' And here I will recommend to my younger brethren pursuing the Art, that whether they follow High Art, or Low Art, let their aim in the Profession be *excellence*, and encouragement will follow as a necessary consequence; let their conduct in life – *their aim, be virtue*, for its own dear sake, as well as *excellence in their beautiful Art for its own sake*. And happy will be the day they make *this* their firm determination; the prize of happiness and glory will be within the reach of minds so constituted; but if neglectful alike of their true honour and that of their noble art, they degrade it and themselves by base views and improper conduct, bitter will be the fruits; if they use the opportunities of an artist for the purposes of vicious indulgence, a miserable mistake will blight their prospects, and the sun of prosperity and hope will cease to shine on their labours.

Specifically on the subject of painting naked women he had only this to say:

As a worshipper of beauty, whether it be seen in a weed, a flower, or in that most interesting form to humanity, lovely woman, in intense admiration of it and its *Almighty Author*, if at any time I have forgotten the boundary line that I ought not to have passed, and tended to voluptuousness, I implore His pardon; I have never wished to seduce others from that path and practice of virtue, which alone leads to happiness here and hereafter; and if in any of my pictures an immoral sentiment has been aimed at, I consent it should be burnt; but I never recollect being actuated in painting my pictures by such sentiment. That the female form, in its fulness, beauty of colour, exquisite rotundity, may, by being portrayed in its nudity, awake like nature in some degree an approach to passion, I must allow, but where no immoral sentiment is *intended*, I affirm that the simple undisguised naked figure is innocent. 'To the pure in heart all things are pure.' My aim in all my great pictures has been to paint some great moral on the heart: 'The Combat', THE BEAUTY OF MERCY; the three 'Judith' pictures, PATRIOTISM, and self-devotion to her country, her people, and her God; 'Benaiah, David's chief captain', VALOUR; 'Ulysses and the Syrens', the importance of resisting SENSUAL DE- LIGHTS, or an Homeric paraphrase on the 'Wages of Sin is Death';

Somehow this doesn't seem quite frank enough: but perhaps that really was all there was to it.[10]

*

The interesting question is not why artists began to notice a feature of the female body that had always been there, but why they only began to notice it in the early nineteenth century. The fact that Etty was the first artist to specialise in nudes *in England* and was therefore, despite two years' sojourn in Italy and France, to one side of the established *European* tradition, may have something to do with it. Since the early Renaissance most painters had been care- fully schooled within a kind of apprenticeship system. The various established conventions of painting and sculpture had been handed down from generation to generation, and since most artists expected (and needed) to earn a living wage from the exercise of their art, experimentation was not particularly encouraged. Later, when state-sponsored academies were established, it became even riskier than before to defy prevailing aesthetic conventions, though this was perhaps least so in England where Sir Thomas Lawrence, of whom Etty was a pupil, rose to the Presidency of the Royal Academy on the strength of his remarkably impressionistic technique as a portrait painter, and where J.M.W. Turner, having shown as a young man his mastery of various conventional styles, continued to obtain respect and admiration for his increasingly indecipherable experiments in depicting light and movement. By the 1800s, in any case, various external challenges had developed to the authority claimed by the academies, and a sudden very rapid expansion of the art profession, so to speak below and to one side of the established system of artistic apprenticeship, came close to blowing away the conventions of art altogether.

The second half of the eighteenth century saw a marked increase in the invention of technical processes and gadgets, many of which – though by no means all – found profitable practical application and thereby provided an incentive to further invention. These inventions included several related to the manufacture of illustrations for books and magazines, notably lithography and steel-engraving. In 1815 there seems to have been one lithographic printer working in London, and in 1820 three, but by 1822 there were more than twenty. Steel-engraving, brought to England from America by Jacob Perkins in 1819, was also established by 1822. Whereas steel-engraving was expensive but commercially attractive for very large print runs, lithography was both cheap – cheaper than copper-engraving – and superior at least to copper-engraving for detail. As early as 1818 Alois Senefelder, the leading pioneer of lithography, discussed the possibility of colour lithographs, but left it up to the artist to 'determine whether it is to resemble a painting, or an engraving printed in colours'. Colour lithographs (chromolithographs) became commercially viable in the 1830s and were to be a central element in high-Victorian kitsch. Improved means of mass-producing increasingly attractive illustrations meant larger markets and consequently more demand for original art-work. The culture of technical innovation itself provided new subjects for illustrations. It had already been pointed out that

> The stupendous effects produced in our manufacturing operations, by the extensive introduction of machinery [and] the circulation of useful knowledge, which distinguishes the period in which we live, has produced an increased demand for the journals of science and the records of those improvements.

Even the preparation and duplication of engineering plans required draughtsmen in larger numbers than in earlier times. The result was the rapid expansion of the art-education industry. George Hamilton claimed, in *The Elements of Drawing in its Various Branches for the Use of Students* (1812) that 'his is the first arranged and comprehensive work on this Art ever published in England'. By 1828 Pigot and Co.'s *London & Provincial New Commercial Directory* listed 580 artists in London alone, and this probably did not include many of the drawing masters teaching other people to draw.[11]

A young man might be trained to draw, perhaps at the expense of an employer, so that he could produce a diagram of a steam engine or a pump, but once he had gained confidence in his pencil there was nothing to prevent him applying his male gaze to more intimate subjects. In 1794 a doctor, Thomas Cogan, had written on the subject of drawing the human body:

> It is also the branch most exposed to the severity of criticism; as grosser faults in the representation of the human form are readily detected, and as numbers, presuming that they have a complete model in their own persons, or competent knowledge from their intercourse with their species, affect the refined connoisseur, and attempt to support the character by searching for minute blemishes.

Cogan's remarks may have been conceived as principally theoretical, and in any case his book only deals with the depiction of heads, but it appears that his younger contemporaries were becoming more aware of what their fellow humans actually looked like.[12]

*

During the eighteenth century, and for some hundreds of years previously, it had not been customary for lovers or even married couples to see each other naked. This is part of the explanation for the curious ambivalence of depictions of the nude in European art from the Renaissance onwards: the nudity is supposed to be idealised and symbolic rather than erotic, yet the pruriently voyeuristic aspect is frequently emphasised, especially in such subjects as 'Susannah and the Elders' (young girl surprised bathing by Biblical dirty old men) or 'The Judgment of Paris' (young stud – in Cranach's version wearing a suit of armour to help preserve his distance – adjudicating between the charms of three Goddesses wearing one veil). One version of Titian's 'Venus and the Organ-player' in the Prado, Madrid, shows above the organ's keyboard a carved mask that stares at the organist, who stares at a naked reclining female behind him, who stares at her little dog – who stares back. It is not altogether clear, but the woman's feet seem to be behind the small of the organist's back. This is definitely the case in two related paintings of apparently later date, 'Venus and the Lute Player', of which one specimen is in the Metropolitan Museum in New York and the other in the Fitzwilliam, Cambridge. The lute players may only be glancing round, but the Prado organist is definitely making a double-take at Venus' crutch over his right shoulder, even though, from the apparent position of her feet, she is lying to his left – a *trompe l'oeil* effect that is no doubt related to Titian's theme of voyeurism.[13]

The sheer unusualness and singularity of female nakedness was related to the fact that women's clothes were cumbersome and difficult to remove – upper-class women were literally unable to dress and undress themselves without the help of a maid. It was moreover the custom, when preparing for bed, either to retain one's undergarments or to replace them with a shift of similar cut, though perhaps longer. People also had very little privacy: the poor lived maybe one room to a family and the rich were hemmed in by servants and impoverished relatives. Yet, paradoxically, though it was difficult to remove garments entirely, it was easier even than today to get unimpeded access to a woman's pudenda. Stockings were secured by coloured garters above the knee, but otherwise nothing at all was worn beneath the shift till drawers began to be fashionable for women in the second decade of the nineteenth century, so there was none of the modern difficulty with regard to extricating legs from the leg-holes of knickers, and of course all those voluminous layers of petticoats were loose enough to be easily lifted aside. John Aubrey tells a story about Sir Walter Ralegh:

> He loved a wench well: and one time getting up one of the Mayds of Honour up against a tree in a Wood ('twas his first Lady) who seemed at first boarding to be something fearfull of her Honour, and modest, she cryed, sweet Sir Walter, what doe you me ask? Will you undoe me? Nay, sweet Sir Walter! Sir Walter! Sweet Sir Walter! At last as the danger and the pleasure at the same time grew higher, she cryed in the extasey, Swisser Swatter Swisser Swatter.

Not the least curious detail of this narrative for a modern reader is that the two wealthy youngsters chose to do it standing against a tree, with the girl's dress and petticoats up around her waist. Yet Ralegh's French contemporary Brantôme argued that that was the best way to make love:

> one should snatch one's moment as quickly as one can, no sooner seen than taken advantage of and done ... the mere thought in such circumstances of how one is forcing one's way under the clothes, treading on cloth of gold and silver canvas and rustling silks with all those pearls and precious stones, crushing, spoiling, flinging down, dragging on the ground, tends to augment and build up one's ardour and satisfaction.

Similarly, in *Fanny Hill*, when Fanny makes love, for the first time, with her beloved Charles, 'his impatience would not suffer him to undress me, more than just unpinning my handkerchief and gown, and unlacing my stays ... my petticoats and shift were soon taken up, and –'. Later Fanny and Charles got into bed together, but though the text clearly states that they were both undressed – 'I found myself undress'd, and a-bed ... Charles ... falls to undressing' – they were evidently not completely nude: 'thrusting up his own shirt and my shift he laid his naked glowing body next to mine.' On another occasion,

> Charles, with a fond impatience, took the pains to undress me ... I was soon laid in bed, and scarce languish'd an instant for the darling partner of it, before he was undress'd and got between the sheets ... [and] after a very short preparatory dalliance, lifting up my linen and his own, laid the broad treasures of his manly chest close to my bosom.

Sometimes the woman herself did the lifting aside: when, in a scurrilous pamphlet of 1723, a lord rolls up the bedclothes covering the woman he had been sleeping with, he 'discovered a most beautiful pair of legs, thighs, and so upwards, to her very Bubbies, for the Good-natur'd Creature had pull'd her Shift up to her Armpits that it might be no obstacle to their Diversions'. But the shift might also ruck up of its own accord, as Camillo found when he crept into Saphira's bedroom in *The History of the Human Heart* and saw that 'the Bed-cloths, as conspiring to bless the happy Lover, left the Nymph quite naked, even her Shift furled itself up above her Middle'.[14]

Undressing, in other words, generally meant removing one's heavy *outer* garments. No doubt the remaining odds and ends got in the way to some extent and after a night of passion a woman could hardly be surprised to find that 'my cap, my hair, my shift, were all in disorder from the rufflings I had undergone'. But even an experienced courtesan like Fanny Hill is described as finding it odd that an impotent client 'would strip me stark naked on a carpet, by a good fire, when he would contemplate me almost by the hour ...'. A short time previously Fanny had attended an evening entertainment where couples took it in turn to perform sexually in front of the other guests. Her partner removed her clothes till,

> dropping my uppercoat [i.e. top petticoat], I was reduced to my under one and my shift, the open bosom of which gave the hands and eyes

all the liberty they could wish. Here I imagin'd the stripping was to
stop,

and she was quite surprised to be asked to take off the rest.[15]

In 1760 much mirth was provoked in Edinburgh by the story that
a worthy citizen had insisted on looking at his wife's vagina after
making love to her, and that while doing so he had dropped his
candle and set fire to her pubic hair. John MacLaurin, an advocate,
later a judge on the Scots bench, even wrote a poem on the subject
entitled *The Keekiad*, 'keek' being Scots for 'peep'. An essential part
of the legend was the wife's outrage and indignation when the
husband first suggests that he should be allowed to look:

> 'Unthinking man,' (the Dame aghast replies,)
> 'For both our sakes, refrain your curious eyes;
> 'Cou'dst thou, unchang'd, the Gorgon's face explore,
> 'Which on her Aegis, Virgin Pallas bore ...?'

Equally crucial to the narrative was the completeness of the husband's fascination at what he saw:

> His eyes insatiate on her beauties pore,
> Each part contemplate and the whole devour;
> His heart and pulse, with doubl'd quickness beat,
> His nerves relax'd, their wonted tone forget,
> His bosom labours, with incessant sighs,
> And all the Man dissolv'd in rapture dies ...

Hence the accident with the candle. No doubt igniting one's wife's
pubic hair is amusing enough, especially to a Lowland Scots sense
of humour, but the whole point seems to be the oddity of wanting
even to look at 'that which is better felt than seen'.[16]

Around 1800 the contemplation of female nakedness became, if
not more respectable, a little bit more normal:

> She was undressing to bathe herself. The long tresses of her hair were
> already bound up. The amorous Monk had full opportunity to observe
> the voluptuous contours and admirable symmetry of her person. She
> threw off her last garment, and advancing to the Bath prepared for
> her, She put her foot in the water. It struck cold, and She drew it back
> again. Though unconscious of being observed, an in-bred sense of
> modesty induced her to veil her charms; and She stood hesitating
> upon the brink, in the attitude of the Venus de Medicis. At this

moment a tame Linnet flew towards her, nestled its head between her breasts, and nibbled them in wanton play. The smiling Antonia strove in vain to shake off the Bird, and at length raised her hands to drive it from its delightful harbour. Ambrosio could bear no more ...

There was some talk of prosecution when the novel from which this was quoted was published in 1796, but nothing came of it and the author was soon afterwards elected to Parliament. Keats was accused by Byron of writing piss-a-bed poetry on account of passages like

> her vespers done,
> Of all her wreathed pearls her hair she frees;
> Unclasp'd her warmed jewels one by one;
> Loosens her fragrant bodice; by degrees
> Her rich attire creeps rustling to her knees,

but Keats' account of how the ardent Porphyro sneaks into Madeline's bedroom and watches from his hiding place as she undresses for bed in due course became a schoolroom classic. Earlier, *Fanny Hill* – which *was* subject to legal proceedings – had contained a passage that suggests a link between this kind of voyeurism and the developing cult of picturesque landscape. Describing her colleague Harriet's 'luscious mouth of nature', 'Fanny' writes: 'the dark umbrage of the downy spring-moss that overarched it, bestowed, on the luxury of the landscape, a touching warmth, a tender finishing, beyond the expression of words.' It was in just such terms that connoisseurs had become accustomed to discuss the paintings of Claude Lorrain and Poussin.[17]

*

We can assume that a culture in which people made love either fully dressed or wearing shifts and night-shirts, merely pulling the garments out of the way of their private parts, did not favour experimentation with regard to body positions during copulation.

Sexual positions are a notable part of wash-room folklore. American movies seem usually to show the woman on top astride the man – no doubt this is Hollywood's idea of political correctness – and David Lodge, formerly Professor of English at Birmingham University, thinks that in Italy it is normal for the woman to crouch on all fours and present her bottom to her lover. It seems however that the so-called missionary position is the one regarded as natural in all European societies and those of European origin. According to Nicolas Venette's English translator, 'The most common Posture is that which is most allowable and voluptuous; we speak Mouth to Mouth, we kiss, caress, when we embrace before.' Taking the woman from behind was supposed to be more effective for impregnation: in the words of Sinibaldi, 'Although the common way of congression be more civil and comely, yet it's less fruitful than that way which nature showed every beast.' As for allowing the woman to be on top:

> Man according to the Laws of Nature, ought to have the Empire over the Woman ... 'Tis beneath his Prerogative to afford such Complaisance ... The Children become Dwarfs, Cripples, Hunch-back'd, Squint-ey'd, and stupid Blockheads, and by their Imperfections fully evidence the irregular Life of their Parents, without putting us to the trouble to search the Cause of such Defects any farther.[18]

Both Sinibaldi and Venette, who borrowed largely from him, lived in the seventeenth century: I have found nothing relating to sexual positions in the medical literature of the eighteenth and early nineteenth centuries, suggesting that the issue was no longer of medical interest. But it was certainly of interest to pornographers.

Vases from classical Greek times show a variety of sexual positions – possibly an indication of the habits of their original purchasers, rather than of the population at large – and the topic obtained some celebrity during the Renaissance owing to a clandestinely circulated set of sixteen prints showing various positions, drawn by Giulio Pippi, commonly known as Giulio Romano, a pupil of Raphael's, and engraved by Marcantonio Raimondi. They were accompanied by rather feeble verses unreliably attributed to Pietro Aretino:

> *Fottiamci, anima mia, fottiamci presto,*
> *porchè tutti per fotter nati siamo*
>
> (Let's fuck, my soul, let's fuck right away
> Since we are all born through fucking)

Despite Aretino's marginal or non-existent connection with the engravings, they are traditionally associated with his name. No complete set of the prints seems to survive, the last known authenticated copy having been destroyed at Dresden on official orders at the end of the eighteenth century, though a set of woodcut copies of fourteen of the sixteen engravings was discovered on a second-hand book stall by Walter Toscanini, son of the famous conductor, earlier this century. The engravings were however relatively well-known in the seventeenth century. In 1674 the fellows of All Souls College Oxford employed the university press to run off an edition of some of the Aretine positions – it seems likely that they did not have a complete set of the originals – but though the printing was carried out in strict secrecy after normal working hours, the Dean of Christ Church, the notorious Dr Fell, who was in overall charge of the press, discovered what was going on and seized both prints and plates. The very free English version of Ferrante Pallavicino's *Whores' Rhetoric*, printed in 1683, has the brothel madam declaring virtuously, '*Aretin's* Figures have no place in my Rhetorick, and I hope will find no place in my Pupils apartment. They are calculated for a hot Region a little on this side Sodom.'[19]

Towards the end of the eighteenth century a little book entitled *L'Aretin Francois par un Membre de l'Académie des Dames* began to circulate. The British Library has a copy, allegedly printed *A Londres 1787*, with French verses, and another, with verses in both French and English, supposedly printed *A Londres 1803*. (The title of this edition has the more modern form *L'Aretin Francais*.) A curious feature of the 1803 edition is that the plates, though showing the same positions and situations as the 1787 edition, have been redrawn and re-engraved, giving the protagonists strikingly sharp 'Grecian' features: a Paris 1825 edition uses a poor copy of these 1803 engravings, but there are also Paris 1829 and Brussels 1830 editions using what appear to be the 1787 plates, now rather worn. The British Library also has a brochure entitled *Les Dessins de Jules le Romain: 22 Planches faite d'après les Origines à Rome par le Professeur Pirolli*. The library catalogue suggests 1860 for the date of this item: it is certainly later than 1824, which is when 'le Professeur Pirolli', otherwise Tommaso Piroli, died at the age of sixty-seven. The drawings are unshaded outlines of a larger format than in the 1803 *L'Aretin Francais* and the majority of the drawings are different compositions though in the same style: but a number correspond down to the faces and the details of the furniture and are evidently either copies or preliminary designs. It seems safe to assume that Piroli, alias Pirolli, executed the 1803 engravings. The 1787 engravings are attributed to François Elluin, after drawings by Antoine Borel. Of the fourteen Giulio Romano designs known

from the woodcut copies found by Walter Toscanini only three have
much resemblance to those in *L'Aretin Francois* and of these only
one seems to be a direct copy, though even here the woman rests
her hand on the man's head whereas in the original her hand is in
the air, striving for balance. Giulio Romano's 'Aretine' drawings are
also known through nineteenth-century copies by Jean-Frédéric-
Maximilien de Waldeck, based on an authentic set of engravings he
saw decades earlier in Mexico. Waldeck's copies include 'La Carriola' (in modern Italian *carriuola*, wheelbarrow) in which a woman
walks on her hands while a man, supporting one of her legs under
each arm, penetrates her at what must have been, for him, a
somewhat uncomfortable angle. In *L'Aretin Francois* an analogous
position is shown except that the girl's legs are above the man's
shoulders, one against his collar bone, the other waving in equilib-
rium, and she supports herself above the floor with a single wheel
with a short axle projecting at either side. This position is described
verbally in *The Genuine and Remarkable Amours of the Celebrated
Author Pietro Aretin*, of 1776, which denominates it as the 'wheel-
barrow fuck': though 'La Carriola' is not among the incomplete set
of sixteenth-century woodcuts discovered by Walter Toscanini, one
would probably be correct in assuming that this was the most
enduringly famed of the 'Aretine' positions.[20]

   Willingness to indulge in variable positions must have encouraged a degree of mutual nakedness. Nevertheless, the quick shunt
against a wall or tree did not go out of fashion: it seems in fact to
have been the normal mode by which one-shilling streetwalkers
accommodated their customers. Though Venette had insisted that
'The Genital Parts of Men are not contrived to Caress standing',
doing it standing – what in vulgar parlance is described as 'having
a knee-trembler' – may even have been a preferred taste. One
supposes for example that sophisticated aristocratic adulterers
would have known how to arrange their encounters as agreeably as
possible, but in the 1780s a witness in a criminal conversation trial
recounted how he had come across the Earl of Peterborough and
Lady Ann Foley making love in a shrubbery at six o'clock one
September evening:

   he first heard Lady Ann cry out, two or three times, 'O dear! you hurt
   me!' which induced him to look that way; and going towards the pales,
   he looked over and saw Lord Peterborough and Lady Ann together
   ... his Lordship had Lady Ann round the middle, and ... her Lady-

ship's coats were up, and, at the same time, he saw her Ladyship's naked legs and thighs round Lord Peterborough's hams; and her arms round his Lordship's neck.

It may of course simply have been a question of the personal preference of the Earl of Peterborough; another witness deposed:

> the said Right Hon. Lady Ann Foley put her back to and leaned against an oak tree, and she then, or the said Lord Peterborough, (but which the deponent cannot say) pulled her petticoats up to her waist, and thereby exposed her naked thighs; and the said Lord Peterborough then pulled down his breeches, and got between her legs and thighs, and carnally enjoyed her.

But if it was simply a matter of individual taste, or the rituals of a particular relationship, it is rather a coincidence that the lover of Lady Ann Foley's sister, Lady Maria Bayntoun, should have behaved in the same way. When the adultery of the latter came before the courts a witness said she had stood on a gate and peering through the upper part of a shuttered window, above the shutters, had seen Lady Maria Bayntoun in the dinner-parlour, 'standing with her face towards Mr Cooper, and *her petticoats up*; and then saw Mr Cooper kiss Lady Maria'.[21]

*

It may even have been that the copiousness of women's clothes made it easier to perform the sexual act standing up: but at just the time of the disgrace of Lady Ann Foley and Lady Maria Bayntoun fashions in clothes began to change.

During most of the eighteenth century fashionable women wore expansive ground-length dresses over bustles or hoops, with their waists pinched in by rigid corseting. About 1790 a simpler, looser style came into fashion. Though often identified with the type of clothing worn in classical times, it seems to have been adapted partly from the style of clothing favoured for prepubescent girls during the previous twenty years, and though stays continued to be worn, the new mode was far less constricting and shape-disguising than earlier styles. The shoulders and arms were bared: it was the first time that elbows and upper arms were put on show, though the forearms were often covered by long gloves. The décolletage became low and wide, and the stays were sometimes arranged to thrust up the breasts, though this provoked adverse comment:

The bosom ... has been transformed into a shape, and transplanted to a place, which deprives it of its original beauty and harmony with the rest of the person –

but of course the commonest objection was on moral grounds:

the libertine, the gross Epicurean, may feast his imbruted gaze upon a form so stripped of decency ... But a man of delicacy, of worth, turns from the couch of sensuality, though Venus herself reposed there; and with celestial rapture clasps to his warm and noble heart the unsunned bosom of the chaste and vestal-enwrapped fair.

It seemed that there was no end to the danger ensuing from exposure of the bosom, 'which from its beauty, its refinement, and its irresistible attraction, was never meant to be exposed to public view'. A correspondent of *The Gentleman's Magazine*, signing himself 'A Layman' even claimed that:

after a young man has passed an hour or two in the company of his mother and sisters undressed, as I have described [i.e. in the latest revealing mode] his passions become elated and untameable; and using or abusing the liberty accorded to young men of going abroad, he rushes into the midnight revels of debauchery, and thus knows nothing of the real merit and delicacy of the female character; he lives diseased, and dies a monument of his own ruin, and of his mother's shame!

There was also, it was suggested, the risk involved in upper-class women passing on their unwanted clothes to their maids who, 'as they are often much the finer-formed women of the two ... have generally more temptation to offer, and as they are weaker in judgment ... are more flattered with the gaze which they attract'.[22]

The new fashion's numerous critics attributed it to the malign influence of French *couture*:

Our youth have received from France the Revolutionary fashions, which were invented, and actually *ordained*, for the purpose of confounding all distinction of rank. And our females have not scrupled to display the shameless modes of Parisian prostitutes;

and a case could be made for suggesting that the new mode had a certain relevance to the new sexual openness of revolutionary France. Fashion does seem to be international, with a capacity to transfer itself across ideological frontiers. On the other hand the new style seems to have originated in England, and flourished especially there, and especially at a time when French ladies of fashion were not spending a lot of money on new wardrobes.[23]

In 1800 a cleric from Jamaica asserted, 'the *Cyprian dress*, and *Cyprian manners*, of the ladies of our times, are far from being calculated to promote their true interest, or to protect their honour'. According to another clergyman,

> Supreme fashion could overturn in the female mind every barrier of chaste love, decency, and sense, and at once rend the veil, already too thin, between modesty and depravity ... Observe the walk, the gait, the air! and, lastly, mind the disgusting, though studied seat! then candidly say is not the common prostitute the more decent of the two, and less danger to be apprehended from her to the morals of the rising generation, than the modish fair?

As if fearing that their apocalyptic vision of an entire moral code overthrown by dressmakers was not convincing enough, critics gave urgent warning of the risk to health involved in up-to-date fashions: 'Many women who, a little while since, shone forth among the loveliest of their sex, are now dressed in their shrouds, because, in an evil hour, they laid aside those parts of their apparel which health, as well as decency, forbade them to relinquish.' Even a doctor as progressive and as widely respected as Thomas Beddoes could claim:

> The last years of the century have seen the land more deeply covered with mourning than any of the preceding. War and pestilence have obviously had a large share in promoting the distress of families: but neither war nor pestilence a larger share, perhaps, than the prevailing modes of female fashion.[24]

Yet these sexually alluring fashions seem to have done little harm to the morals of Jane Austen or of most of the young girls she wrote about. One of her older contemporaries even suggested that the new fashion was related to an *improvement* in moral standards:

Ladies of old, 'twas understood,
Were poor frail creatures, flesh and blood!
Too prone their virtue to surrender
To ev'ry saucy, bold pretender ...
Yet anxious to continue chaste,
With whale-bone they secur'd the waist;
Which, stiff with buckram, lac'd and twisted,
The fierce invader's force resisted:
Thus armed with stays and female pride,
Her lovers many a nymph defy'd.
But now, like angels chaste and pure,
With rigid Virtue's shield secure,
The gate's thrown open, cautions cease,
The nymph enjoys herself in peace.

And though it was alleged that the ultra-modish were leaving off their chemises and stays, it is doubtful whether very many did so: one notes, however, a curious prefiguring of the twentieth-century axiom that a woman should never go out of doors without clean knickers:

The *Chemise*, (now too frequently banished,) ought to be held as sacred by the modest fair, as the vestal veil ... There are circumstances which might occur to her, wherein the want of this decent garment might subject her to a shame never to be forgotten by herself or others. Let her think of accidents 'by flood, or field, or fire,' and I trust she will never again subject herself to the chance of such unwomanly exposure.

In fact, after 1810, a garment came into fashion for women that offered even more effective protection from prying eyes and intrusive fingers, penises, etc. than the chemise: silk drawers. These, however, were initially regarded as involving a sexual display rather than sexual modesty: Princess Charlotte, daughter of the Prince Regent, was once accused of showing her drawers when she got in or out of a carriage, and of wearing them too long, to which she pertly replied, 'the Duchess of Bedford's are much longer, and they are bordered with Brussels lace'. In the end one suspects that the real issue was not modesty or immodesty, but simply the unacceptability of novelty. Nevertheless there is one aspect of women's fashions 1790-1810 which deserves particular attention.[25]

*

In 1940 an obscure scholarly journal produced by the University of California published an article by Jane Richardson and A.L. Kroeber analysing the variation in the length and width of skirts, height and width of waists, and the depth and breadth of décolletages in England since the mid-seventeenth century. Richardson and Kroeber found that the years 1650-60, 1787-1820 and from 1920 onwards were periods of 'pattern strain, rapid change and variability'. Most of the extremes of measurement occurred during these phases of variability, for example women's waists were at their highest in 1807, at their lowest in 1926, but the important phenomenon was the extent of the change from year to year. The upheavals of the French Revolutionary and Napoleonic Wars, the aftermath of the First World War, and also probably the Civil War in England in the mid-seventeenth century, coincided with and evidently stimulated statistical maximums of changeability and instability in women's fashions.[26]

Richardson's and Kroeber's object was to demonstrate the variableness of fashion in periods of social and cultural stress. They did not claim that the rapid changes in fashion had any overall direction or logic. In fact it seems there *is* a particular pattern. In around 1615 fashionable women wore large farthingales and high-necked dressed finished off with closed ruffs. By the middle years of the century they were wearing looser, higher-waisted, lower-necked dresses without major internal structures to disguise the body shape. Tight corsets began to come in during the 1650s, and by the 1680s fashionable women were tightly-laced and wore bustles to disguise their body profile, together with long trains to impede their walking. Rigid corseting and bustles or hoops remained in fashion until the pseudo-classical style came in about 1790, and came back when the pseudo-classical style began to go out after 1810; by the mid-nineteenth century fashionable women were well covered up and loaded down with constricting, shape-disguising wrappings. Though there was a movement against tight-lacing, and propaganda in favour of more practical underclothing, in the era of the late-Victorian 'New Woman', the turn towards looser, less disguising, less constricting garments really only occurs at the time of the First World War. The hobble skirt worn by the Suffragettes (and other ladies of fashion) *circa* 1910-14 was a kind of paradoxical last lurch in favour of constriction. 'I freed the bust, but I shackled the legs', boasted the influential designer Paul Poiret: but within half-a-dozen years women were working in munitions factories, driving buses to free men for the Western Front, and wearing trousers.[27]

There have been counter-swings, of course, but the overall movement of women's fashions since 1914 has been in the direction of physical liberation. The 1950s torpedo-chested bottle-blonde, with her sheath skirt and wobbling stiletto heels, was only a passing phase, whereas unisex has lasted over twenty years and shows no sign of going away.

A key theme in the process of freeing women's bodies from restrictive clothing, whether in the mid-seventeenth, late-eighteenth or later-twentieth century, has been the restoration to visibility of the outline of the bottom. When the farthingale, which disguised the shape of the whole lower body, faded away under James I it was replaced by 'bum rolls' which simply disguised the buttocks. These went out of fashion in the 1630s and for fifty years dresses hung more or less naturally on the lines of the body. When the reverse movement back to disguising the shape began, it was the bottom that was the first thing to be disguised. A hundred years later, when hoops went out, the bottom continued to be modified by bustles for a further fifteen years or so, and when the movement towards liberation was again reversed the first thing to be reintroduced was the bustle. For much of the present century the natural body line was disguised not by bustles but by longer corsets: 'foundation garments' only really went out in the 1960s. In the middle of that decade mini-skirts both emphasised the wiggle of the backside and enabled onlookers to glimpse the junction of the upper thigh and gluteus maximus, and later on the widespread adoption by women of slacks and jeans (sometimes home-altered for tightness) involved the display of the entire profile of the buttocks.

The possibility that such changes in fashion involve a revaluation of female sexuality, or at least of female sexual characteristics, is suggested by the fact that periods of fundamental change in female fashion generally coincide with revolutions in male modes. The coming in of simpler, less discommoding women's clothes around 1650 coincided with the beard going out of fashion and moustaches becoming thinner (they disappeared about 1685 and only came back after the Crimean War). Wigs for men, which came in alongside tight-lacing for women with the Restoration of Charles II, went out of fashion at about the same time as the adoption of the gauzy neoclassical style for women's gowns. Soon afterwards, as if to balance the plunging necklines of the women, men's stocks started becoming higher and tighter, though perhaps the most fundamental change of all was in the replacement of knee-breeches and stockings by trousers after 1807. Again, in the 1960s the mini-skirt revolution for women was followed within a couple of years by the revival of beards and long hair for men.

As far as women's fashions are concerned, it is surely more than a coincidence that the 1800s, which were one of the periods when rumps were highly visible, at least in outline, also saw the establishment of flagellation as a major component of the commercial sex industry.

Flagellation – achievement of sexual arousal by beating, or being beaten, on the buttocks – has a long and obscure history. In 1629 a German doctor, Johann Heinrich Meibom, had published a pamphlet entitled *De flagrorum usu in re veneria* which, despite its appearance of being a spoof in the style of Rabelais, was a serious analysis of classical and humanist writers on the subject. An English translation by George Sewell, *A Treatise of the Use of Flogging in Venereal Affairs. Also of the office of the Loins and Reins* was published in 1718 by Edmund Curll: in 1725, when Curll was prosecuted for publishing various obscene works, *A Treatise of the Use of Flogging* was included among the offending titles. It was reprinted for clandestine circulation in 1761. The book's status as a collector's item is indicated by the number of Latin editions issued in the eighteenth century. A Paris edition of the Latin text of 1757 had the imprint 'Londini, 1665' and another edition with the imprint 'Londini, 1770' was probably also the work of a continental printer, but there was also a genuine London edition of the Latin text in 1784. A French translation appeared in 1792: what appears to have been the fourth edition of this version, printed at Besançon in 1801, also had a false London imprint. It seems that flagellation was already identified on the continent as an English speciality.[28]

The standard explanation of flagellation's popularity with the English upper-classes, that one acquires a taste for it from being caned at Public School, dates at least from the reign of Charles II: in Thomas Shadwell's play *The Virtuoso* (1676) Snarl says, 'I was so us'd to't at *Westminster*-School I cou'd never leave it off since.' (Richard Busby, headmaster of Westminster School from 1638 to 1695, obtained such legendary fame for his predilection for flogging his pupils that he is alluded to on the title page of a flagellationist pamphlet of the 1800s, *Manon La Fouetteuse: or, the Quintessence of Birch Discipline. Translated from the French by Rebecca Birch,*

late teacher at Mrs Busby's Young Ladies' Boarding School.) Flagellation is mentioned as a recourse for the impotent in John
Armstrong's *The Oeconomy of Love*:

> Thence what desperate Toil
> By Flagellation and the rage of Blows,
> To rouse the *Venus* loitering in his Veins!

and it is described in *Fanny Hill*, but pornographic works dealing
primarily with flagellation – including women whipping other
women – seem to have begun to circulate only in the 1770s. *The
Exhibition of Female Flagellants* probably dates from 1777 and Part
the Second of the same from 1785: in the latter an introductory letter
by Philopodex ('arse lover') states, 'to see the representation of an
agreeable young Lady having her petticoats pulled up, and her
pretty pouting Backside laid bare, is amusing enough'. The 1793
edition of *The Exhibition of Female Flagellants* was apparently
printed at the expense of Theresa Berkley, whose establishment,
latterly at 28 Charlotte Street, Portland Place, London, made her
queen of the profession. A reprint of *Venus School Mistress, or,
Birchen Sports* issued apparently in the late 1830s – the first
printing had been *circa* 1808 – contained a respectful account 'of the
late Mrs Berkley'. Another noted madam of a London flagellation
parlour was Mrs Collett, at Tavistock Court, Covent Garden, later
at Portland Place, and ultimately at Bedford Street, Russell Square,
who was allegedly patronised by King George IV. Other people
found flagellationist delights in institutions established for other
purposes, notably schools. *The Cherub: or, Guardian of Female
Innocence* (1792) recounts how an 'old debilitated Croesus, of Broad-
street' had an arrangement with the mistresses of two girls'
boarding schools, one near Hackney, the other near Stratford (now
in the London Borough of Newham). When girls were to be punished
he would hide in a closet, would watch the girls being 'flogged upon
their bare posteriors', and would eventually emerge from hiding
to have a closer look with his pocket glass and to deliver the final
couple of blows: the girls would be unable to detect his presence
because, while being beaten, they were 'stretched upon a long low
table, made for the purpose'. In 1816 there was a notable scandal
when General Sir Eyre Coote KB was found to have been paying
1/6d or 2/- to fifteen- or sixteen-year-old boys at Christ's Hospital,
first to let him beat them, and then to beat him. Although one

pupil testified that after Coote gave him six stripes with a cane, he also 'gave me two slaps on the backside with his bare hand', and although one of the boys involved had the unusual forename Paulette, it does not seem that there was any more conventional homosexual intent: but despite a testimonial signed by the Director of the General Army Medical Board, several peers and MPs, and other respectable gentry, stating that from their knowledge of Coote his behaviour 'proceeded from insanity alone, and therefore they cannot impute it to any vicious or criminal intention or propensity whatever', he was struck off the Army List and stripped of his Knighthood of the Bath.[29]

The first heyday of the flagellation parlours was also the period in which prosecutions for sodomy became more numerous, as will be described in a later chapter. For the moment it may suffice to suggest that buttocks were becoming a valued sexual feature, which in earlier days with bustles and hoops and front-to-front sex they may not have been. Even a clandestinely circulated pornographic novel like *Fanny Hill* might contribute to this process:

> She presented a full back view of her person, naked to the waist. Her posteriors, plump, smooth, and prominent, form'd luxuriant tracts of animated snow, that splendidly filled the eye … Sometimes he took his hands from the semi-globes of her bosom, and transferred the pressure of them to those larger ones, the present subjects of his soft blockade, which he squeez'd, grasp'd and play'd with, till –

The chronology is not easy to sort out but it does seem that during the eighteenth century women's bodies as a whole, and previously undervalued parts of them, were acquiring a new significance as erotic objects. How far this involved any degree of sexual or moral or social liberation for women will be discussed in the next two chapters.[30]

2

The Waning of Female Lust

Until the first half of the eighteenth century it was generally assumed that sexual appetite was stronger in women than in men. In his essay 'On some verses of Virgil' Montaigne cited classical authorities on this point and recounted the story of the Queen of Aragon, to whom a Catalan woman once complained of 'the too assiduous efforts of her husband':

> after mature deliberation with her council, this good queen, to give for all time a rule and example of the moderation and modesty required in a just marriage, ordained as the legitimate and necessary limit the number of six a day, relinquishing and giving up much of the need and desire of her sex, in order, she said, to establish an easy and consequently permanent and immutable formula.

In London and among the scholars of Oxford in the mid-sixteenth century it was commonly said of women, 'though they be the weaker vessels, yet they will overcome two, three or four men in the satisfying of their carnal appetites'. Giovanni Benedetto Sinibaldi, part of whose *Geneanthropeia* of 1642 was published in English in 1657 under the title *Rare Verities. The Cabinet of Venus Unlocked and Her Secrets laid open*, noted that 'Caelius Rodiginus thinks (and that upon good grounds) that a woman is ten times more inclined to, and delighted in copulation than a man', and that 'A Woman swelling with lust is not easily satisfied, for the tasting of those sweets makes her the more desirous of them', though he also suggested that 'Women are more lustful in the Summer, but Men in the Winter'. Sinibaldi had a wider circulation on the continent than in England, but an English-language abridgement of Nicolas Venette's *Tableau de l'amour consideré dans l'estat du mariage* of 1687, a work based partly on *Geneanthropeia*, became a bestseller under the title *Conjugal Love Reveal'd*. The ninth chapter of the English version (corresponding to Part II, Chapter IV, Article III of the French original) was devoted to the question 'Which is the most Amorous, the Man or the Woman?' and claimed:

> Women are by far more lascivious and more amorous than Men ... as Sparrows do not live long, because they are too hot, and too susceptible of Love, so Women last less time; because they have a devouring heat that consumes them by degrees.

This did not, of course, imply any superiority, as was explained with another simile: 'their Passion is more violent, and their Pleasure of longer continuance, as Fire kept in green Wood, through the weakness and fickleness of their Judgement.'[1]

Because they accepted the premise of women's lustfulness, both the expert medical opinion and the folklore of the time seem more modern in their understanding of female sexual responses than the orthodoxy established in the nineteenth century. The female orgasm (though originally conceived as an ejaculation similar to that of the male) was considered to be normal: the Spanish Jesuit Tomás Sánchez (1550-1610), whose *Disputationum de sancto matrimonii sacramento* went through more than thirty editions between 1605 and 1754, even discussed the question whether it was permissible for two lovers to achieve orgasm at different moments: though indeed the idea that women produced a seminal emission similar to that of men was going out of favour by 1700. There was also a general recognition of the role of the clitoris in female sexual response: according to *Conjugal Love Reveal'd*: 'There Nature has placed the seat of Pleasure and Lust ... there is Leachery and Lasciviousness established', or, as Bernard Mandeville put it, 'all our late Discoveries, in Anatomy, can find no other Use for the *Clitoris*, but to whet the Female Desire by its frequent Erections'.[2]

In a culture that frowned on extra-marital sexual activity by women this acknowledgement of their natural sexual appetites must have fostered women's confidence in their own sexual responsiveness within marriage, but wives who lacked notable enthusiasm for love-making are unlikely to have been exceptional. Fears of pregnancy, discomfort caused by vaginal infections, physical distaste for a husband chosen because of social and financial pressures rather than on account of his personal attractiveness, male selfishness and lack of consideration, the unrecognised or unacknowledged peculiarities of individual sexual needs, are frequent reasons for unsatisfactory sexual relationships in the twentieth century, and if anything such factors must have operated with even more force three hundred years ago. The stereotype of the sexually voracious female, like any other stereotype, was as much a denial as a recognition.

It is not the intention here to examine the origin and evolution of this belief. Coelius Rhodiginus and Montaigne in the sixteenth century had already traced it back to classical antiquity but, since one of the themes of this book is the changes in ideas about sex in the century or so after 1700, it would be inconsistent to assume that beliefs about the sexual voraciousness of women were constant and immutable across the whole spectrum of ethnic cultures comprising European civilisation for the two millennia before 1700. Such beliefs might derive from fear of women, disapproval of possible signs of independent will, or suspicions of female fidelity – Montaigne suggested that sexual continence had come to be regarded as particularly the duty of the female precisely because of the belief in her greater appetite, but this may have been simply a reversal of the sequence of connection in men's minds, a not unusual psychological process. These beliefs may have had something to do with male uncertainties about the quality of their own performance in bed – this seems implied by a passage in *Conjugal Love Reveal'd*:

> how can a Man be fit to do his Duty, in regard of his Affairs Domestick and Foreign, after being exhausted in excess of Conjugal Embraces? ... The Man has far greater Occasion than the Woman to excuse himself from the Duty of Wedlock.

They might derive from the diminished status of women in classical times, reinforced by the misogyny of medieval Catholicism. Whatever the origin of the doctrine of female lustfulness, the fact is that it was strongly entrenched as late as the third decade of the eighteenth century, when, quite rapidly, it gave way to the opposite conviction.[3]

*

At some point in the 1730s there appeared a revised edition of a medical manual, *The Ladies Physical Directory*, which had first appeared in 1716. The amended text rejected the notion that 'in celebrating the Rites of Love a Woman is too many for a Man, and capable of tiring him quite down', though it pointed out that women,

because taking longer to arouse, and in many cases being pene-
trated before they were quite ready, often remained unsatisfied
after 'a frequent Repetition of such imperfect Enjoyments'. The
anonymous author was categorical in dismissing the earlier orthodoxy regarding women's greater sexual appetites:

> This silly Notion seems to infer that Women are warmer in their
> Nature, or more desirous than Men, which is absolutely false in Fact,
> for as the *Female Sex* are of a finer Make, more tender Constitution,
> and much weaker in Body [they are] of a much colder Temperature
> than Men, and of course much less inclin'd to Venery than the Male
> Sex are; nor are they able to bear Coition (to full Satisfaction) half so
> often as Men.[4]

Nothing could be more subterranean than shifts in popularly held
prejudices. It seems unlikely that *The Ladies Physical Directory*
invented a new view of female sexuality: and it is even less likely
that it helped materially to disseminate this view, for despite at
least eight editions the book had a relatively limited circulation: all
surviving editions state on the title page that it is 'sold ... at the
gentlewoman's at the Two Blue Posts' – the eighth and probably last
edition says 'sold ... only at the gentlewoman's at the Two Blue
Posts' – which suggests that it was printed and offered for sale as
part of the business of some otherwise unknown pioneer sex-coun-
sellor, and would therefore have come directly into the hands of no
one outside her circle of clients. And while the 1742 edition is the
last known printing of *The Ladies Physical Directory*, Venette's
Conjugal Love Reveal'd, disseminating the contrary view of
women's sexual drives, continued to be reprinted: a version retitled
Conjugal Love; or the Pleasures of the Marriage Bed, purportedly
the twentieth edition, came out *circa* 1750. One might also mention
an unpublished essay preserved in Edinburgh University Library,
written about 1761 by Robert Wallace, a royal chaplain and former
Moderator of the General Assembly of the Church of Scotland, which
states:

> by a false, unnecessary, unnaturall refinement some would deny that
> there is any lust in modest women & virgins, whereas every woman
> during certain seasons and a certain period of life is incited to lust &
> would gladly suffer the Venereal commerce with the other sex, unless
> there is something uncommon in her constitution or she is sickly and
> under a bad habit of body ... the most bashfull virgin or chastest

matron has often more lust or inclination to Venery than the greatest prostitute, who often has an aversion to her trade & only consents & submits to the drudgery of the Act in the view of money.

But perhaps the main point about Wallace's essay was that he decided not to publish it. Possibly he recognised how much it was out of tune with prejudices that had been establishing themselves during the previous two decades.[5]

By 1789 another Scots worthy, Dr Robert Couper, was writing: 'To many women, the embraces of the male are extremely, perhaps completely, indifferent, and to some they are disagreeable; yet even these women were prolific.' But it seems that even this was not quite clear or forceful enough: by 1797 Couper had altered the phrasing to: 'It is well known, that to many women the embraces of the male are extremely, perhaps completely, indifferent, and to some they are even disagreeable.' In 1812 an English writer (not it seems medically qualified) stated:

the libertine is fond of inculcating the notion that all women are by nature libidinous ... on the contrary, all women would be chaste, if they were not corrupted by men, or their imaginations polluted by the loose conversation and filthy enticements of depraved women.

In their natural, uncontaminated state, it was supposed that women would avoid libidinous promptings almost by a reflex process, as the poet Coleridge explained:

a virtuous woman will *not* consciously feel what she ought not, because she is ever on the alert to dicountenance and suppress the very embryos of Thoughts not strictly justifiable, so as to prevent them remaining long enough in their transit over her mind to be even remembered.

Perhaps the classic statement of this point of view appeared in *The Westminster Review* in 1850, somewhat after our period, but worth quoting for its patient elaboration of what would nowadays be regarded as complete nonsense:

In men, in general, the sexual desire is inherent and spontaneous, and belongs to the condition of puberty. In the other sex, the desire is dormant, if not non-existent, till excited; always till excited by undue familiarities; almost always till excited by actual intercourse. Those feelings which coarse and licentious minds are so ready to attribute to girls, are almost invariably *consequences*. Women whose position and education have protected them from exciting causes, constantly pass through life without ever being cognizant of the promptings of the senses. Happy for them that it is so! We do not mean to say that uneasiness may not be felt – that health may not sometimes suffer; but there is no consciousness of the cause. Among all the higher and middle-classes, and, to a greater extent than would commonly be believed, among the lower classes also, where they either come of virtuous parents, or have been carefully brought up, this may be affirmed as a general fact. Were it not for this kind decision of nature, which, in England, has been assisted by that correctness of feeling which pervades our education, the consequences would, we believe, be frightful. If the passions of women were ready, strong, and spontaneous, in a degree even remotely approaching the form they assume in the coarser sex, there can be little doubt that sexual irregularities would reach a height, of which, at present, we have happily no conception. Imagine for a moment, the sufferings and struggles the virtuous among them would, on that supposition, have to undergo, in a country where, to hundreds of thousands marriage is impossible, and to hundreds of thousands more, is postponed till the period of youth is passed; and where modesty, decency, and honour, alike preclude them from that indulgence which men practise without restraint or shame. No! Nature has laid many heavy burdens on the delicate shoulders of the weaker sex: let us rejoice that this at least is spared them.[6]

After about 1740 the only situation in which women were represented as enthusiastic about sex was in pornographic fiction. In the seventeenth century, when normal women were thought to be at least as libidinous as men, it was possible for sexually knowing men to admit the likelihood that prostitutes faked their enthusiasm. Thus in *The Whore's Rhetorick* of 1683 the (male) authors have the brothel madam advise the novice tart:

let your caresses, and ecstasies be sometimes inclining to violent, sometimes slow and remiss; but still such as may seem natural, without any artificial constraint, that so he may believe you ravished beyond your self; and be thought, not only to feed him with your body, but to have given him likewise your very Soul.

Sixty or seventy years later, when a great deal of openly published fiction was based on the premise that women were naturally chaste and virtuous, the kind of literature that had to be peddled surreptitiously was full of young girls perpetually ready and eager for intercourse and easily brought to orgasm. Even the still-virgin Tonzenie, in *A New Atlantis for the Year One thousand seven hundred and Fifty-eight*, masturbates with a dildo through which 'her French maid, well skilled in such practices, would in the moment of rapture, dart a warm injection'. Orgasm is described in *Fanny Hill* as 'the melting swoon', when, 'whilst in the convulsive grasp of it, [I] drew from him such a plenteous bedewal, as, join'd to my own effusion, perfectly floated those parts'; *The Genuine and Remarkable Amours of the Celebrated Author Peter Aretin* refers to 'the critical minute' or 'critical period', when 'nectar gushed forth in streams to mingle in one flood'. Medical experts, however, did not refer to orgasm at all, though Dr Robert Couper did admit with evident pain, and only with regard to a contingent possibility, 'it is proper that the animal instinct, which prompts the reproduction of the species, should not be disappointed in its gratification; however brutal these sensations may appear to the purified philosopher'.[7]

The corollary of the belief that normal women did not enjoy sex was that women who enjoyed sex were not normal, and the term *nymphomania* came into use to describe the medical disorder they were suffering from. The term first appears in post-classical times in *A Treatise on all the Diseases Incident to Women*, an unauthorised edition, in English, of lectures given in Paris by a leading French physician, Jean Astruc. This work, published in 1743, states that 'The Antients called this Affection *Nymphomania*, thinking that the *Clitoris*, which they called *Nympha*, was its only seat'. Astruc himself preferred the terms *Furor Uterinus* or *Metromania* and in the authorised version of his work, published in Paris in 1761 and in English translation, as *A Treatise on the Diseases of Women*, in London 1762, he wrote that he had the authority of later classical authors for '*Nymphomania*, which means the mania of the clitoris ... or *Erotomania*; which is *Mania amoris*. But we have avoided employing these terms because they are not received into common use.' *Nymphomania* was, however, adopted as the principal term in a medical manual written in Latin, entitled *Synopsis Nosologiae Methodicae*, by William Cullen MD, published at Edinburgh in 1769: metromania, and also hysteromania, theligonia, nymphotomania, andromonia, nymphocluia and entelipathia being offered merely as synonyms. Then in 1771 a French doctor named J.D.T. Bienville published a work entitled *La Nymphomanie, ou Traité de la fureur uterine*. This appeared in an English translation, by Edward Sloane Wilmot MD, as *Nymphomania, or, a Dissertation*

Concerning the Furor Uterinus, in 1775. In his Preface Bienville commented, perhaps a little ironically, on the fact that in Astruc's authorised French text of 1761 the relevant chapter had been written in Latin:

> The celebrated *Astruc*, at the end of his treatise *des maladies des femmes*, hath given us a short Latin essay, which seems to have escaped, with difficulty, from the modesty of his learned pen; he hath written in this language, in order to conceal his sentiments from the eyes of the vulgar, and to impart them only to enlightened readers.

But Astruc's modesty was most convenient for Bienville as it enabled him to pass off Astruc's research as his own. The discussion of classical authorities was paraphrased from the 1761 text of Astruc's work, and Astruc's sober account of the symptoms of the complaint was simply reproduced in more highly-coloured language:

> They perpetually dishonor themselves in secret by habitual pollutions, of which they are themselves the unfortunate agents, until they have openly passed the bounds of modesty, but when impudence enlists itself on their side, they are no longer fearful of procuring this dreadful, and detestable pleasure from the assisting hand of a stranger ...
> ... soon the excess of their lust having exhausted all their power of contending against it, they throw off the restraining, honorable yoke of delicacy, and, without a blush, openly sollicit in the most criminal, and abandoned language, the first-comers to gratify their insatiable desires.

Bienville's book, though not precisely a best-seller in English, established itself as a medical classic, cited, for example, as an authority in Alex P. Buchan MD's *Venus Sine Concubitu* of 1818; an abridged version appeared as late as 1840 under the title *Nymphomania!* Though the *Critical Review* regarded both Bienville and Wilmot as 'wretched smatterers in physic', they were undoubtedly responsible for establishing the term *nymphomania* in the English language. And, of course, an easily recognisable term made it easier to recognise the complaint referred to. Perhaps Bienville's most interesting remark – adapted, once again, from Astruc – is his confession of surprise that 'the most celebrated writers of antiquity, inhabitants of southern climes', never mention the disorder: it seems not to have occurred to either Astruc or Bienville that doctors in Greek and Roman times, with their different expectations of women, may not have even noticed that the problem existed.[8]

*

Perhaps the most striking evidence of the changing perception of women's sexuality is to be found in contemporary fiction. Leaving aside *Robinson Crusoe* and *Gulliver's Travels*, both of which were quickly marginalised as specifically suitable for children, two of the most popular, and perhaps the two most influential novels of the eighteenth century were *Pamela* and *Clarissa* by Samuel Richardson. The eponymous Pamela is a maid-servant, Clarissa a girl from a genteel family: both are abducted by upper-class males who attempt to rape them. In *Pamela* (1740), the villain finally relents and makes an offer of marriage, which is gladly accepted: in *Clarissa* (1747-8) Lovelace succeeds in violating the heroine, who falls into a decline and dies. Earlier novels had dealt with abduction and rape, notably those of Mrs Eliza Haywood, with her phoney situations, phoney names – Cleomira, Lysander, Alovysa, D'Elmont, Melliora – and her phoney rhetoric:

Melliora: I do Conjure you, even by that Love you plead, before my Honour, I'll resign my Life! Therefore, unless you wish to see me Dead, a Victim to your Cruel, fatal Passion, I beg you to desist, and leave me.

D'Elmont: I cannot – Must not ... what, when I have thee thus! Thus naked in my Arms, Trembling, Defenceless, Yielding, Panting with equal Wishes, thy Love Confest, and every Thought, Desire! What cou'dst thou think if I shou'd leave thee? How justly wou'dst thou scorn my easie Tameness; my Dulness, unworthy of the Name of Lover, or even of Man!

Richardson's leisured, painstaking accounts of men's attempts to bully young women into yielding their favours strike a quite different note. His novels contain many layers of meaning and implication. In both *Pamela* and *Clarissa* the heroines are attracted by the men who lay siege to their virtue. In *Pamela* the eponymous maid-servant is initially flattered by her employer's kindness and, when, after he has abducted and imprisoned her and frequently attempted to assault her, he finally admits that 'I was just upon resolving to defy the Censures of the World, and to make you my wife', she seems to have no difficulty in forgiving his monstrous behaviour:

I found to my Grief before, that my Heart was too partial in his Favour; but *now*, with so much Openness, so much Affection, nay, so much *Honour* too, (which was all I had before doubted, and kept me on the Reserve) I am quite overcome ... Love is not a voluntier Thing.

Some contemporaries – notably Henry Fielding, who wrote a spoof of Richardson's novel entitled *Shamela* – suspected that the moral of Richardson's narrative was that if a poor girl held out against the blandishments and threats of a rich man who merely wanted to sleep with her, there was a good chance he would eventually come across with an offer of marriage and respectability. The sub-title of *Pamela – Virtue Rewarded –* was consonant with this interpretation. In *Clarissa*, it is the heroine's attraction to Lovelace which causes her to place herself in his power, and which provides an additional tension to the account of his attempts to get between her legs. In neither case therefore is the issue a woman's right to reject a lover whom she dislikes. In *Pamela*, after Squire B.'s surprising offer of wedding bells, and throughout *Clarissa*, it is made clear that if lawful marriage is added to physical attraction, then sexual intercourse can go ahead.[9]

Richardson's novels are so rich in psychological and social insight that it seems disappointing to have to conclude that the moral principle which is at the heart of their drama is simply the wrongness of premarital sex. In any case the moral aspect of the extra-marital exploits of the predatory males is given a very secondary importance, in contrast to seventeenth-century discussions of sexual morality which attach equal significance to the continence of men and women. One also notes that in the sixteenth and seventeenth centuries the concepts of female honour and chastity were equally applicable – and, it seems, in practice more frequently applied – to married as distinct from not-yet-married women: Shakespeare's Lucrece, for example, is able to boast

> Immaculate and spotlesse is my mind,

even though she is a wife and mother. In *Pamela* and *Clarissa* on the other hand the question of 'virtue' seems to have narrowed down to a question of virginity.[10]

Male concern for female virginity is another phenomenon that has a long history in western Europe. There is a possibility however that our understanding of the concept of virginity in England in the sixteenth and seventeenth century is coloured by eighteenth-century emphases that have remained embedded in our culture even after two hundred years. Before Richardson a literary scenario that turns on the unmarried and sexually quite innocent status of a heroine is less usual than it became after the 1740s. Perhaps the best-known example is Shakespeare's *Measure for Measure*. Isabella, the play's principal female character, has to be unmarried because she is a novice in a nunnery, and is going to end up marrying the Duke Vincentio, but her objections to sleeping with Angelo, the Duke's deputy, as the price of her brother's life do not seem entirely to relate to her anxiety about her maidenhead as such: in fact one is struck by the lack of consistency in the reasons she gives at various times for not sleeping with Angelo:

> were I under the terms of death,
> Th' impression of keen whips I'd wear as rubies,
> And strip myself to death, as to a bed
> That longing have been sick for, ere I'd yield
> My body up to shame.

> Better it were, a brother died at once,
> Than that a sister, by redeeming him,
> Should die for ever.

> had he twenty heads to tender down,
> On twenty bloody blocks, he'd yield them up
> Before his sister should her body stoop
> To such abhorred pollution:
> Then Isabel live chaste, and brother die:
> More than our brother is our chastity.

I had rather my brother die by the law than my son should be unlawfully born.

In the first passage it is a question of her honour, in the second it is her immortal soul, in the third it is the question of the pollution of her body, in the fourth she is worried about illegitimate offspring. In the 1750s Charlotte Lennox commented, '*Isabella* is a mere Vixen in her Virtue. How she rates her wretched Brother, who gently urges her to save him.' Modern criticism has tended to move away from the unsympathetic view implied by Charlotte Lennox, that Isabella has some sort of neurotic revulsion against sex, and one might, for example, conceive that she is, under extreme pressure, merely saying the first things that come into her head because of her difficulty in finding words to express a more fundamental and more complex conviction: but in any case, whether or not she has a considered moral objection to Angelo's offer of her brother's life in exchange for her virtue, it is clearly not her virginity as such that is at issue.[11]

In Milton's *Comus* (1634) the female protagonist is again unmarried, partly because the masque was written in order to be acted by the Earl of Bridgewater's unmarried daughter and her younger brothers – the story is supposed to have been suggested by the children having been lost at night in a wood, while travelling home from a visit, a short time previously – and partly because of 'The Lady's' role as the very epitome of chastity, an aspect of her character that is underlined by the fact that the defenders of her honour are her two younger brothers, both young enough to be assumed to be themselves quite pure and sexually unawakened: a husband to defend her honour would have introduced a more sexual element. But it is unclear how precisely Comus, an enchanter, son of Bacchus and Circe, apparently the personification of Self-Indulgence, poses a threat to the Lady: it seems he wants her to do something, rather than wanting to do something to her. It is difficult in any case to see Milton's hymn to chastity as relating to the normative sexual behaviour of human beings:

> What was the snakey-headed Gorgon shield
> That wise Minerva wore, unconquered virgin,
> Wherewith she freezed her foes to congealed stone
> But rigid looks of chaste austerity ...

One is uneasily aware that Milton himself probably took the notion of absolute sexual purity seriously at this stage of his life, but even if he was exploiting the opportunities of the highly artificial and unrealistic masque tradition to ventilate some of his private obsessions, his awareness of his audience, and his evident success in giving them what they expected, suggest that it would be unwise to read too much of a narrowly sexual ideology into his highly abstract and allegorical confrontation of virtue and temptation.[12]

It is in the eighteenth century that one detects a growing preoccupation with the act of defloration itself, exemplified equally by a pamphleteer's description of a brothel madam 'Cursing, Rending and Roaring at her Maids and Drawers, to drown the Cries and

Groans of *departing Maidenheads'*, by Lovelace's remark in *Clarissa*, 'is it not very impudent of her to think I will be any man's *successor*? ... I have been always aiming at the merit of a first discoverer', and by John Wilkes' flourishing reference to seeing

> with equal Eye, as God of all,
> The Man just mounting, and the Virgin's fall,
> Prick, cunt, and bollocks in convulsion hurl'd,
> And now a Hymen burst, and now a world.

In some instances the subject merely provided scope for worldly-wise comment:

> Women have naturally a Tenderness and Affection for the Person who spoils them of their Virginity, and there is nothing more common than when they have gratified the Inclinations of the Man they love, to permit him to reiterate them as frequently as he desires, especially if he has exercised himself strenuously.

Such comments implied that the women's complicity involved a degree of sexual appetite, and the novels of Eliza Haywood were sometimes quite unambiguous on this point:

> full of Desires and tender Languishments before, his glowing Touch now dissolv'd my very Soul, and melted every thought to soft Complyance – in short I *suffer'd* – or, rather let me say I could *not* resist his proceeding from one Freedom to another, till there was nothing left for him to ask or me to grant. The guilty Transport past, a thousand Apprehensions all at once invaded me; Remorse and Shame supply'd the Place of Ecstasy ...

But in *Pamela* and *Clarissa* the eponymous heroines are above the promptings of physical urges, and the relationship between Pamela and Squire B., between Clarissa and Lovelace, at first subtle and ambivalent, becomes progressively simpler and starker, till it is reduced to a kind of obsessive ballet in which one character constantly tries to snatch, and the other as constantly tries to preserve, the particular virginity which has become the real protagonist of each book. In an Eliza Haywood novel the contest of wills might be won and lost by p. 22:

> What was now the Distraction of this unhappy Lady, waked from her dream of Vanity to certain ruin! Unavoidable Destruction! She rav'd,

she tore, did all that woman could, but all in vain – In the midst of Shrieks and Tremblings, Cries, Curses, Swoonings, the impatient *Ferdinand* perpetrated his Intent, and finished her Undoing.

Pamela's virtue, on the other hand, stands siege for more than three hundred pages and Clarissa's for most of five volumes.[13]

What was happening was a kind of diminution of sex. The whole physical equipment of female sexuality was reduced to one totem, and that an entity of problematic physical existence – it was realised that not every virgin had an intact hymeneal membrane – and the complexities of female sexual response were reduced to one preliminary act, defloration. Characteristic of this attitude was the practice of referring to female virginity in terms more applicable to a physical, conveyable object. Moll Flanders' remark *circa* 1722, that 'being forsaken of my Virtue, and my Modesty, I had nothing of Value left to recommend me, either to God's Blessing or Man's Assistance', is still on the borderline of metaphor and literal statement, but Pamela already seems to see her virginity as a distinct object with exchange value when she writes, 'to lose the best Jewel, my Virtue, would be poorly recompensed by those you propose to give me', and a contemporary parody of Richardson's novel refers to 'that Jewel, on which all her Hopes of living great in the World depended'. Another favoured simile was of a flower or blossom, as in *Fanny Hill* where 'my virgin flower was yet uncrop'd', though the two images might be used together, as in *The Adventures of a Rake* where the protagonist 'robbed her of her Virgin Treasure, and cropped the Rose that would not bloom again'. Also employed was the more anatomically suggestive metaphor of the mine: 'I was still mistress of that darling treasure, that hidden mine, so eagerly sought after by the men, and which they never dig for, but to destroy', or 'he was a Novice in the Art of working the Maidenhead Mines'. Other forms of real estate were implied in Eliza Haywood's account of the lover who 'ravag'd each sweet charm about her, and left her only the Ruins of a Virgin'. For other writers however the maidenhead was merely a toy: 'the toy you covet.' The term *money* meanwhile became common slang for the private parts of pubescent girls, as in the warning: 'Take care miss, or you will shew your money.'[14]

A moment's reflection will suggest that, if a couple make love repeatedly, the very first time they do so will be overlaid, in memory and in the private mythology of their mutual sexual explorations, by subsequent bouts of love-making. Slightly more problematic is the question of how much satisfaction a woman gives, and receives, on the very first occasion she goes to bed with a man. Some women confess to having been hurt and confused; others boast of having discovered an immediate genius for sexual intercourse. Still, it seems very probable that people who have made love previously perform better, and have more fun, than people who are trying it for the first time. The pleasures of 'a first discoverer', in Lovelace's phrase, almost certainly do not relate to appreciation of the full range of a woman's sexual response. On the other hand, supposing the woman has no capacity for sexual response at all, every experience of making love to her will be about the same, and the first time will therefore be distinguished, partly by being the first, and partly by being the only one necessary to explore the full extent of the woman's sexuality. No subsequent trial would be necessary. 'What would you more?' Antonia asks Ambrosio in *The Monk* after he has raped her. 'Is not my ruin compleated? Am I not undone, undone for ever?' An obsession with defloration was the natural corollary of the denial of women's sexual responsiveness.[15]

Even in clandestinely circulated pornographic works, where the girls are always randy and ready, the authors show a steadfast preoccupation with the loss of virginity: in *Fanny Hill* the main entertainment at the party held to celebrate Fanny's installation as one of the team in a bawdy house consists of the other tarts recalling the first time they had sex, and *A Cabinet of Amorous Curiosities* of 1786, a volume now known only from the description by Henry Ashbee, is made up of a series of separate stories involving defloration under slightly implausible circumstances: two country girls taking their heifer to bull are raped while watching the operation; another village maiden is seduced by a quack who is pretending to explain to her the method used to rob her grandmother, and so on.[16]

Of course it was not always easy to tell if a woman was a virgin or not, as Venette pointed out in his discussion of the question 'If there be any Signs of a Maiden head':

> fris'd and curl'd Hair in the amorous Parts, a moist and open Chink, absence of the Membrane Hymen, flaggy and discolour'd Nymphae [i.e. pendulous and discoloured wrinkles on the labia], the interior of the Womb widened, and the Voice changed is no sufficient Evidence of the Woman's being a Prostitute.

Traditional wisdom, as represented by a chap-book that was notably popular with less educated readers in the provinces, suggested that the answer to the question 'How to know whether a Female be a pure Virgin' was a piece of alabaster, burnt, beaten to powder, sifted through a piece of fine lawn, and slipped into the girl's drink while she was not looking, but among the more sophisticated classes a woman's reputation for chastity generally depended on her ability to maintain an appearance of being entirely uninterested in sex. In 1804 the judge stopped the trial of the brothers Lockhart and Loudoun Gordon, indicted for the abduction of Rachel Lee, illegitimate daughter of Lord Despenser, when the allegedly injured woman stated in evidence:

> in the chaise on the road to Uxbridge, she had said to Loudoun Gordon, that she found it useless to make further resistance, and tearing from her breast a gold locket and a camphire bag, she exclaimed, 'the charm that has preserved my virtue hitherto is dissolved', (adding, as she threw it away) 'now welcome pleasure'.

It seems that it was not merely the suspicion that Rachel Lee had *wanted* to be abducted which disturbed the judge: it was her apparently pleased anticipation of what would happen afterwards. *Now welcome pleasure* was not the kind of thing male judges wanted to hear from women.[17]

3

Seduction

In view of the masculine anxieties which probably lay behind the denial of women's sexuality it is not surprising that the establishment of the new orthodoxy regarding women's lack of libido coincided with a growing obsession with the protection of their sexual purity. The threat to female chastity was seen as having two related forms: an innocent woman might unthinkingly expose herself, without suspecting the sexual implications of a particular situation, or she might be seduced, i.e. somehow persuaded against her real wishes to yield to the sexual importunities of an unscrupulous adventurer. These two dangers were posed, for example, by men-midwives, or accoucheurs, who were subject to an extraordinary outcry in the final third of the eighteenth century.

Part of the objection to male accoucheurs was their excessive – often dangerous – fondness for the obstetric forceps and other newfangled instruments, but the aspect of their practice given most emphasis by critics was the sheer immorality of allowing one's wife to be mauled around in private by another male:

> I desire every man who loves his wife, or regards his own honour, seriously to figure to himself a smart man-midwife, locked into his wife's apartment, lubricating his finger with pomatum, in order to introduce it into his wife's *Vagina*!

Even moving a woman into a different position in her bed was seen as dangerous:

> It is the duty of every *man* in the bloom of life, to call the patient's husband (if not in the room) to do this, in order that his *own* bosom may not be *fired by touching his neighbour's wife* in parts unaffected by the labour pains: for I appeal to husbands to determine, whether *they* could *coolly* walk upon *hot* coals; in other words, whether they could coolly turn, twist, and *touch* a new and beautiful object? And whether the man is lost in the term, *Doctor*?

Any suggestion that women in an advanced state of pregnancy might be less than physically appealing was dismissed with impatience: 'a fine woman ... can appear in no situation, except in the act of death, but such as may stir the most unconquerable of passions.' But the crux of the matter was the impossibility of mere professionalism being stronger than the natural urges of men, especially while carrying out a digital examination: 'Is it possible for a Man *in Health*, to range over a pretty Woman thus – and not be inflamed almost to Madness?!' It was obvious that 'A man once admitted to such a liberty, knows not himself ... If men-midwives under these circumstances stand unmoved, they are a part of the human species I am a stranger to!' In short,

> does the Man's being called, *Doctor* ... obliterate the Idea in *her* Breast – does it obliterate the Idea in *his* – that she is, a Woman – and that he is, a Man? – Can it remove those natural Sensations, to which it is no more in our Power to be insensible, than to add to our Height?[1]

Nor did the danger end there: for once the Doctor's self-control had gone, the disappearance of his patient's self-control would inevitably follow:

> agitated himself, he will *wish to agitate the pretty Woman, who has set all his Pulses in an uproar* – He cannot help it ... he is no longer a free Agent ... Under Pretence that *it is necessary to dilate*, before he can properly decide on her Situation, he may *digitate* ... till infallible Symptoms leave no Room for Doubt, but that *the Lady's free-Agency is as much destroyed, as his own.*

It was reported that there had been several prosecutions of 'these Touching Gentry': in fact there had been a couple of prosecutions which had failed, but even after more than fifty years references were made to the two doctors having been 'tried for ravishing their obstetric patients'. In any case, the damage was not confined to the period of medical attendance. 'When the Lady is recovered, can he look at her, *without remembering her Person, and the Liberties she permitted him to take with it*?' John Blunt, who described himself as 'A Student Under Different Teachers, but not a practitioner of the art', had heard accoucheurs talking about 'the hidden charms of their *fair* patients to their pot companions'. And the effect on the woman might be even more lasting:

Accustomed to the licentious Familiarities of *one* Man, (not her Husband) a *Path* has not only been *opened*, but made smooth, and easy for another ... What is it to me whether my Wife has been polluted by her Midwife-Doctor in her Dressing-Room – or by a Libertine, in a Bagnio?[2]

A frequently cited objection to the employment of male accoucheurs was that it was a custom imported from the continent. The defenders of English virtue were generally more than ready to denounce foreign influences: '*Lascivious* Dances', for example, 'are *out of Character*, in England, and fit only for the *Levity* of France.' John Blunt posed the question:

is it more incumbent on us to teach our daughters to understand the fulsome flattery of a Frenchman, to shine in a ballroom so as to attract the attention of a seducer; or to play an Italian air on the harpsichord? ... [or] to teach them ... how to preserve their own life and health ...?

This xenophobia was of course reinforced by the French Revolution and the outbreak of war with the French Republic, and William Windham, a highly respected politician of the day, even argued that the virtue of English womenfolk would be placed at risk by making peace with the French Revolutionists:

I cannot but imagine to myself the circumstances of one of the Regicides and Septembrizers opening his house in London as Ambassador of the Republick and finding it crowded (as he certainly will) by the Wives and Daughters of the first nobility and Gentry of the Country; who will be initiated there in the doctrines of Revolutionary Morality; and be ready to take lessons in the practice from the numberless able and agreeable professors, who will attend there for that purpose.

Another commentator drew a suggestive parallel between the conduct of male accoucheurs and that of the Catholic clergy, whose sexual adventurism in Spain, France and Italy had long been a by-word among the Protestant Anglo-Saxons:

Many of these modest-looking doctors, inflamed with thoughts of the well-shaped bodies of the women they have delivered, handled, hung over for hours, secretly glorying on the privilege, have to their patients, as priests to their penitents, pressed for accommodation: and driven to adultery and madness, where they were thought most innocently occupied.

Clearly the sexual paranoia of the time was merely one aspect of a
general culture of anxiety that also expressed itself in the political
and ecclesiastical sphere. We shall return to this question later.[3]

*

'It is a melancholy reflection that infidelities are much more frequent among people of elevated rank, than those of less exalted
station', wrote a pamphleteer in 1785. They were certainly much
better publicised. At this period the only means of obtaining a
divorce that would permit remarriage was by private Act of Parliament, usually preceded by a trial for criminal conversation which
would prove in court the guilt of the party to be divorced – who, as
the law then stood, could only be the wife. Both parts of the process
were expensive so that only the rich could afford to end their
marriages in this way. Contemporaries exclaimed at the frequency
of divorces, though in fact they averaged fewer than three a year
except in the 1790s when they averaged 4.3 a year. A criminal
conversation suit consisted of a husband prosecuting another man
for damages on account of his adultery with the prosecutor's wife:
women, even if they could afford to, were not entitled to prosecute
other women for adultery with their husbands, and the general legal
opinion was that:

> Forgiveness on the part of a wife, especially with a large family, in
> the hopes of reclaiming her husband is meritorious; while a similar
> forgiveness on the part of the husband would be degrading and
> dishonourable.

The evidence produced in crim. con. trials was widely publicised, in
newspapers and pamphlets, but it seems that a significant number
among the social classes that were financially in a position to afford
crim. con. suits and private Acts of Parliament were considerably
less worried by questions of marital fidelity than most of their fellow
countrymen. We find for example that the Duchess of Devonshire
was quite open in having an affair with Charles Grey, later the
second Earl Grey, prime minister 1830-34, and that the Duke of
Devonshire meanwhile had an affair with Lady Elizabeth Foster,
whom he married after his first duchess's death. The sister of
Charles Grey's duchess, the Countess of Bessborough, had an affair
with Lord Granville Leveson, who later married her niece. The

Countess of Bessborough's daughter by the Earl of Bessborough,
Lady Caroline, married the Hon. William Lamb and had a well-
publicised affair with Lord Byron. Lamb, when he became prime
minister (as Lord Melbourne) probably did *not* have an affair with
the Hon. Mrs George Norton, but her husband sued for crim. con.
nonetheless. Lamb's sister, Emily, Countess Cowper, had a long-
standing affair with Melbourne's cabinet colleague Lord
Palmerston, whom she eventually married after burying Earl Cowper. The illegitimate offspring of such relationships, though rarely
provided with any considerable share of the family properties, were
not necessarily social outcasts. In 1824 the Countess of Bessborough's daughter by Lord Granville Leveson, Harriet Arundel
Stewart, married George Godolphin, afterwards eighth Duke of Leeds,
at the British Embassy in Paris, Lord Granville being at that time the
ambassador. Robert Montagu, one of Martha Reay's sons by the Earl
of Sandwich, became a full admiral, and of the two illegitimate sons
of the Hon. Edmund Nugent (himself the son of a viscount) one,
Charles Edmund Nugent, became Admiral of the Fleet and the other,
George Nugent, became a field marshal. George III refused
Knighthoods of the Bath to both George Nugent and General William
Keppel (son of a younger brother of the third Earl of Albemarle) on the
grounds of their illegitimacy, but the less squeamish Prince Regent
granted them this honour in 1813. The Prince Regent's eventual
successor, William IV, even made his eldest illegitimate son an earl.[4]

The runaway marriage also obtained a degree of acceptability.
Gretna Green became a popular locale for marriages without paren-
tal consent in the second half of the eighteenth century, after the
tightening up of legal requirements effectively curbed clandestine
marriages in England. Scottish law regarded mutual declarations
in front of witnesses as a legal marriage, and Gretna was conven-
iently close to the most accessible part of the border. Joseph Paisley,
the 'parson' at Gretna 1753-1810 (popularly characterised as the
village blacksmith, but only because of his practical endorsement of
the proverb 'strike while the iron is hot') made a regular trade of
Scots marriages. In 1810 Robert Elliott, the husband of Paisley's
granddaughter, took over the business and by 1839 had married, he
claimed, over 3,000 couples in a specially reserved wedding room at
the local inn, with a bedroom for consummating the marriage right
next door. Among the couples wedded by Paisley were the Earl and
Countess of Westmorland: the Earl was one of three members of the
cabinet in office 1807-12 who had married their wives after success-

ful elopements, the other two being Lord Eldon, the Lord Chancellor, and Spencer Perceval, Chancellor of the Exchequer, later prime minister. Lord Erskine, Lord Chancellor in the previous government, was married twice at Gretna Green: the first time, a genuine runaway match, when he was twenty in 1770, the second time in 1818 when he turned up disguised as an old woman to marry his housekeeper, hoping thereby to elude the vigilance and vengeance of a young lady who was threatening to sue him for breach of promise.[5]

*

These adventurous goings on were not however exactly typical of English social customs, more an indication of the increasing moral and psychological isolation of the governing classes. Among the much more numerous middling classes the actual number of individuals involved in elopement, adultery and the procreation of bastards was almost certainly greater than among the aristocracy, but little publicised, and such behaviour was becoming increasingly marginalised as exceptional, irregular and socially unacceptable.

The marginalisation of sexual immorality advanced in step with the increase of masculine nervousness regarding female frailty. The combined process may be observed even in successive editions of the eighteenth century's most popular handbook on pregnancy and childbirth, *Aristotle's Master-piece*. The first edition of 1684 had printed a certain amount of nonsense about what happened to fertile women when they were denied sexual intercourse:

> the Seed derogates to a venomous quality; and from the effects thereof arise the Swarth and Weasel Colour in Maids, when they begin to be in Love, and desirous of Copulation; as also their short Breathings, Tremblings, and Pantings of the Heart.

The second edition of 1690 simplified this to:

> a due Use of these Enjoyments being deny'd to Virgins, very often produces very dismal Effects, as green and Weasel-Colour, short Breathings, Tremblings of the Heart.

This was the text followed till 1728 when a further amendment was introduced:

And the Use of these so much desir'd Enjoyments being deny'd to
Virgins is often follow'd by very dangerous and sometimes dismal
Consequences, precipitating them into those Follies that may bring
an indelible Stain upon their Families, or else it brings upon them
Green-sickness, or other Diseases.

'Follies that may bring an indelible Stain upon their Families'
undoubtedly refers to elopement with, or becoming pregnant by, an
unsuitable lover.[6]

The problem of seduced maidens had been discussed by Samuel
Johnson, in an article in *The Rambler* which was quickly reprinted in
the larger-circulation *The Gentleman's Magazine*, in 1751, but it seems
to have owed its popularity as a topic of discourse, and as a subject for
outpourings of moral outrage, to literary fashion. Oliver Goldsmith's
best-selling novel *The Vicar of Wakefield* of 1766 featured a daughter
who runs off with a heartless squire but is reconciled to her grieving
family after 'the monster had the assurance to offer me to a young
Baronet of his acquaintance'. Henry Mackenzie's *The Man of Feeling*
of 1771, also a major success with the public, contained a classic
account of a girl who is seduced, abandoned and driven to prostitution.
Both novels were key texts in the fashion of sentimentality which
prevailed during the 1770s and 1780s, a phenomenon that owed
something to Rousseau but much more to the consolidation of a
leisured middle class whose womenfolk, in particular, had little to
do, apart from giving instructions to household servants, besides
read, write and worry. Oddly enough, though the audience for
pronouncements on the topic of seduction seems to have been identified as largely female, the individuals making the pronouncements
seem to have been predominantly male. Most women writers seem
to have steered clear of the subject of sex, and the few who did not
seemed inclined to suggest aspects of the topic which would not
quite fit into the consensual view that was being established on the
subject. Thus Mary Wollstonecraft's posthumously published novel
The Wrongs of Women has a character who, as a servant girl raped
by her master, complains, 'I have since read in novels of the blandishments of seduction, but I had not even the pleasure of being
enticed into vice', and Elizabeth Inchbald's *Nature and Art* (1796)
which, anticipating Tolstoy's *Resurrection*, shows a judge trying a
woman whose life of crime stemmed from his having seduced her as
a young man, focuses more on the issue of the man's moral corruption. Male writers preferred to stress the plight of the seduced

females and the anguish of their parents – usually, by coincidence,
their fathers. Not that the emphasis on fathers was purely a literary
convention, for it was legally possible (though not very common) for
an outraged father to sue his daughter's seducer for damages, in
respect of the loss that the father, rather than the daughter, was
deemed to have suffered. In one such case the barrister retained by
the father argued:

> She was now not of a shilling value – she was worse than valueless
> – but this constituted the very claim of a heartbroken parent, mourn-
> ing over the ruin of his child. He [the counsel for the plaintiff] asked
> the jury to give – not present value but what she was worth when the
> blessedness of innocence was in her heart, and its blush on her cheek.

In this instance the plaintiff put the value of £500 on his daughter's
innocence: the jury decided to allow him £2.[7]
The emphasis on the seduced maiden's family in much of the
literature has led one modern scholar to suggest that the preoccupation with seduction originated in the breakdown of ecclesiastical
sanctions against immorality, which had hitherto tended to protect
the values of the family. The problem might also be seen as arising
from the pressures of an increasingly mobile population at a time
of urbanisation and industrial change. Seduction was seen as specifically a vice of urban society: 'The Seduction of Women is a Crime
so common in the Metropolis of this Kingdom, and daily spreading
its baneful influence so rapidly through every Part', wrote Edward
Relfe, and Hannah Cowley in her poem *The Scottish Village: or
Pitcairne Green*, contemplating the establishment of industrial civilisation in a hitherto unspoilt part of rural Scotland, wondered:

> And shall the mighty woes of hapless love
> Be here unfelt; the heart not here be torn?
> Oh no! in all their violence they'll rove –
> Swains shall betray, and maidens *feel* their scorn.
> Already sure, the dismal sounds I hear,
> The broken vow accus'd, the rending sigh –
> Ah see! the love-lorn stretch'd upon her bier,
> Rent from all joy, she only knew to die!

Young women from the country who had recently arrived in town
in search of employment were seen as especially vulnerable:

> The town being overstock'd with *Harlots*, is entirely owing to those Numbers of *Women-Servants*, incessantly pouring into it from all Corners of the Universe, and those Debaucheries practis'd upon 'em in almost all the Families that entertain them: *Masters, Footmen, Journeymen, Lodgers, Apprentices*, &c are for ever attempting to corrupt; and few young Creatures now-a-days are endow'd with a Stock of Virtue sufficient to hold out against all their Attacks.

The notorious rake Colonel Francis Charteris, who is depicted in the first plate of Hogarth's 'Harlot's Progress' as lurking on the look-out for girls arriving in London from the country, instructed his 'Procurators and Purveyors' to seek out 'none but such as were *strong, lusty, and fresh Country Wenches, of the first size, their B-tt-cks as hard as Cheshire Cheeses, that should make a Dint in a Wooden Chair, and work like a Parish Engine at a Conflagration*'. Charteris evidently had a particular taste for large muscular women: he even initially rejected Sarah Williams, later one of his favourites, because though 'rather above six Foot', he feared '*she seemed not to have Strength or Substance enough to go through the Fatigue of his Business*'. But the main attraction of country girls was less their muscularity than the fact that they did not know their way round a city where there were 'almost countless numbers who were vigilant, artful depredators on the charms of innocence'. In 1801 a group of philanthropists established an 'Institution for Enabling Young Women who have left the Country to get Places in London to return to their Families, so as to prevent them from Vicious Courses', but as late as 1807 there was a riot in Ropemaker Street, near Finsbury Square on the edge of the City of London, after two men lured to a house of ill fame a 'young country girl' who 'innocently told them, that she had come to town in order to get into service, and that she wished very much to be engaged'; on guessing the nature of the premises to which she had been enticed, she screamed for help, attracting a large crowd which stormed the building: 'The furniture was torn to pieces, and not a window was left standing.' But though changes in the structure of employment and of the family no doubt contributed to the sense of a growing problem, a reading of the contemporary literature suggests that there was a great deal in the later eighteenth century's preoccupation with seduction that cannot be explained merely in terms of communal misgivings with regard to new socio-economic conditions.[8]

*

Seduction, defined by one commentator as 'the art of tempting, deceiving, and corrupting', was thought to consist of inducing a young lady to do something she knew to be wrong, in such a way that the moral responsibility and the guilt remained with the seducer: the young lady, though making a decision to co-operate of her own free will, was essentially a victim:

> Unhappy maid, who, innocent as fair,
> A victim falls to dark Seduction's snare,
> She in whose bosom Vice has not effac'd
> The beauteous tints that Virtue's hand had trac'd.

Earlier in the eighteenth century it was assumed that the young woman might simply be carried away by the excitement of the moment working on her natural instincts:

> when Temptation is strong, Desire inflam'd, Youth pressing, and Opportunity inviting, 'tis no easy matter to resist the *critical Minute*, especially when Virtue, which should have guarded, has deserted Love's *Portal*.

What might happen was described convincingly enough in Hugh Kelly's novel *Memoirs of a Magdalen*, published in 1767:

> The extatic tenderness with which she received my embrace entirely destroyed my recollection; and a cursed sopha lying most conveniently ready to assist the purpose of my rashness, I proceeded from liberty to liberty till she was actually undone.

The woman in this case, needless to say, was immediately overcome with shame and remorse, but:

> At last, I succeeded pretty well in re-assuring her: she ventured to look up with an air of some confidence, condescended to play with my fingers, and even once went so far as to honour my hand with her lips – I need scarcely inform you what the consequence was – the tide of passion swelled to its customary height – and every impulse of recollection was again swept away upon the couch.

By 1767 however it was already unusual to admit that a young woman had any sexual passions to arouse, and the emphasis was chiefly on *verbal* persuasion. *The Gentleman's Magazine* suggested that what usually happened was that

> young and inexperienced women ... have been assailed by all the arts of fraud and oratory, allured by personal beauties and accomplishments, deceived by magnificent promises confirmed by the most solemn oaths, and perhaps betrayed by love.

John Moncreiff, probably the first versifier to take up the theme of Johnson's discussion of seduction in *The Rambler* and *The Gentleman's Magazine* in 1751, complained:

> As soon as Beauty's early Blossom blows;
> While yet the Mind nor Fraud nor Falsehood knows;
> By Snares, which scarcely wiser women shun,
> The Novice falls; by specious Snares undone.
> In artful Guise, a Crowd of Foes appear,
> Who buzz Esteem and Passion in her Ear.
> ... Young, open, with a honest Heart,
> She falls a prey to the Seducer's Art;
> To Shews of Honour, which deceitful prove,
> To Rakes, to Sharpers at the Game of Love.

Another writer described seducers as 'cringing, flattering and protesting':

> Thus are you deified for a Time. But for what purpose? That your Votaries may, like the Devil, your grand Deceiver, find your Brain intoxicated, your Passions inflamed, your Reason lost, your Guards dismissed.

The author of *Serious Thoughts on the Miseries of Seduction and Prostitution with a Full Account of the Evils that Produce Them* referred scathingly to 'the honey toned persuasions of a mellifluent tongue, with a ready volubility of words', and the seducer in a poem in 1803 was characterised as

> A base destroyer, on whose tongue
> Poison more rank than Java's hung.

Excessive fluency was clearly something to be wary of: the novelist Eliza Parsons told her readers, 'the air of respect, the awe and faltering tongue characterise the real lover, not the "rattling tongue of saucy eloquence" '.[9]

The idea that seduction was achieved primarily by feats of verbal persuasion obviously focused on the cunning and sinister motivations of those who

> with artful wiles betray,
> And luring Virtue to your guileful snare,
> In ruin plunge the trembling shrinking fair.

An anonymous pamphleteer of 1792 protested:

> One would think it scarcely possible that there would be found in the world, a man so far lost to all sense of justice and honour, as to be capable of forming a deliberate plan to ensnare and ruin an innocent and helpless woman.

In fact the heartless seducer seems to have become a stock character that had an irresistible appeal to the horrified imaginations of late-eighteenth-century readers:

> And did'st thou, barbarous monster! did'st thou dare
> Consign to shame the violated fair;
> To loathsome penury and death consign,
> Her whom thy flattering tongue had call'd, divine?
> Did'st thou not skill and artifice employ,
> To lure the hapless maid, and then destroy?
> What kind persuasion woo'd her soften'd sense,
> What cunning falsehood, and what fair pretense,
> What fond endearments, mingled with the kiss,
> That promis'd constancy, and nuptial bliss!

It was supposed that some of these villains were merely unfeeling cynics: 'To delude a modest virgin, and then brag of it, and turn her upon the town, seems to be a necessary qualification for Admittance into the Society of gay Acquaintance', Edward Relfe noted in 1780, and Harriet in Thomas Holcroft's play *Seduction* (1787) jeers at another character as 'A man of honour among men, the ruin of woman he thinks as necessary to his fame as to his pleasure'. But it was also suggested that seducers were agents of an international conspiracy:

The directors of the nefarious Illuminati were so sensible of the political influence of women, that it was in their particular orders to the devilish emissaries, to use every method possible to undermine the moral rectitude of the fair sex ... From this opinion entertained of womenkind by the Illuminati, I really believe the present vile system of female education has originated.[10]

But of course the archetype of the diabolically cunning male owed much of its appeal to its congruence with the notion of women as weak-headed and in need of male protection:

Is it not most disgraceful and unjust, that when, from ignorance and inexperience, they are totally unequal to cope with the craft of a designing debauchee, they are left an unprotected prey to any man whose lascivious desires their persons excite? Seduced by such under the most captivating professions of affection, under the most solemn vows of constancy, to leave their natural guardians, they are often hurled in a few weeks from plenty to want.

It was not necessarily a question of the victims being ignorant of moral principles or of the facts of life. The pioneer feminist Mary Wollstonecraft claimed that 'many innocent girls become the dupes of a sincere, affectionate heart, and still more are, as it may emphatically be termed, ruined before they know the difference between virtue and vice', but the majority – male – opinion was that women could be easily persuaded to forget the difference between virtue and vice even when they knew it. 'The prudence, the virtue, and the religious education of a young girl are but poor defence, when opposed to the art and cunning, the flattery, and delusive promises of treacherous man', explained one expert: 'modesty, gentleness, good behaviour and even good sense, cannot repel the base insidious arts of systematic seduction', claimed another:

Some tempers are so impotently ductile, that they cannot refuse any thing to repeated solicitations ... The Debauchee's Language is, 'Poor Fool, she loved me, and therefore could refuse me nothing.'[11]

In any case the failure to distinguish between right and wrong was tragically easy: 'Narrow is the boundary frequently between vice and virtue, and a moment may decide her fate and character forever.' Evidently it all happened incredibly rapidly: 'how quick must be the Transition from deluded Virtue to shameless Guilt, and from shameless Guilt to hopeless Wretchedness.' Only very occasionally was there a last-minute reprieve: 'A conscientious man has

been known to lose his powers on finding the woman he was going
to be connected with unexpectedly a virgin.' But generally the
catastrophe simply, somehow, came to pass, for as the poet
Wordsworth wrote:

> The road is dim, the current unperceived
> The weakness painful and most pitiful,
> By which a virtuous woman, in pure youth,
> May be delivered to distress and shame.[12]

*

It seemed obvious to writers on this subject that 'Lawless pleasure
is but a poor and short compensation for the loss of innocence and
character,' and that

> The first period of unhappiness commences from the instant a poor
> girl has yielded to the art of the seducer, when her soul, exhausted
> with the conflict of passion, is suddenly alarmed with terrors of
> detection.

The dishonoured woman's agonised realisation of her irretrievable
loss was a favourite theme. According to one poet:

> From that dire Moment Hell and Horrour rise:
> Peace from her violated Mansion flies.
> Hourly with Sighs the troubled Bosom heaves;
> Which Hope, Life's latest Consolation leaves.
> Succeeds, in chearful Innocence's room,
> An everlasting, a remorseless Gloom.

According to another:

> The miserable victim, now alone,
> Knowing that her honour is for ever gone,
> Bedews with tears the bed of lust and shame,
> And sighing ev'ry breath, her Maker's name.

Having been seduced – or 'ruined', another favoured word – it was
hardly likely that the poor girl could be safely married off. In
Clarissa the eponymous heroine tells Lovelace, 'my Uncle Harlowe
when he knows how I am, will never wish any man to have me', and
Lovelace himself acknowledges, 'there is now but one man in the

world whom she can have – And that is *Me*'. But Anna Rivers, in Eliza Parsons' novel *The Errors of Education*, though grateful that her seducer's mother wishes for their marriage, insists, 'I never would pollute the vows of hymen, nor by the specious name of marriage screen myself from the censure of the world, and give an unworthy daughter to my generous benefactress.' And even seducers might have scruples about marrying the women they had seduced: thus Sir Robert Harold in Hugh Kelly's *Memoirs of a Magdalen*:

> It is to me a fixed principle, that the same woman who suffers even the man she doats upon to distraction, to take advantage of an unguarded moment, will have her unguarded moments with other people – Passion will, in all probability, often supply the want of inclination; and the same warmth of constitution which originally betrayed her into an indiscretion with him, is but too likely to make her guilty of an indiscretion with every body else.

Hugh Kelly, as already noted, may have been a little behind the times in supposing that any normal woman's libido could be on such a hair-trigger, but his basic premise was widely accepted. Ultimately it was not a question of the nature of the ruined woman's error because her intention in the matter was of no relevance in any case. In seduction the guilt remained with the seducer: but the woman was just as much ruined if, instead of being conventionally seduced, she was brutally raped. Thus Antonia, in M.G. Lewis' *The Monk*, having been raped and fatally wounded, with her dying breath tells Lorenzo, her one and only true love:

> had She still been undefiled, She might have lamented the loss of life; But that deprived of honour and branded with shame, Death was to her a blessing. She could not have been his Wife, and that hope being denied her, She resigned herself to the Grave without one sigh of regret.

As a female character in Robert Bage's novel *Mount Henneth* says of her loss of virtue, 'all crimes but this may be expiated: no author has yet been so bold as to permit a lady to live and marry and to be a woman after this stain'. And women were not backward in endorsing the words placed in their mouths by men, possibly because, as one man explained, 'those, who had envied their superior attrac-

tions, are now delighted to point at them with fastidious disdain'.
Miss Hatfield, for example, wrote that after yielding up her virginity

> The unhappy victim, unable to re-gain the sacred path from which
> she once strayed, finds its barriers surrounded by those awful frowns,
> dreadful as the flaming sword that guarded those of Paradise.

Such attitudes were even satirised by Jane Austen in *Pride and
Prejudice* where the sententious Mary Bennet says of the seduction
of her young sister:

> 'we may draw from it this useful lesson; that loss of virtue in a female
> is irretrievable – that one false step involves her in endless ruin –
> that her reputation is no less brittle than it is beautiful ...' Elizabeth
> lifted her eyes in amazement.[13]

But disqualification for marriage was not the worst penalty
suffered by young women who had been 'ruined'. What particularly
worried the various commentators was the supposedly inevitable
progression from seduction to prostitution:

> a deplorable multitude of unhappy females, beautiful and lovely
> daughters, who gladly would have returned, had that been permitted,
> as humble penitents to the bosom of parental clemency, are now
> prowling about the streets.

The heartless seducer would of course quickly abandon his victim:

> Since he I lov'd disdain'd my ermine fame,
> Cropt the young flow'ret of my blooming name,
> And sated, cast my sallied charms aside
> To pine unsweet, unlovely, unallied.

Once separated from the protection of parents or of a respectable
employer, a young woman could soon find herself in a desperate
financial plight:

> Left soon by Poverty, Derision, Shame;
> Oblig'd to prostitute herself for Hire,
> The Sport of Drunkards and of lewd Desire.

The process of destitution would, it was supposed, invariably be
accelerated by 'pregnancy, the natural consequence of the illicit

amour'. In vain did William Hale, on the basis of 'the extensive acquaintance which I have had with the lower orders of society', argue in a pamphlet published in 1809: 'there is not one instance in a hundred of a woman who becomes a prostitute in consequence of seduction, although it is *their constant plea of defence*', in vain did the same William Hale produce a revised statistic in another pamphlet in 1812: 'not one instance in a thousand of a *virtuous* woman who becomes a prostitute in consequence of seduction'; the stereotype of the young woman who sinks through the intermediate stages from seduction to streetwalking was altogether too persuasive:

> Cast off from him by whom she was undone,
> Behold the course of Sorrow, she must Run;
> Compell'd to drudge for Bread, in Public Stews –
> When lo! – Disease and Misery ensues –

One commentator even claimed that 'the perfect impunity with which *Seduction* is allowed to be practised in this country' was a principal cause of prostitution.[14]

Patrick Colquhoun, a metropolitan stipendiary magistrate who was generally acknowledged to be the leading expert on prostitution in London in the 1800s, was sure that streetwalkers were mainly recruited from the lower classes and was able to reassure his genteel readers that

> under the circumstances incident to their situation they cannot be supposed to experience those poignant feelings of distress, which are peculiar to women who have moved in a higher sphere, and who have been better educated.

There was even some notion that seduction was something done by males of better-class families to females of respectable but socially inferior rank. The seduction of a tenant's daughter by the squire, or his son, was a stock scenario that appears in Goldsmith's *The Vicar of Wakefield* of 1766, in an anonymous novel of 1783 that was probably written by a woman, *Female Sensibility; or, the History of Emma Pomfret* (where Mrs Dormer succours a starving girl who reveals that 'though I am the daughter of one of his best tenants, farmer Grove's only child ... 'Squire Dormer, madam, is my cruel seducer'), in a short story by Jane Austen's elder brother Henry, published in 1790, in George Walker's *The Vagabond* of 1799, and even in George Eliot's *Adam Bede* as late as 1859 – the latter novel apparently being based on a real incident in 1802. The young man courting the milkmaid in 'The Bashful Maid', a street ballad of the 1780s, also seems of a superior class:

> HE
> Well met, pretty maid
> Nay don't be afraid
> I mean no mischief I vow:
> Pshaw! what is it you ail?
> Come give me your pail
> And I'll carry it up to your cow.
>
> SHE
> Pray let me alone
> I have hands of my own,
> Nor need yours to help me – forbear!
> How can you persist,
> I won't sir, be kist
> Nor teazed thus – go trifle elsewhere.

The final stanza, and the woodcut of a pair of breeches which illustrates the ballad, sufficiently indicate the sequel. In 'The Milk Maid', a street ballad circulating in Scotland in the 1800s – the British Library has one copy printed at Stirling in 1805 and another printed at Greenock in 1810, though it is probably of English origin – the social status of the young blade who seduces the milkmaid is specified:

> Coming home with my milk, the young 'Squire I met
> Who said, Polly, love, set down your pails ...
> To oblige him, and 'cauoo that I would not be cross
> I presently quitted my pails:
> He pull'd me gently down, in a bed of green moss,
> And kissed me – I should not tell tales.

Of course a literary tradition is not evidence of the frequency with which such liaisons occur, but they do indicate the frequency of people *thinking* they might occur. Samuel Johnson claimed in 1751 that

> Many of the beings which are now rioting in taverns, or shivering in the street, have been corrupted not by acts of gallantry ... but by fear of losing benefits which were never intended, or of incurring resent-

ment which they could not escape; some have been frightened by masters and some have been awed by guardians into ruin.

A similar awareness of the class-dimension was apparent in *The Gentleman's Magazine*'s sarcasm regarding schemes of seduction in 1788: 'Why, such a plan, no doubt would have been disgraceful and infamous to have attempted upon a woman of *rank* and fashion! — but to an ordinary girl, and below one's rank, Lord! where's the harm?' But nearly all the debate about seduction seems to have been on the part of the middle classes, who showed themselves much more concerned for the virtue of their own daughters than for the virtue of the lower-class girls who really did become streetwalkers. One pamphleteer found it absurd that:

> A woman who is entitled to property, either immediately or at her parents' death, is deemed by the law of this land not to be capable of taking proper care of it, until she is twenty-one years of age, but of her virtue she is left completely mistress after twelve.

But perhaps the whole point was that the virtue of teenage girls belonging to families who had no property was of interest to the middle classes only insofar as it touched on their own immediate concerns, as employers and as trustees of charities.[15]

*

Needless to say, little attention was given to the opinion of women who had first-hand experience of being seduced. Perhaps those who were prepared to write about it were inclined to take an inappropriately casual tone in any case:

> I shall not say why and how I became, at the age of fifteen, the mistress of the Earl of Craven. Whether it was love, or the severity of my father, the depravity of my own heart, or the winning arts of the noble lord ... does not now much signify;

or to take undue advantage of the opportunity for covert boasting:

> At the early age of sixteen I fell victim to my own inexperience, and the impassioned solicitations of a man, one of the handsomest and most accomplished of the age;

or to show inappropriate cynicism on the subject of innocent maidens preyed on by conscienceless Lovelaces:

> Notwithstanding all the many melancholy stories told about forlorn run-away maidens by captains, rakes etc., I say many, even of these damsels, have, before their beauish acquaintance, disposed of their first favours to their father's clerks, apprentices, or serving men.

Perhaps the most elaborate discussion of seduction from the woman's point of view is a work entitled *The Victim*, published in 1800, which begins as a temperate examination of the question whether seduction is more heinous than continuing an illicit sexual connection afterwards, for men as well as women, but suddenly changes tack towards the end, and after a highly-coloured account of the writer's anguish at the death of her father, and a reference to 'the remembrance of my degeneracy and guilt!' continues:

> those caresses, which were considered as expressions of fondness, and which your munificence so amply rewarded, were not the result of either attachment or esteem. I was conscious of being neither loved nor respected – that I was retained in finery and in pomp merely to gratify your licentious appetite; and believe me, Sir, in the midst of all my sprightliness and gaiety, I passed a life without endearment, and secretly detested myself for the crimes you basely hired me to commit, and which I had not the virtue to forsake: and had it not been for the death of him whom my vices and ingratitude have hurried to the grave, I should still have remained the slave of caprice and of lust, and have continued to requite your munificence with the semblance of gratitude and rapture, while, from my heart, I detested your embrace,

and finishes with the wish that

> you will remove me from the scenes that have witnessed our atrocities; and where my person and my infamy are equally unknown – that the remainder of my days may be spent in imploring from the benignity of Heaven, that forgiveness without which I am lost for ever!

But the anonymous author of this heart-rending document turns out to have been William Giles, a banker who had established himself as a writer on morality with his bestselling *Guide to Domestic Happiness* more than twenty years earlier. Perhaps significantly one discussion of seduction which was genuinely written by a woman and which was printed in a volume intended as a manual on the raising of teenage daughters dealt with the seduction of a *married* woman, possibly because the seduction of *unmarried* girls was regarded as too explosive a subject to be brought to the attention of teenagers. It was apparently a male author who wrote, 'I do not hesitate to aver, that the seduction of unmarried females is more practised, and more openly practised, in Great Britain, than in any other civilised state in the world.' Whatever the objective realities, the seduction of innocent virgins clearly had an irresistible attraction for the male imagination in this period.[16]

4

Rape

Rape was a much less popular subject of discourse with men than seduction, but though the female victims of rape have left much more testimony on record than the victims of seduction it is generally in the prosaic, almost elliptical language of the witness box:

> he took up my petticoats, unbuttoned his breeches, and put something up the inside of me ... afterwards he gave me a red and white handkerchief to wipe me with ... he put his private parts quite inside me ... I could not make water for five days.

> he took up by petticoats; he put his private parts into me, and when he had done he wiped me with his handkerchief.

> he took me into the parlour, and locked the parlour door; he then *downed* me on the bed, which was in the parlour, and I got up again; then he forced my legs open with violence, and entered my body with violence; after he had his will of me, he wanted me to lay hold of his private parts.

> he threw me down on the bed, and he took and got upon me, and he entered my body, and he hurt me very much indeed, and I tried to halloo out, and he clapped his hands before my mouth, and he told me if I made any disturbance he would cut my throat, and then after he had done he said he wanted some tea and sugar.

Perhaps the hard facts embodied in the judicial statistics are more eloquent, especially when compared with the statistics produced by our own more intensively policed society. Between 1805 and 1818 the courts of England and Wales found 76 men guilty of rape. In the same period, 229 people, men and women, were found guilty of murder. As far as the legal system was concerned, there was only one rape for every three murders. In 1997 the police recorded 650 homicides in England and Wales and 6600 rapes. This works out as 10 rapes for every homicide.[1]

The failure of rape victims to report is a familiar issue. As a result of publicity given to the question in the mid-1980s the number of rapes recorded by the police rose 72.4 per cent between 1984 and 1987, and it is still widely believed that the crime is seriously under-reported. There are several indications that under-reporting was on an even larger scale, percentage-wise, in the early nineteenth century. First of all it was extremely difficult to obtain a conviction: between 1810 and 1818, 63.1 per cent of all persons prosecuted for serious crimes were convicted, but only 17 per cent of persons prosecuted for rape. Nearly half (46.6 per cent) of rape cases never went beyond the preliminary Grand Jury stage, at which prosecution evidence was briefly outlined before the case went forward to trial. Women who claimed to have been raped did not always make convincing witnesses, of course:

Elizabeth Bocock:	They all three ravished me, one after another, whether I would or no, for I desired them to let me alone, but they would not; and I was afraid to cry out, for there were a thousand Men in the House –
Judge:	A thousand Men? Remember you're upon your Oath, and mind what you swear.
Elizabeth Bocock:	I believe there might not be quite a thousand Men, but I am sure there was nine or ten, and they all wanted to ravish me, but I would not let 'em; tho' I don't know but they might have done it too, if Charles Cook had not been so kind as to stand by me, and fight my Way out of the room, for, I'll say that of him, he was a mighty civil Man, though he was one of the three that ravish'd me.
Judge:	But what Resistance did you make?
Elizabeth Bocock:	I did what I could, for when I found they had a Design upon me, I fell down upon my Knees, and told them that I was a poor innocent Girl, that lived at the *Anodyne Necklace*, by *Temple Bar*; but they minded nothing that I could say, for they would not be satisfy'd till they had all three ravish'd me; but I believe in my Conscience that every one of them got me with Child, for I was never so serv'd in all my Days. And I went home and told my Mother, and she put them into the Hands of a *Lawyer*.

But the forensic abilities of alleged rape victims were not the only problem. T.E. Tomlins' *Law Dictionary* (four editions 1797-1835) quoted the bland remark of the great seventeenth-century judge

Matthew Hale: 'though rape is a detestable crime, it is an accusation easily made, and hard to be proved', and it seems that the difficulty with regard to corroborating evidence was the major reason for the number of unsuccessful prosecutions. Prosecutions for assault with intent to commit rape were much more likely to be successful, presumably because a frequent reason why intended rapes failed to proceed beyond the stage of intention was that the victim was assisted by third parties who were available to give evidence against the attacker.

1810-1818	% Convicted	% Acquitted	% No Bill returned by Grand Jury	No. of cases
All crimes	63.1	20.6	16.3	75,081
Rape	17.0	36.4	46.6	283
Assault with intent	61.8	12.5	25.7	272[2]

The number of unsuccessful prosecutions for rape could hardly have been encouragement for potential prosecutors, especially as they had to put up the money for the prosecution themselves – and these costs were refundable only if there was a conviction. In the County Palatine of Durham, with ten prosecutions for rape between 1805 and 1818, the Grand Jury refused to find a true bill in nine cases, and the tenth ended in an acquittal: after that it would have been hardly surprising if Durham rape victims had concluded that their best remedy was to keep quiet, especially if they came from families too poor to afford legal fees.

Moreover though rape was a capital offence – 47 of the 76 men convicted 1805-1818 went to the gallows – it benefited from a certain degree of social acceptance. In 1763 troops had to be sent to prevent the rescue of a condemned rapist due to be executed on Kennington Common. The principle that a woman's previous sexual history was not a relevant issue in a rape prosecution was established in this period, at a judges' meeting in January 1812, but the previous good character of the accused might on occasion lead the judge to recommend a free pardon. And even a custodial sentence did not necessarily involve a lasting stigma. In 1806, for example, Henry St George Tucker, accountant general of Bengal, was convicted in the

Supreme Court at Fort William, Bengal, of assault with intent to commit rape on the wife of one of his closest friends. The judge, Sir Henry Russell, announced, 'we have been guided more by the lenity of the precedents to be found in English Courts than by any circumstances of mitigation in your case', and sentenced Tucker to six months in jail and a 4,000 rupee (i.e. £400) fine. Though he was a controversial and by no means universally popular figure, this disgrace did Tucker no professional harm at all: as soon as he came out of gaol he was appointed to the commission for the settlement of ceded and conquered territories, and in 1808 became a supernumerary member of the Board of Revenue. He eventually became Chairman of the East India Company, which was almost as respectable as being Lord Mayor of London, but more remunerative.[3]

The corollary of social acceptance of men guilty of sexual assaults was communal hostility against persons involved in prosecuting rapists. In 1817, when Thomas Flemings was prosecuted at Bedford Assizes for raping fifteen-year-old Sarah Gardener, a mob of two hundred people gathered outside the Gardeners' house, threw stones and exhibited effigies. It has been suggested that this incident was linked to a case decided at Bedford Assizes a few months previously: the Rev. Robert Woodward, vicar of Harrold, was jailed for two years, and his daughters Sarah and Susannah each for one year, for conspiring to bring a false accusation of rape against James Harris. It seems unlikely however that the exposure of the Woodwards in itself raised doubts as to the truth of Sarah Gardener's claims to have been raped, as the details of the two cases, and the social positions of the protagonists, have nothing in common: it seems more plausible to suppose that the Woodward case simply helped confirm what many people already suspected about individuals who took it upon themselves to forward rape prosecutions.[4]

Another feature of the statistics is the relative frequency of prosecutions for rape on girls below the age of consent, which had been fixed at twelve years as far back as 1275. On the Norfolk circuit between 1805 and 1818, two out of the seven trials for rape involved girls under twelve: the returns subsequently published do not specify the age group of victims in most other parts of the country, but in County Durham, following the ten failed rape prosecutions mentioned previously, a man was sentenced to death for raping a girl under twelve in 1819. It has been calculated that 19 per cent of rape cases heard at the Old Bailey 1730-1830 involved girls under ten, including the case of one of the first blacks to be executed in

England, John Caffin, hanged in August 1817 for raping a seven-year-old. *The Times* had commented on the frequency of such crimes as far back as 1789. There seems to have been a belief current among certain classes that, if one was suffering from venereal disease, the most effective way to get rid of it was to have sex with an uninfected person, to whom it would be automatically passed on, though this could hardly have been the only reason for sexual assaults on very young children. Provided the judge was satisfied that younger rape victims understood the meaning of the oath, their evidence on oath was admissible, but they inevitably made unsatisfactory witnesses, and one notes, for example, that in the winter sessions at the Old Bailey in 1804-1805 the jury acquitted in two separate cases of child-rape. It does seem however that attacks on under-age girls were more likely to lead to prosecution, if reported, than attacks on older women, so that the apparent prominence of child-rape cases is a function of the under-prosecution of sexual attacks on adults.[5]

*

The relative indifference of English society at this period with regard to rape is of course in marked contrast to the excitement aroused by the subject of seduction. The anonymous author of *The Rape: a Poem* (1768) saw seduction as the commendable norm against which the rapist foolishly and tastelessly offended:

> Say, what could prompt a libertine to stray
> From soft persuasions soul-enchanting way:
> Alien to mighty love, why have recourse
> To savage violence and brutal force?

This would hardly have been an acceptable viewpoint a generation later: in fact, while seduction became the subject of innumerable diatribes, rape scarcely figured at all in print. It was certainly not felt to be a suitable subject for novels, despite the precedent of Richardson's *Clarissa*. The most lurid literary rape of the period after 1750 was of Antonia in M.G. Lewis' *The Monk* (1796); the rapist was in holy orders and was also his victim's long-lost brother, the action supposedly took place in a Roman Catholic country, and the novel was widely abused for its salaciousness: clearly it had only an eccentric relation to normative sexual behaviour in the Home Counties. Attempts at rape in novels set in England generally ended in failure. In Robert Bage's *Barham Downs* (1784) the heroine is rescued in the nick of time by a Quaker. In Thomas Holcroft's *Anna St Ives* (1792) Coke Clifton, having kidnapped the heroine, dare not rape her by daylight as he is intimidated by her magnificent virtue: he attempts instead to assault her in the dark but, 'Blundering idiot as I was I had forgotten to remove a chair, and tumbled over it'. One rather feels that Coke Clifton's reluctance to confront his intentions by daylight is a reflection of the embarrassment of the author: it was no longer possible for an author to be either as explicit or as realistic in the depiction of personal sexual tragedy as Richardson had been forty years earlier. Similarly, in Amelia Opie's *Adeline Mowbray* (1804) the heroine's stepfather needs to prime himself with liquor before he dares make a pass at her: 'Bold as he was in iniquity, he dared not in a cool and sober moment put his guilty purpose into execution'; as a result Adeline is able to push him over so that he stuns himself 'against the brass edge of one of the sofas'.[6]

*

In the 1740s Samuel Richardson had given a unique emphasis both to the socio-economic factors that might underlie rape and seduction and to the possibility that what would normally be regarded as a seduction might in reality be consummated by physical violence. Especially in *Pamela*, the potential relationship between sexual exploitation and class exploitation is clearly indicated. It seems that in the 1740s both Richardson and his intended readers might identify equally with Pamela, the servant girl, and with Clarissa, apparently the daughter of an affluent bourgeois family, but, no less than Pamela, the victim of a scion of a morally decadent land-owning aristocracy. A real-life case along the lines of a Richardson novel received considerable publicity in 1768: assisted by various employees, Frederick, sixth Baron Baltimore, abducted, held prisoner and raped a young milliner, but when brought to trial he was acquitted, though he found it advisable to go abroad following his release. But even in 1768 the focus of public interest was on the already notorious aristocratic rake rather than his lower-class victim. By the 1790s, the English middle classes were still alert to the moral decadence of the aristocracy, but they no longer cared to identify themselves with lower-class persons like Pamela, so that when latter-day Pamelas were raped there was little market for published accounts of the resulting trials; yet the pamphlet-buying public showed an

avid interest in transcripts of crim. con. trials, which related to the
sexual behaviour of the rich and noteworthy, and in 1790 a man
named Rhynwick Williams obtained nationwide notoriety, under
the denomination 'The Monster', for stabbing at the legs of three
young women who, though themselves lower-class, happened to be
in streets also frequented by the wives and daughters of respectable
citizens. Despite their horrified disapproval of upper-class immorality, the middle classes were realigning themselves psychologically
with the upper classes in order to confront the threat allegedly posed
by the French Revolution. In fact even the more extreme political
reformers of the 1790s tended to accept the inviolability of private
property, and to be committed to the standard self-image of Britain
as an unusually open and socially mobile community. The degree to
which differences of economic status determined the style of most
inter-personal transactions outside the immediate family had become something that could no longer be acknowledged. And this was
nowhere more so than in the sphere of illicit sexual relations.[7]

As already suggested, social class is something of a missing factor
in the discourse on seduction. It is somewhat more evident in the
material on rape. Anna Clark has produced figures suggesting that
in the years 1800 to 1829, 30 per cent of rapists brought before the
courts were middle- or upper-class as compared to only 16 per cent
of victims; and with a significant number of rapes going unreported,
one imagines that the middle- and upper-class rapists were pro-
portionately more successful in evading prosecution than the
lower-class ones. There is not the same reason for supposing the
proportion of middle-class victims to be understated. According to
one author,

> A rape of violence is by no means so dangerous in society as that of
> seduction, because women of modest and delicate dispositions, are
> seldom in situations liable to abuse ... A rape of violence is both
> morally and religiously less hurtful on society than a rape of seduc-
> tion, because the latter, in its progress, generally subverts the mind,
> as well as dishonours the person and character of the sufferer.

Evidently the 'women of modest character and delicate dispositions'
who never found themselves in exposed situations and whose un-
subverted minds were of such importance to the writer did not
include working-class girls from 'poor but honest' families, but this
is not stated in so many words. As shown in the previous chapter,

it was something of a literary convention that younger members of
the squirearchy practised their amorous skills on the daughters of
their tenantry. Household servants were another species of convenient prey. At Eton upper-class schoolboys desirous of losing their
virginities regularly made use of the maid-servants: it was recalled
of the abnormally chaste Lord Henry Conway, 'When at Eton, Eden
would lock Conway up for hours with Polly Jones but nothing ever
happened between them.' William Hickey, at a private school at
Streatham in the 1760s, made use of Nancy Dye, one of the maids,
'a fine luscious little jade'. Institutional communities may however
have been a more practicable hunting ground than private homes:
a family would hardly retain its social respectability if the maid-
servants were known to be in danger from the *paterfamilias* or his
sons. Nevertheless Anna Clark has calculated on the basis of Assize
depositions from the years 1800 to 1829 that in north-eastern
England just under a fifth of rape victims were domestic servants
who had been attacked in the house where they were employed.
Often the perpetrators were fellow-servants: but not always.
Dorothy Stevenson, aged seventeen, a nursery maid, giving evidence before the Court of Arches in the divorce proceedings brought
by the Countess of Strathmore against Andrew Robinson Bowes,
formerly MP for Newcastle, told of how on the second night of her
employ in the Bowes family, Bowes crept into the room which she
shared with Mrs Houghton, the wet-nurse, and climbed into the
latter's bed: soon afterwards 'the deponent heard Mrs Houghton's
bed make a great creaking as if there were therein two persons in
the act of carnally knowing each other'. About a fortnight later Mrs
Houghton left the household, and Dorothy Stevenson later heard it
was because she was pregnant. About a month or six weeks after
that Bowes invaded Dorothy Stevenson's bed, and when she
screamed 'immediately crammed a handkerchief, or corner of a
sheet, or something of that kind, into the deponent's mouth, and
forced a carnal connection with the deponent'.[8]

The vulnerability of girls of the servant class to exploitation by
people like Bowes is illustrated by the evidence of another witness
in the same case. Elizabeth Waite had become a nursery maid at
the age of sixteen, but, on leaving her job, was 'obliged to submit to
prostitution'. She was desperate to go straight, however, and, on
hearing that the Bowes family were on the look-out for a maid, went
to their house in Grosvenor Square. Bowes 'did at that time take
improper liberties with the deponent's person' and also promised to

pay her father's debts so as to release him from confinement as a debtor at the King's Bench. The poor girl visited her father in prison, but he warned her 'that such offer had been made with a view of seducing the deponent'. Elizabeth Waite returned to the Bowes house two or three days later and repeated to Bowes what her father had said. Bowes denied any such motive, gave her half a guinea, and instructed her to come back a few days later to see if the incumbent maid had left. On the next visit, Bowes sat with the girl for some time under pretext of waiting for his wife, offered her wine, took more 'indecent liberties' with her, and finally 'threw her down by force on a sopha which was in the said room, and the said Andrew Robinson Bowes did then and there have carnal knowledge of the deponent'. He then told her to come back later for 'a present'. She stayed away for about two weeks, at the end of which, having had to sell nearly all her clothes, she went once again to Grosvenor Square. Bowes refused to give her anything, and she was forced to apply for admission to the Magdalen Hospital.[9]

Another case is that of the Rev. Dr Edward Drax Free, rector of Sutton in Bedfordshire. The reverend doctor engaged as a servant one Maria Crook, spinster, late in 1810; she stayed in his employ about six months and bore his child in August 1811. Catherine Siggins, spinster, engaged as a servant in late 1812 or early 1813, bore the reverend doctor a child in November 1813. Margaret Johnston, spinster, engaged at the beginning of 1814, produced another of the reverend doctor's offspring in August 1814: she later returned, became pregnant again, was turned away, gave birth and returned twice more. One notes that Dr Free allowed himself very little time to get used to his servants before making them pregnant, though the triple return of Margaret Johnston does suggest that he did not actually force her to do anything she did not want. Ann Taylor, widow, another servant, found Dr Free importunate but not unmanageably so: he 'took indecent liberties with her person, and several times urged her and endeavoured to form a criminal intercourse and connection with her'. Despite this she remained in his employ four years. Of course her remaining so long may have had less to do with the delicacy and moderateness of the rector's sexual attentions than with her anxiety to keep her job: there was no shortage of maid-servants at this period and a woman discharged without a reference might well find herself unemployed for a long time. That might be especially awkward if, like Margaret Johnston, one had a bunch of illegitimate children to support. Perhaps after all Margaret Johnston's putting herself three times in the way of being made pregnant by the rector had less to do with compliance than with overwhelming desperation. Incidentally, these details of the private life of the rector of Sutton come from the proceedings taken to deprive him of his parish, so one is not to suppose that such conduct was regarded as altogether proper and normal, but neither Free nor Bowes were indicted for rape as such: the way in which they abused their power over their servants only came to light incidentally, in the course of legal proceedings initiated on other grounds.[10]

*

One may assume that other men who unscrupulously exploited their economic and social power over women were sometimes unscrupulous enough to use force. Similarly one may assume that some of the men who cynically persuaded girls to run away with them, or to meet them in places where they would not be interrupted, took the opportunity to achieve physical intimacy rather more speedily than the girl in question intended: though it might not have been literally true that 'when once a girl condescends to admit private meetings with a man, her heart is in his hand, and he may do with it what he pleases'. Once a young woman had placed herself in a compromising position with a man there was very little she could do to stop him making the most of the situation:

> Strongly belov'd, confided in, esteem'd;
> Nay the Protector of her Honour deem'd:
> Who, thus intrusted, in an evil Hour,
> Half steals, half ravishes fair Virtue's Flow'r,
> Blasts her that loves him with a lewd Embrace,
> And robs her of her dearest Jewel, Peace.

There was at least one trial (concluding in an acquittal) of a man who took advantage in this way of a girl he had promised to marry, and Jonathan Swift, for example, seems to have regarded it as a more or less routine occurrence, writing in one of his political allegories of a female personage 'undone by the common Arts practised upon all easy credulous Virgins, half by Force and half by Consent, after solemn Vows and Protestations of Marriage'. As one fictional victim of seduction exclaimed,

O, let no young woman ever think she stands secure, or permit private interviews and unguarded freedoms! let modesty and delicacy be the guardians of her honour, or she is lost for ever!

Of course the precise details of what might happen were usually only hinted at: thus in *Pride and Prejudice*, when Lydia Bennet runs off with Wickham, Jane Austen writes of Elizabeth Bennet:

> though she did not suppose Lydia to be deliberately engaging in an elopement, without intention of marriage, she had no difficulty in believing that neither her virtue nor her understanding would preserve her from falling an easy prey.

It might be a question of what Germaine Greer has called 'petty rape', in which reluctant consent extorted by bullying, or silence, or merely failure to resist, are construed as permission for the man to go ahead. The eighteenth century was certainly familiar with the concept, which features in one of the most enduringly popular of Restoration plays, Thomas Otway's *Venice Preserved*:

Pierre: Patience guide me!
He used no violence?

Jaffeir: No, no! out on't, violence!
Played with her neck; brushed her with his grey beard.
Struggled and towsled, tickled till she squeaked a little
May be, or so – but not a jot of violence –

A would-be seducer might choose to believe that the woman's resistance was merely an act. 'Not to mention the actual Pleasure a Woman received in struggling, it is a Justification of her, in the Eye of the Man, and a kind of *Salve* to her Honour and Conscience that she never did fully comply, but was in a Manner forc'd into it.' This theory was familiar even to young women attempting to depict seducers in their first novels:

> 'Oh my love,' said he gaily, 'none of your hypocrisy; such conduct as mine all women love, for it spares their blushes, and, making resistance ineffectual, gives them the glory of a triumph, without the mortification of a conquest; for you know,' added he, boldly looking in her face, 'that, however you may talk, or outwardly behave, your wishes concur but too easily with ours, not to make your success a self-denial.'

Or it might be that the woman changed her mind at the last moment, without the man bothering to register the fact save as an additional erotic detail:

> Yes, Thornton, she *did* fall upon my bosom; and I reaped the rewards of my insinuations, and of my address, in her arms – 'Tis true, she returned not the embrace – What of that? I was wrought up in the crisis, and her strugglings only answered the ends – and served as the sweet succedaneum of writhing the limbs in the transports of taste.[11]

It seems indeed that at one level contemporaries did not really distinguish between being seduced and being raped. Though Richardson's Clarissa, for example, acknowledges that being raped 'has not tainted my mind, it has not hurt my morals', she seems to feel that she has been just as much dishonoured as if she had willingly surrendered to Lovelace's advances. The phrase 'a fate worse than death' as a euphemism for rape belongs to this period: Edward Gibbon wrote in 1781 that 'The matrons and virgins of Rome were exposed to injuries more dreadful, in the apprehension of chastity, than death itself', but by 1810 Jane Porter could refer to 'a worse fate than death' as if the concept was already a cliché; and yet, as generally understood, the phrase refers not to rape as such, but to the loss of virginity. The fact of defloration was more important than how it took place. According to Edward Relfe, 'Whoever robs a woman of her Innocency, despoils a poor defenceless Creature of *All* that makes her valuable.'[12]

The evolving mythology of seduction which emphasised the inferiority and helplessness of women as moral beings was an inevitable part of the period's overall mythologisation of the social and sexual nature of women: the objective reality of women's vulnerability to the abuse of men's physical and economic superiority was played down precisely because of the obfuscation of the nature of male dominance that was implicit in the whole process of mythologisation. Seduction involved women who had supposedly said 'yes': rape involved women who had said 'no'. With the limitation of female identity and female sexuality to a once-only disposable maidenhead, the distinction between seduction and rape was evident mainly in the way that ostentatious concern for the tragic predicament of those who had said 'yes' served to divert attention from those who had asserted their moral autonomy by daring to say 'no', and afterwards complaining publicly of having been abused.

TABLE I

Numbers convicted of murder and rape in England and Wales 1805-1818

	1805	1806	1807	1808	1809	1810	1811	1812	1813	1814	1815	1816	1817	1818
Murder	10	5	17	8	10	15	8	19	29	25	15	30	25	13
Rape	5	4	3	7	9	2	5	3	5	5	12	8	6	2
(Of whom executed)	5	2	2	3	4	1	3	3	4	3	7	4	5	1

Source: *Parl. Papers* 1819 XVII, pp. 302-3.

TABLE II

Numbers proceeded against for all crimes, for rape, and assault with intent to commit rape, England and Wales 1810-1818

	Tried & convicted			Tried & acquitted			No Bill at Grand Jury		
	All crimes	rape	assault, etc.	All crimes	rape	assault, etc.	All crimes	rape	assault, etc.
1810	3158	2	16	1130	6	4	858	16	3
1811	3163	5	15	1234	16	1	940	5	3
1812	3913	3	13	1494	13	–	1169	13	9
1813	4422	5	15	1451	12	4	1291	18	11
1814	4025	5	17	1373	9	3	992	14	14
1815	4883	12	27	1648	11	7	1287	12	8
1816	5797	8	22	1884	11	3	1410	17	8
1817	9056	6	25	2678	12	6	2198	29	11
1818	8958	2	18	2622	13	6	1987	8	3

Source: *Parl. Papers* 1819 XVII, pp. 306-12.

1. Quality control in a condom warehouse, 1744. The man behind the table is a clergyman, apparently blessing the merchandise.

2. From Govard Bidloo's *Anatomia Humani Corporis*, 1685. The pose is based on that of the Medici Venus.

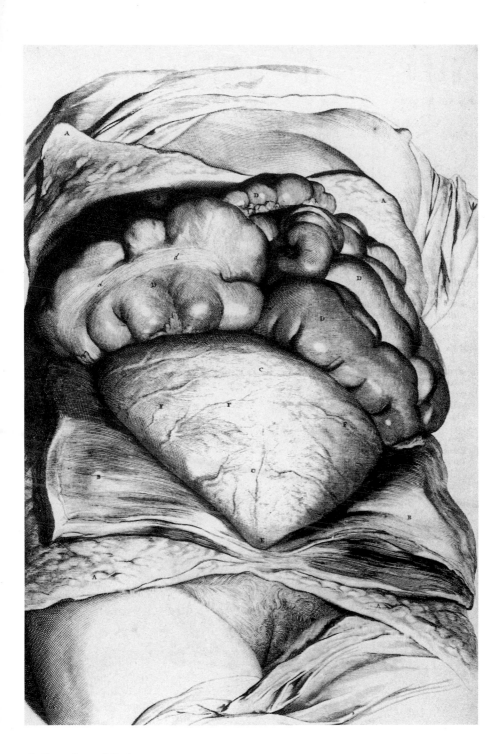

3. From Govard Bidloo's *Anatomia Humani Corporis*. The almost photographic fidelity to nature of the drawing does not extend to the nipple, which appears unpigmented. See p. 11.

4. Nell Gwyn, with juvenile-sized areoles, by Sir Peter Lely, *circa* 1667. See p. 11.

5. Hans Baldung Grien's 'The Seven Ages of Woman', 1544. See p. 12.

6. Lady Henrietta and Lady Elizabeth Finch by Charles Jervas, *circa* 1730, showing the fashionable sloping shoulders of the period. See p. 15.

7. Nude by William Etty.

8. 'Nude Woman with a Crucifix and Skull', presumably a Magdalen, by William Etty.

9. 'A Nude Reclining and a Woman Playing the Piano', by Henry Fuseli, *circa* 1799-1800 – a picture based on Titian's 'Venus and the Organ Player' pictures. See pp. 21-2

10. Mary Paterson, an eighteen-year-old Edinburgh prostitute murdered by Burke and Hare in 1828. Her body was sold for £8 to Dr Robert Knox for use in his anatomy school, and it was recalled that 'students crowded around the table on which she lay, and artists came to study a model worthy of Phidias and the best Greek art ...'.

11. Vertical sex, al fresco, by Thomas Rowlandson. The title 'Meditations among the Tombs' is borrowed from a well-known devotional work by the Rev. James Hervey (1746).

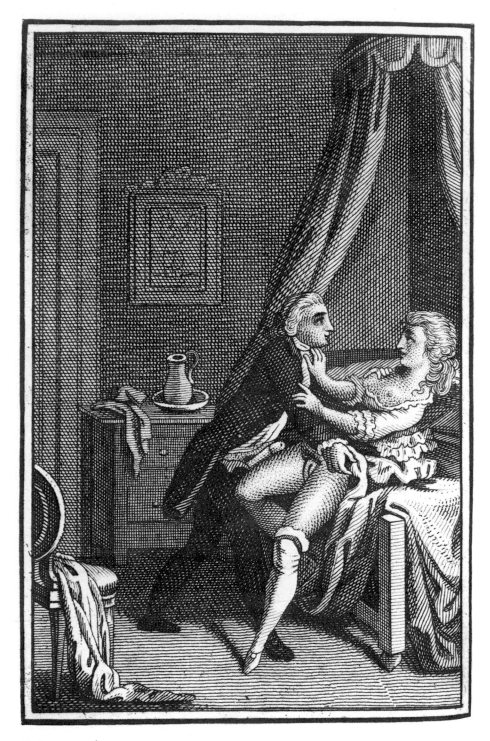

12. From *Les Épices de Vénus*, printed with the 1803 edition of *L'Aretin Francais*, probably by Tommaso Piroli. Before the invention of knickers women had very little protection once their outer garments were lifted aside.

13. 'Sometimes he would strip me stark naked on a carpet, by a good fire, when he would contemplate me almost by the hour, disposing me in all the figures and attitudes of body that it was susceptible of being viewed in': illustration, probably by Hubert François Gravelot, from the 1766 edition of *Fanny Hill*.

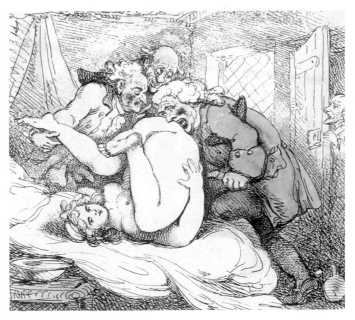

14. 'Cunnyseurs', by Thomas Rowlandson. Although this drawing probably dates from after 1810 the men are depicted in the fashions of the 1790s – knee breeches, large cuffs, a tricorne hat, long hair tied with a black ribbon – the object being no doubt to emphasise the age, conservatism and respectability of the men in contrast to the youth and unsophisticated complaisance of the girl.

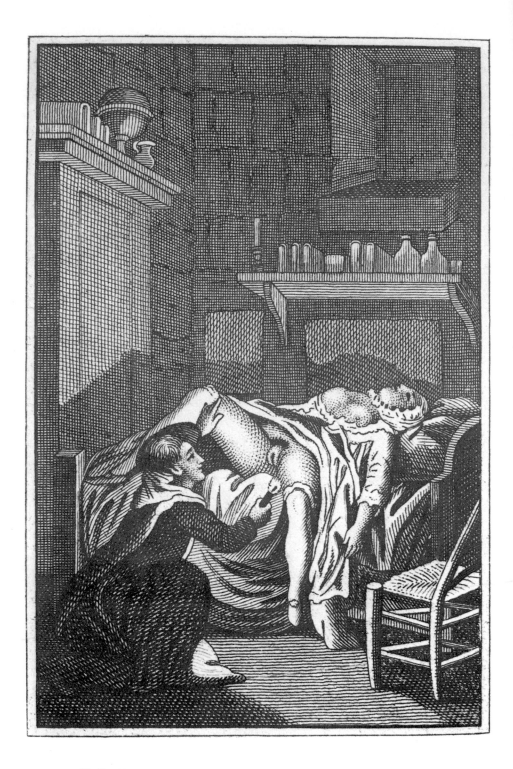

15. Keeking by candlelight, probably by Tommaso Piroli. See p. 24.

16. *La Carriola*, the wheel-barrow, from the 1803 edition of *L'Aretin Francais*, probably by Tommaso Piroli. See p. 28.

17. Another position from *L'Aretin Francais*, corresponding to one of the sixteenth-century series, except that the woman steadies herself by placing her hand on the man's head whereas in the original her hand is in the air.

THE WILLING FAIR, OR ANY WAY TO PLEASE.
The happy captain full of wine,
Forms with the fair a new design:
Across his legs the nymph he takes,
And with St George a motion makes:
She ever ready in her way
His pike of pleasure keeps in play:
Rises and falls with gentle ease,
And tries her best his mind to please.
Ah! happy captain, charming sport!
Who would not storm so kind a fort?

18. The woman on top again, by Rowlandson. The detail of the dog stealing left-overs from the table is borrowed from plate VI of Hogarth's *Marriage à la Mode*. Such references to other, perhaps more serious-minded, artists are common in Rowlandson's erotic drawings.

19. 'Mr. B———s and the Magdalen': Andrew Stoney Bowes raping Elizabeth Waite, who is depicted with a half-smile, as if she is enjoying every minute. Her testimony in court suggested otherwise. See p. 83.

20. From Alexander Hogg's *A New and Complete Collection of the Most Remarkable Trials for Adultery, &c.*

21.'Behind the Stone, Before the Stone,
The Taylor was with her alone.'

John Motherhill, a tailor, raping Catharine Wade in the churchyard at Brighton in
September 1785. Bathing machines are visible in the background. The Motherhill case is
unusual in that there were at least four editions of the trial. The one from which this
illustration is taken dates from 1806 and Motherhill is shown dressed in the style of the
1800s rather than of the mid-1780s.

22. 'A Corner, near the Bank; – or – An Example for Fathers', by James Gillray, 1797.
The elderly roué eyeing up the streetwalkers is believed to be a portrait from life of a
notoriously lecherous clerk at the Bank of England. Protruding from his pocket is a
volume labelled *Modest Prints*, presumably containing erotic drawings.

23. Young debauchees admiring their friends' sexual technique. From the 1766 edition of *Fanny Hill*.

24. Fanny Hill being touched up by Phoebe Ayres, her 'tutoress'. See pp. 111-12.

25. Three women enjoying the company of a man disguised as a nun. From the *Les Épices de Vénus* section of the 1803 edition of *L'Aretin Francais*.

26. 'The Arse Bishop Joslin[g] a Soldier – or – Do as I say, not as I do.' A contemporary print, probably by Isaac Robert Cruikshank, showing the arrest of the Right Rev. Percy Jocelyn, Bishop of Clogher in July 1822. See pp. 137-8.

27. The most explicit of the 'divers wicked lewd impious impure bawdy and obscene Prints' in Alexander Hogg's *A New and Complete Collection of the Most Remarkable Trials for Adultery, &c.*

28. A woman being burnt at the stake during the reign of George II. In the background male bodies hang from the gallows.

5

The Desperate

The convention that young girls who had been seduced inevitably
gravitated towards prostitution may in part have been a rationali-
sation of a linguistic usage: the consciously virtuous were ready to
apply the term prostitute and its synonyms to any unmarried
woman who had mislaid her virginity. Thus Louisa Mildmay in
Hugh Kelly's novel *Memoirs of a Magdalen* becomes the 'Magdalen'
of the title simply in consequence of two turns on the sofa with Sir
Robert Harold; and in 1800 Lord Chief Justice Eldon, later Lord
Chancellor, told the House of Lords:

> Suppose a poor helpless girl was robbed of her innocence, what would
> a private man say? Why, that he was very sorry for it: but what did
> the law say? That she was to be regarded as a prostitute – Why? that
> others should be deterred from following her example.

Nevertheless there were undoubtedly large numbers of women in
London, and in other cities, who were prostitutes in the most limited
sense of the term, in that their principal source of income was from
selling casual sex. James Boswell, who took care to be well-informed
on the subject, thought there were 'free-hearted ladies of all kinds:
from the splendid Madam at fifty guineas a night down to the civil
nymph with white-thread stockings who tramps along the Strand
and will resign her engaging person to your honour for a pint of wine
and a shilling'. He might also have mentioned the tart he coupled
with in Hyde Park on 31 March 1763 – 'She was ugly and lean and
her breath smelt of spirits' – or the woman who stole his handkerchief from his pocket while he was having it off with her in Whitehall
Gardens and then vehemently denied the theft, causing him, by the
time he got home, to feel 'shocked to think that I had been intimately
united with a low, abandoned, perjured, pilfering creature'. A shilling – a twentieth part of a pound, equivalent to a day's wages for
the lowest-paid workers in the eighteenth century – seems to have
been the going rate for streetwalkers, though the satirist John

Wolcot ('Peter Pindar') referred to gatherings where 'every woman is accomplished, every woman is handsome … and … more than a half of those Cleopatras are to be purchased for half-a-crown'. Sometimes, however, casual sex was provided for free, out of high spirits and a sense of adventure: Boswell, cruising in Covent Garden, 'met two very pretty little girls who asked me to take them with me'. Having explained that he had no money to give them, he screwed them both in a private room at *The Shakespeare Head*. Covent Garden and the Strand were the most notorious locations for meeting loose women, but Boswell once picked up 'a strong, jolly young damsel' outside St James's Palace and had her on Westminster Bridge – 'The whim of doing it there with the Thames rolling below us amused me very much' – and five weeks later did business with 'a fresh, agreeable young girl called Alice Gibbs' whom he encountered in Downing Street.[1]

Other women occupied 'that most miserable situation of a *Bawdy-house Prostitute*', sitting up till 5 a.m. with customers in brandy shops till the latter allowed themselves to be inveigled into bed: 'if any part of a strumpet's life is more wretched, more pitiable than another, sure it is this', recorded a woman who had tried it. But brothels, though they have always figured largely in pornography and folklore, seem never to have represented a very large part of the industry. Between December 1719 and November 1720 the Societies for Promoting a Reformation of Manners, operating in London, prosecuted 1,189 persons – mainly streetwalkers, though also men who exposed themselves or had sex in public – for 'Lewd and Disorderly Practices' as compared to fourteen persons for 'Keeping Bawdy and Disorderly Houses'. There are no comparable statistics for exactly a hundred years later, but in the year ending 29 September 1857, 8,771 women were arrested for prostitution in England and Wales under the Vagrant Act, and 44 men and 80 women were indicted on account of 106 disorderly houses. Not all of the latter would have functioned primarily as brothels: in 1817 the Secretary of the Society for the Suppression of Vice complained to a committee of the House of Commons about disreputable public houses and premises where dances were held in violation of licensing regulations:

These places are generally the resort of the daughters of petty tradesmen, of men and maid servants, in and out of place, of apprentices, and of shopmen, where they mix in association with people of abandoned characters, and with thieves and sharpers, who soon establish intimacies, which (independent as to maid servants, of their tendency to prostitution) not infrequently, it is probably, prove subservient to those robberies in private houses, which are so frequently heard of through the newspapers.

Before 1817 eleven premises were prosecuted by the Society for the Suppression of Vice as 'disorderly houses', though only two were alleged to be brothels as such: the others had committed such heinous crimes as opening too late at night and serving alcoholic refreshment during the hour when churches were holding their Sunday morning services. In Edinburgh in the late 1830s it was calculated that the city had 800 full-time prostitutes, of whom 600 or so lived in 203 disorderly houses, including ten licensed taverns, 25 ginger-beer shops (often public houses that had lost their licences) and 97 eating and lodging houses, i.e. 132 premises that undoubtedly provided accommodation for young women but equally undoubtedly required their services as barmaids, waitresses and cleaners: the extent to which the same women also served as prostitutes may not have been as clear-cut as was claimed at the time, and one begins to wonder what credence should be given to the disorderly status of the other 71 premises listed. Similar arithmetical doubts are raised by the claim that in the parish of St Paul's Shadwell, in the London port area, with a population of 9,855 in 1,682 houses, there were 1,000 prostitutes and 200 disorderly houses in 1816: this would have meant not only that nearly half the adult female population were prostitutes but also that every house with more than two adult female occupants was a disorderly house.[2]

The smallest but most affluent category of prostitutes were those who accepted the protection and the living arrangements of a single lover, though according to one such kept mistress, it was normal for these ladies to have, in addition, 'a gentleman or two whom they used to meet privately, and from whom they used to receive very handsome presents'. Occasionally such lovers – even well-known public figures – might marry their kept mistresses; Charles James Fox married Mrs Elizabeth Armistead in 1796, after ten years of cohabitation, though he waited another seven years before making the marriage public: in 1776, as Elizabeth Cane, she had been mentioned in *The Town and Country Magazine* as 'that celebrated Thais' and in 1783 the same publication numbered her among the 'impures of the ton' – in modern parlance, high-class tarts – and she had clearly had a considerable reputation as a courtesan before settling into domesticity with the Whig leader. Less notorious, at least initially, was Emma Lyon, whom Sir William Hamilton, ambassador to the court at Naples, took over from his nephew in 1785 and whom he made Lady Hamilton in 1791. Perhaps the best-known kept mistress of the day was Dorothea Jordan – generally known as Mrs Jordan, though she was never married. As a young actress she had a relationship with her manager which left her with a child. Next she lived with a barrister named Richard Ford, later the chief magistrate at Bow Street, and had three children by him. In November 1790 she commenced a relationship with HRH the Duke of Clarence, the third son of George III, and lived with him as his acknowledged mistress from October 1791 till December 1811. They had ten children together, but the Duke of Clarence was so insolvent that Mrs Jordan had to persist with her stage career to help meet their household bills. At the end of 1811 the Duke cast Mrs Jordan off as he had high hopes of marrying a Miss Catherine Tylney-Long who, as well as being pretty and much younger than Mrs Jordan, was heiress to a fortune said to be worth £40,000 a year. When the Duke eventually succeeded to the throne as William IV, a decade and a half after Mrs Jordan's death, he created their eldest son Earl of Munster and gave their younger sons title and precedence as the younger sons of a marquis: four of their daughters married lords. Nowadays of course a woman like Mrs Jordan would not be regarded as a prostitute at all: on the other hand, since William IV's time no royal has admitted to having had illegitimate children.[3]

*

In 1813 it was claimed that 'It is a truth, dishonourable to the British nation, that the dreadful sin of prostitution is more prevalent among us than in countries immersed in superstition and idolatry'. Patrick Colquhoun, stipendiary magistrate at the Queen Square Office, Westminster, in the sixth edition of his *A Treatise on the Police of the Metropolis* (1800), having acknowledged that the number of prostitutes 'certainly exceeds credibility', produced a figure of 50,000 in London alone. He broke the figure down as follows:

1.	Of the class of Well Educated women ...	2,000
2.	Of the class composed of persons above the rank of Menial Servants ...	3,000
3.	Of the class who may have been employed as Menial Servants, or seduced early in life ... who live wholly by Prostitution ...	20,000
4.	Of those in different ranks in Society, who live partly by Prostitution, including the multitudes of low females who cohabit with labourers and others without matrimony ...	25,000

In another of his works Colquhoun claimed that there were 100,000 'lewd and immoral women' in the whole of England and Wales, 'taking into account the prodigious number among the lower classes who cohabit together without marriage, and again separate when a difference ensues'. It is clear that Colquhoun's round and sweeping estimates incorporated a lot of women who had never dreamt of offering sex for money, including many who, with the more liberal divorce laws of a later age, might have obtained divorces from uncongenial first husbands and have remarried. But statistics have an allure which often seems in direct proportion to their bogusness. The anonymous author of *Fund of Mercy: or an Institution for the Relief and Employment of Destitute and Forlorn Females* (1813), having cited Colquhoun's estimate of 50,000 prostitutes in London, suggested that even if there were only half as many, it could be supposed that each year they enticed into sin '50,000 of our unwary youth', of whom '20,000 contract that deplorable disease, from which few of these women are free', and that of the 'unwary youth' thus infected, perhaps a quarter would never properly recover, a third of these – 1,666 – dying annually and another third lingering on for some years before dying 'of what are termed cold, consumptions, and decline'.[4]

Another authority put the number of women in London who 'make a practice of prowling the streets' at about 1,000. The difference between this estimate and Colquhoun's 20,000 'who may have been employed as Menial Servants ... who live wholly by Prostitution' is to be explained, partly by Colquhoun's commitment to large, round figures, and partly by the social and sexual norms of what was, by modern standards, an enormously brutal and competitive society. The cities of London and Westminster were thronged by destitute persons of both sexes, by poorly paid household servants

and girls working in trades that employed women, such as milli-
nery. The area east of the City of London was the greatest port in
the world, and many of the women dwelling there had husbands or
live-in lovers (to use the coy modern parlance) who were away at
sea. There were thousands of men, by no means all of them sailors
from other ports, who were looking for sex, and not all of them could
be bothered to wait till it was openly on offer. Starving girls shiver-
ing in doorways, chambermaids tidying beds in hotels or
flop-houses, milliners' assistants on the way home from work might
be accosted and might find it more convenient to comply when the
alternative might be physical violence or, in the case of maid-
servants, the loss of a job. A better-off man might give a handsome
tip afterwards: even the standard payment of a shilling might make
a lot of difference to an unemployed girl from the country with no
home or prospects. This casual and almost unintended, or at least
unpremeditated, prostitution was still prostitution in the eyes of
people like Patrick Colquhoun.[5]

Statistics compiled by the Metropolitan Police in 1837-8 tend to
confirm Colquhoun's earlier surmise that active prostitutes were
mostly 'women who have been in a state of menial servitude'.
According to the police statistics, of 3,103 prostitutes examined,
only 85 could read and write with ease, of whom four 'had received
a superior education'. This is far below any comparable statistics
for literacy: even among prisoners passing through Norwich Castle
between 1826 and 1843, 28 per cent could read and write. Yet
commentators persisted in arguing that the principal reason why
women of the poorest classes resorted to prostitution was the fact
that they had fallen victim to the wiles of seducers. Despite the
assertions of people like William Hale to the contrary (see above,
p. 70) the standard view was that 'Young women, having been
seduced, deserted, and banished from their friends, are frequently
left without other resource than that of entering the recesses of
debauchery'. Even Colquhoun supposed that:

> Many of them perhaps originally seduced from a state of innocence
> … seem to have no alternative, but to become instruments of promot-
> ing and practising that species of seduction and immorality, of which
> they themselves were the victims.[6]

This emphasis on seduction was important to early nineteenth-
century society's self-image: if seduction of innocence was the main

source for the recruitment of prostitutes, there was no need to worry about other possible causes of destitution among women of the poorer classes. Colquhoun himself believed:

Poverty ... is the state of every one who must labour for subsistence ...
Poverty is therefore a most necessary and indispensable ingredient in society, without which nations and communities could not exist in a state of civilisation. It is the lot of man – it is the source of *wealth*, since without poverty there would be *no labour*.

Employment prospects in a large and growing urban centre like London were probably better than elsewhere, and as the *London Chronicle* had pointed out in 1758, 'The great disproportion of the births and burials in this metropolis, sufficiently demonstrates the necessity of frequent supplies of servants and labourers from the country'; but in a society with only limited provision for jobless people hiccups in the labour market meant that there were always large numbers of people destitute and desperate. In addition, marital breakdown, or for unmarried girls, the cruel treatment of parents or, perhaps especially, step-parents might drive young women from their homes. A never-ending supply of people desperately seeking work was a wonderful lubricant for the economy: but steady recruitment for vice and crime was an inevitable side-effect.[7]

Though a standard part of the seduction scenario was rejection by one's family and friends, cutting the victim off from economic support, the fact that many prostitutes came from families that were incapable of providing economic support was invariably glossed over. Along with the abandonment of the disgraced girl by her outraged relatives, the blackmail and physical menaces of pimps were invented as an explanation of why originally virtuous girls persisted in their evil ways:

Their Sighs, and Tears, and Groans, are criminal in the Eye of their Tyrants, the Bully and the Bawd, who fatten on their Misery, and threaten them with Want or a Goal [gaol], if they shew the least Design of escaping from their Bondage.

Equally there was a tendency to exaggerate the youth of prostitutes, probably for dramatic reasons: a sixteen-year-old straight out of school has an appeal to a wide range of fantasies quite lacking in a thirty-year-old mother of three. William Dodd, chaplain of the Magdalen Hospital, wrote of prostitutes as

abandon'd to infamy, and in the very last stages of distress, when for
the most part, not exceeding *twenty years*; to which indeed few arrive,
the generality being thrown out much younger, and many corrupting
away piece-meal, at an age, when few are esteem'd women!

A young creature perhaps is debauch'd at fifteen, soon abandon'd,
quickly common, as quickly diseas'd, and as quickly loathsome and
detested!

But a sample of 111 prostitutes reported on by the Guardian Society
for the Preservation of Public Morals found only one aged fourteen,
35 aged from sixteen to twenty, 23 aged twenty-one to twenty-five
and 36 aged twenty-six to thirty, and the Metropolitan Police in the
late 1830s found that out of 2,194 prostitutes only three were under
fifteen, 414 were aged from fifteen to twenty, and 872 aged from
twenty to twenty-five: nearly half the 2,194, therefore, were of the
age at which women normally married, or older. These were women
who had made themselves sufficiently noticeable to get themselves
arrested by the police. Statistics supplied by the Lock-Hospital at
Edinburgh at roughly the same period tell a different story: of a
thousand women admitted because suffering from venereal diseases, 42 were under fifteen and 662 more under twenty. But these
were girls frightened enough to ask to be enrolled for a VD cure and
seemingly contrite enough not to be turned away, of whom many no
doubt had contracted gonorrhoea after sexual relations with only
one man. The Edinburgh Lock-Hospital statistics are much less
likely than the figures from London to represent a cross-section of
what might be regarded as hardened streetwalkers: most of the
Guardian Society's sample had been working as prostitutes for at
least two years, and they cited two other women, one of whom had
been imprisoned eighteen times and another more than thirty times
on vagrancy charges connected with prostitution.[8]

The emphasis on seduction as the cause of women becoming
prostitutes also embodied a statement about the nature of female
morality and female psychology. As already noted, in their talk of
'fallen women' and 'Magdalens' contemporaries were not overscru-
pulous in distinguishing between women who had had sex with one
man for love, and women who had had sex with several men for
money, and to assume that seduction led to prostitution was a
means of conflating the two. Admittedly Colquhoun suggested that
seduced women could be rescued from prostitution if caught in time
by people who shared his views: 'It is in the first stage of Seduction,
before the female mind becomes vitiated and depraved, that Asy-

lums are most useful.' If on the other hand, the poor girls were left to themselves, 'the general consequences ... are increasing wickedness, a ruined constitution, a premature death, and, as far as we can see, everlasting destruction'.[9]

Socially aware people in the later eighteenth century were totally convinced of the readiness of the young, the lower-class, and females of all descriptions, to be corrupted, polluted and contaminated. Their image of the prostitutes who 'throng our streets, lie in wait for the incautious, and corrupt the rising generation' seems to tap the same depths of paranoia that would later be teased by films like *The Invasion of the Body Snatchers* and *Night of the Living Dead*. In the end it is this aspect of eighteenth-century prostitution that is most distinctively characteristic of its period: its status as an ideological construct brought into play to bolster various aspects of a complex code of social and sexual repression.[10]

*

The underlying ambivalence of the impassioned attacks on seduction has already been noted, and it is similarly significant that amidst all the discussion of prostitution and immorality so little was said about the single most important cause of prostitution, the willingness of males to pay for sex. Men like James Boswell were easily able to justify their own commerce with prostitutes: 'Surely,' he confided to his journal, 'in such a situation, when the woman is already abandoned, the crime must be alleviated, though in strict morality illicit love is always wrong –.' However even Boswell on occasion felt something like remorse, as when, after recording a ten-minute transaction with 'a young Shropshire girl, only seventeen, very well-looked, her name Elizabeth Parker', he added, 'Poor thing, she has a sad time of it!' William Dodd, chaplain of the Magdalen Hospital, an institution established to rescue prostitutes from their miserable state, announced

> That in the present disordered state of things, there will always be *Brothels* and *Prostitutes*, is a fact but too indisputable, however unpleasing. Any attempt to prevent this evil, would be no less impossible than impolitic, in the opinion of many; absurd in itself, and productive of the worst consequences.

At first glance Dodd may have seemed to be endorsing the scandalous opinion of Bernard Mandeville, in his *A Modest Defence of Public Stews* of 1724, that prostitution was the best safeguard of the virtue of women who were not prostitutes, but it seems from the writings of one of Dodd's associates that their fears lay in a quite different direction:

> Great care ought to be taken, that while we hastily remove one evil, we do not render the remedy worse than the disease by introducing a greater ... The imagination of the writer is not so filled with the idea of reforming that he should suppose it practicable totally to suppress whoring; the consequence of which, were it possible to effect it, might be the increase of a horrid vice too rife already, though the bare thought of it strikes the mind with horror.

In other words, close the brothels and the lads would begin screwing, not one another's wives, but *one another*. The same idea surfaced again nearly forty years later:

> Indeed all undue restraints on that intercourse [i.e. intercourse between men and women] do mischief. They lead to commission of unnatural crimes, and to the formation of connexions which prove injurious to the dearest interests of society.

Nevertheless it was clear from a scurrilous publication of 1782 that Mandeville's argument was still recalled: the Dedication to Lady Grosvenor (whose affair with George III's brother had led to a crim. con. prosecution) begins

> It is become a maxim in these refined times to consider female prostitution as a political good. In that light we may look up to your Ladyship, as the most distinguished character among the political conveniences of the present age.

Mary Wollstonecraft also referred to this line of argument in *A Vindication of the Rights of Women*: discussing prostitution she acknowledged, 'I may be told that ... [prostitution] only affects a devoted part of the sex – devoted to the salvation of the rest.'[11]

In fact some attempt at repression was made, both at the beginning and at the end of the period under discussion. A society for the suppression of bawdy houses was founded in Bethnal Green in 1690, and another in the Strand in 1691, and the publicity obtained by such vigilante endeavours led first to a letter from Queen Mary II to the Middlesex justices urging enforcement of the laws against immorality, and then, in 1698, to a Royal Proclamation on the subject. Societies for Promoting a Reformation of Manners were formed all over the London area. In practice they functioned as branches of a single organisation and almost nothing is known about individual societies, but in conjunction with one another they obtained a grand total of 101,683 convictions for various offences against morality and public decency by 1738. They were evidently behind the prosecution of a homosexual coterie in 1726 which led to three men being hanged, but their normal targets were prostitution, Sabbath-breaking, swearing and drunkenness. From December 1708 to November 1709 prosecutions were brought against 794 persons for 'Lewd and Disorderly Practices' – mostly, one supposes, streetwalkers – 132 keepers of 'Bawdy and disorderly houses' – which would have included gambling dens and premises famed for brawling and loud music – and 1,523 tradesmen who opened for business on Sunday. From December 1719 to November 1720 1,189 were prosecuted for 'Lewd and Disorderly Practices', 14 for keeping 'Bawdy and disorderly houses' and 615 for 'exercising their Trades on the Lord's Day'. Thereafter the Societies' efforts seem to have been concentrated more and more on persecuting Sabbath-breakers: from December 1729 to November 1730 251 were prosecuted for 'Lewd and Disorderly Practices' as compared to 424 for Sabbath-breaking, and from December 1737 to November 1738 52 for 'Lewd and Disorderly Practices' as compared to 493 for Sabbath-breaking. It may have been that the sanctity of the Lord's Day was a higher priority with the kind of people who joined these societies than the suppression of sexual immorality, but it may also have been that both magistrates and constables were more sympathetic to prosecutions for Sabbath-breaking than for streetwalking. In any case since many prostitutes had no fixed abode they would have had to be arrested and detained pending trial, and there would have been a problem securing witnesses: a commercial premises which outraged the neighbours by opening on Sundays was a much more convenient target. The Societies went into a decline during the 1730s, which in itself suggests lack of widespread support for their activities: a similar campaign launched in 1757 by an ad hoc alliance of Methodists and Dissenters soon ran into legal trouble. When the vigilante movement was finally relaunched in the 1780s under the denomination of 'The Proclamation Society', and later 'The Society for the Suppression of Vice', prostitution was not targeted, the chief object being now the suppression of obscene literature.[12]

In 1812 a group of respectable citizens in London formed an organisation called 'The Guardian Society for the Preservation of Public Morals'. Probably its most important work was in maintaining a refuge for repentant prostitutes – its full title was 'The Guardian Society for the Preservation of Public Morals, providing temporary Asylums for Prostitutes, removed by the operation of the Laws from the Public Streets, and affording to such of them as are destitute employment and relief' – but they persuaded the Lord Mayor of London to issue a proclamation against streetwalkers. The City of London's Court of Common Council appointed a committee to investigate prostitution in the capital and later petitioned the House of Commons to urge that:

> such humane, salutary and efficient Laws be provided, and such an active and vigorous system of police be established, as shall render this metropolis as distinguished for its public decency and decorum, as it already stands pre-eminent for its extent, its wealth, and its magnificence.

Partly as a result of such initiatives there was a tightening up of the enforcement of the laws against vagrancy, which led to a renewed assault on the streetwalkers themselves. Details are available in the *Parliamentary Papers* of the number of vagrants arrested in England and Wales between January 1820 and January 1824, though as usual in this period the returns have no consistent format. Those from Middlesex are incomplete, and show that of 7,342 individuals committed to four London prisons those accused of sex-related offences numbered only 369: 110 men committed for 'indecently exposing their persons' and 259 for deserting their wives and children 'whereby they became chargeable to the parish'. The returns from the provinces on the other hand supply almost the first authoritative data we have on the extent of prostitution outside London, though the figures provided clearly have little consistent relation to the objective situation owing to differences in the practice of law enforcement in different areas. Of 200 vagrants committed between January 1820 and January 1824 to the City of Chester House of Correction, 153 were prostitutes: of 469 committed to the City of Gloucester House of Correction, only 89 were prostitutes, of whom 60 were committed in the year 1823 alone; of 74 committed to the Bedfordshire House of Correction, only two were prostitutes. Clearly the operation of laws against an offence so common and (from some viewpoints) innocuous as prostitution was likely to be a hit-and-miss affair: arguably it still is, even today.[13]

*

The fading away of the Societies for Promoting a Reformation of Manners may have encouraged prostitutes to conduct their business with greater openness: in 1758 a commentator wrote of the number of well-dressed streetwalkers patrolling Fleet Street and the Strand as if it was something new. It has also been suggested that a growing paranoia on the subject of homosexuality led to a comparative increase in resort to prostitutes, because more and more men felt the need to advertise their masculinity. There is, however, no way of assessing the possible increase or decrease in the number of prostitutes in this period, and the most important initiatives in combating prostitution in London in the mid-eighteenth century, the Lock-Hospital and the Magdalen Charity, are to be best understood not as a response to a new problem but simply as an instance of the middle class's interest in mobilising private and communal charity for the establishment of useful institutions such as schools and general hospitals: Guy's Hospital (founded 1722), St George's Hospital (1733), the London Hospital (1740) and the Middlesex Hospital (1745) are merely the most notable of the London hospitals founded in this period: in addition at least four lying-in – i.e. maternity – hospitals opened in London between 1745 and 1765.[14]

The Lock-Hospital, established in 1746, specialised in the cure of venereal diseases. Although it did not readmit anybody 'who had been discharged for irregularity, or has again received the infection', its rehabilitative function was purely incidental, and in fact it dealt with a larger number of men than women. The Magdalen Hospital, for the rehabilitation of prostitutes, opened its doors in 1758. The Asylum for Female Orphans, established in the same year at the Lambeth end of Westminster Bridge, claimed a similar function, for as the chaplain later explained:

> we diminish the number of female profligates, who, in the metropolis and its neighbourhood, bear a proportion to the whole sex, which I dare not mention. When, therefore, we shelter a female orphan, in her most defenceless years, in her greatest distress, and, perhaps, at the decisive moment of her life, we, in all probability, prevent one from adding to the number.

A number of institutions modelled on the Magdalen Hospital were founded a generation or so later, including the Lock-Asylum for the Reception of Penitent Female Patients when discharged from the Lock-Hospital, in 1787, the Refuge for the Destitute in 1805, the London Female Penitentiary in 1807, the Guardian Society for the Preservation of Public Morals in 1812 and the Fund of Mercy, or an Institution for the Relief and Employment of Destitute and Forlorn Females in 1813. Institutions of the same type were also established outside London, in Edinburgh, Glasgow, Plymouth, Liverpool, Bristol, Hull, Leeds, Norwich, Colchester and Oxford: that at Oxford, opened in 1832 may have been one of the last such foundations.[15]

These institutions represented only a small fraction of the energy going into charitable organisations in the 1800s – other initiatives of the period include the Society for Superseding the Necessity of Climbing Boys (i.e. chimney-sweepers' boys), the Society for Promoting the Civilisation and Improvement of the North American Indians, the Society of Friends of Foreigners in Distress, the City of London Truss Society for the Relief of the Ruptured Poor and the London Society for Promoting Christianity among the Jews – and in numerical terms they barely scratched the surface of the problem. On 25 March 1802 the Lock-Hospital had 79 inmates, of whom fewer than half were women (and some of these were no doubt women of the poorer classes infected by their husbands); the Lock-Asylum had 24 inmates. In 1807 the Magdalen Charity had 67 inmates. In 1811 the London Female Penitentiary had 48 women in its house in Pentonville and claimed that in the previous four years it had had 523 applications from women, of whom 133 had been admitted. In January 1820 the female department of the Refuge for the Destitute, in Hackney Road, had 61 inmates, mostly recently discharged prisoners or women recommended by the magistrates in lieu of committal proceedings, though eight of the new admissions in 1819 had been listed as 'Seduced and deserted' and others may have been streetwalkers. In 1827 the Guardian Society had 51 women in its asylum in New Road, St George's in the East. In 1813 these institutions were said to house a total of 244 women, though 'many hundred unfortunate females have applied to them for admittance during the last year', and the chaplain of the Asylum for Female Orphans had earlier felt justified in boasting:

We may consider ... this house like Noah's ark floating upon the waters, as preserving a few souls safe and unpolluted from the torrent of dissipation and vice, which overflows the world.[16]

Of the 390 applicants for admission to the London Female Penitentiary between 1807 and 1811 who were not 'received' it is probable that many were not actually rejected, but had last-minute second thoughts. It is clear that not all the inmates of these refuges were made to feel perfectly comfortable. Between 1807 and 1811, 85 women entered the London Female Penitentiary and subsequently left. Five had been carried away in coffins, and 56 had been put out to service or 'reconciled to friends'. Eleven had been discharged – i.e. thrown out – three had left amicably, being counted separately, and ten had 'eloped'. At the Magdalen Hospital, of 2,415 women admitted between 1758 and 1784, 293 are listed as 'Uneasy under Restraint, and [discharged] at their own Desire', 52 'Never returned from Hospital, to which they were sent to be cured' and 333 were discharged 'For Faults and Irregularities'. According to a later calculation, of 3,437 women who passed through the Magdalen Hospital up to 1802, 2,230 had been 'reconciled to their friends, or placed out to service', but 449 had been 'discharged at their own request' and 476 'discharged as incorrigible'. At the Bristol Penitentiary, established in 1802, of 54 women who passed through up to 1809, five had died 'real penitents', eight had 'Returned to their friends', 17 had been placed in service ('twelve of whom have given satisfaction to their employers') six had been 'Dismissed by their own desire', four 'Ditto for bad behaviour', four 'Ditto being pregnant', and ten had 'eloped'.[17]

The names of these institutions certainly conjure up an image of joylessness and repression, of charity marred by sermonising, sourness and self-righteousness. Initially the Magdalen Hospital announced, with regard to its inmates:

> In their Work, as in every other Circumstance, the utmost Care and Delicacy, Humanity and Tenderness will be observed, that this Establishment may not be thought a House of Correction or even of hard Labour, but a safe Retreat from their distressful Circumstances

By 1769 the relevant passage in the 'Rules' had been revised to:

> In their work, as in every other circumstance, the utmost propriety and humanity are observed; and all loose or idle discourse, sluttish-

ness, indolence, or neglect of moral or religious duties, are closely attended to.

At the same time the girls were warned:

> Our Charity stands on this foundation: that quarrelsome, sullen, idle, sluttish, careless, and indecent young women are not the fit objects of it.

Great emphasis was placed on the need for due gratitude:

> Consider then, Young Woman, of how great value to you this House of refuge is; as being the only one, to which you could fly, the only place where you could have any possibility of attaining present or future Bliss.
>
> Surely then you must greatly prize it; and feel the utmost Gratitude for the worthy Governors and Supporters of it.
>
> This Gratitude we would wish you to cherish, as it will ever be a motive to the very best Conduct.

The Lock-Asylum seems to have had even stricter rules than the Magdalen Hospital. At a time when opinion on a wide range of matters within the Church of England was becoming increasingly polarised between the Evangelical and the High Church camps (sometimes referred to respectively as the Clapham Sect and the Hackney Phalanx), the Magdalen Hospital maintained a notably ecumenical committee, including many Evangelicals but also High Church laymen like Lord Kenyon and Joshua Watson, who acted as stewards at the annual sermon in 1815 and 1817 respectively: in May 1811 one of the stewards was Viscount Folkestone, who only subsequently became known as an Evangelical and who at that time was chiefly celebrated for having had an affair with the recently discarded mistress of HRH the Duke of York, who had been commander-in-chief of the Army till forced to resign because of a hugely publicised scandal – in which the said ex-mistress figured prominently – in 1809. The Lock-Asylum on the other hand seems to have been totally under Evangelical control, with William Wilberforce, John Venn and Charles Simeon all involved in its management. The London Female Penitentiary seems to have aimed to be much less repressive than the earlier institutions, promising

> The seduced and unfortunate female who is solicitous to forsake the paths of vice ... shall be received in a manner least calculated to

wound her feelings; and be afterwards treated with the utmost delicacy and kindness.

This attitude of leniency provoked the antagonism of religious hardliners, partly on the grounds that to suggest that women in need had no alternative to prostitution except where provision was made for charitable refuges, was 'to libel the parish officers' but chiefly because

> Prostitutes who apply to the Penitentiary, cannot be supposed to give evidence of genuine penitence, because they are not required to submit either to penance, or to hardship ... there is no period whatever, in which an Harlot undergoes disgrace.

It was claimed that the Penitentiary would attract the vilest whores: 'the only necessary qualification will be, to add to their numerous crimes, the sins of hypocrisy and falsehood.' The doctrine that a reform in outward behaviour was not the same as, and not a substitute for, the kind of spiritual transformation involved in genuine repentance, was of course basic to the kind of Puritanism which had flourished in the seventeenth century and which was experiencing, with the Evangelical movement and its echoes among the nonconformist congregations, a considerable revival in the 1800s. Exponents of these views, with their belief that human beings had an infinite capacity for evil, eagerly resurrected the Puritan idea that prostitutes were not so much unfortunate victims of social and economic necessity as 'actuated either by lust, idleness, or avarice' and led to 'pursue their desperate career from awful depravity, from idleness, avarice, shameless profligacy, unbridled lust ... from a principle of lust, idleness, profligacy or avarice.' It was later claimed:

> The number of females who follow a life of prostitution for the gratification of sexual desire alone, is comparatively limited; but it is found in combination with other causes, and may be said to be a conspicuous feature in the character of the great majority of prostitutes. It is scarcely possible to conceive that any female could give herself up to unrestrained indulgence in this respect, without having some inclination to it.

Since sexuality in normal women was regarded as non-existent, its manifestation in streetwalkers might be considered as evidence of their depravity: but the basic issue was the degree of severity that was appropriate when dealing with such women.[18]

Even an institution organised on the principle of kindness and leniency might be a strain on the nerves of the inmates. From its foundation the Magdalen Hospital made it a rule to give 'all possible Discouragement ... to every Kind of Discovery that the Parties themselves do not chuse to make'; by 1816 this regulation had been redrafted as 'no enquiry into names or family is permitted; but all possible discouragement given to the making any discovery of them'. This was evidently not the rule at some of the refuges established later. A broadsheet of 1835 entitled *Most Wonderful Appearance of a Ghost at the Penitentiary, Earl's Mead, Bristol* gives some curious sidelights on the atmosphere of this particular institution in the 1830s: when the phantom was reported, the matrons, suspecting 'a spirit of another and more dangerous description' – i.e. gin – caused the house to be searched, despite the lateness of the hour, and then sent for some of the patrons, who after enquiries decided to sit up all night with the inmates:

> The gentleman, in order to improve the time, was questioning the unfortunate girls with reference to their past lives ... [in one case] asking her if she had ever known of the commission of murder, the guilty perpetrators of which were never brought to justice.

Evidently the only medal for tact which this charitable gentleman would be likely to obtain would be one he awarded himself: the girls, not surprisingly, were at last reduced to 'begging, as a favour, that they may be ironed, and sent to Bridwell'.[19]

At the same time, one wonders to what extent these institutions were less friendly and oppressive and rule-bound than the average middle-class household where these women might hope to find employment as domestic servants. Perhaps the point was that many of the inmates did not *want* to be domestic servants. The Guardian Society, from whose refuge 385 out of 1,015 inmates had withdrawn or been expelled between 1812 and 1827, reported that the majority of the women they had attempted to help were in difficulty as a result of 'the combined effects of ignorance, idleness, and insubordination'. One could well imagine that, driven to seek assistance as a result of a particular accumulation of problems – venereal infection or other illness, being robbed or beaten up, a succession of unremunerative evenings on the prowl – many of these women regretted their decision to be 'rescued' once their natural vitality and high spirits had been restored. One courtesan down on her luck recorded:

> My sighs were like those of a stript gamester: I was mad at my misfortunes, but never intended to leave off my former practices. I grieved for my change of circumstances but it was a grief which proceeded from pride, not an affliction from the horrors of a misspent life, but chagrin occasioned by my knowing that I was deprived of the means of making the same figure in town as formerly.

Even at their most desperate, not all such women were desperate enough to apply to charitable institutions. When in February 1816 a sub-committee of the Guardian Society visited 130 women 'who had been removed from the streets' and confined in Bridewell, then the main London prison for women, only 45 of the prisoners were even willing to speak to their visitors, and of these 'only twenty-one expressed a desire to be rescued from their vicious associates'. For the members of the sub-committee this was horrifying proof of the corrupting effect of evil company and debauched habits: an alternative interpretation might be that these women, even when provided with enforced leisure for reflection, preferred the style of life they had chosen to any practicable alternative, but this was an interpretation that the middle classes were reluctant to make. They preferred to talk of 'that want of principle, which too much distinguishes the lower part of the Inhabitants of large Cities'.[20]

Septimus Hodson, chaplain of the Asylum for Female Orphans in Lambeth, announced, 'we are to enquire into the motives of our Benevolence', and in the end it seems possible that the real function of the Magdalen Hospital and similar institutions was to effect some sort of transfer of responsibility, to make some sort of moral statement by a cunning shift of perspective. In 1769 the Magdalen Hospital announced, 'This House of repentance may be also considered as a signal to warn unwary youths, from splitting on the rocks of vice, where they are so often allured by the vanity of dissipation', yet this view of itself was addressed much more to potential subscribers than to potential seducers. In fact nearly all the thousands of pages written on the subject of prostitution and seduction were by people who abhorred illicit sex and consequently had little direct knowledge of it, but this is not to say they had no personal interests at stake. William Hale, who claimed that to suggest that women in want had no existing means of assistance was 'to libel the parish officers' was himself a parish treasurer. His argument that no woman was ever under the economic necessity of prostituting herself was praised in the *European Magazine*, in a review that was probably by Patrick Colquhoun's colleague Joseph Moser, metropolitan stipendiary magistrate at the Worship Street Office, round the corner from Finsbury Square. Since prostitution was traditionally regarded as the last resort of destitute females, to claim that nobody had ever been forced into prostitution by poverty was tantamount to suggesting that nobody had ever suffered the extremities of destitution, a convenient maxim for those whose job it was to defend the legal and social *status quo*. The controversy about the London Female Penitentiary in 1809 involved at least nine pamphlets attacking the views which William Hale had put forward in *An Address to the Public upon the Dangerous Tendency of the London Female Penitentiary*, a reply by Hale entitled *A Reply to the Pamphlets Lately Published in Defence of the London Female Penitentiary: with Further Remarks Upon the Dangerous Tendency of that Institution*, a pamphlet on his behalf by the Rev. John Thomas, pastor of the Independent congregation of which Hale was deacon – this publication was entitled *An Appeal to the Public; or a Vindication of the Character of Mr William Hale, from the Calumnious Aspersions of the Reviewer in the Evangelical Magazine* – and articles in the *European Magazine*, the *Evangelical Magazine* and the *Christian Guardian*; one cannot but suspect that these exchanges were fuelled as much by self-importance, and a desire to shine within one's particular circle, as by an urgent determination to do one's best for London's outcasts. The self-importance of the do-gooders was remarked upon at the time. One critic of charities for the relief of prostitutes claimed:

> a number of these charities are only known to, or heard of by the public at the annual meetings, when a flaming report is made, a dinner had, and a fresh subscription for their support entered into.

Some of those involved seem to have been motivated by a hypocritical desire to cover up, or perhaps exorcise or expiate, their own lascivious proclivities. The Rev. Benjamin Russen, master of the charity school in Bethnal Green, took one of his pupils, aged fifteen, to attend divine service in the chapel of the Lock-Hospital and raped her in the coach on the way home, explaining to her 'there was no harm in it, as he was a minister'. At the Old Bailey, where he stood trial for this and for rapes on three younger pupils, his defence was that the girls were the tools of neighbours who had conspired to secure his dismissal after he had told the curate 'that the man who lives next door to me lives with another man's wife; that the reverend Mr D. [evidently another local curate] had a bastard child'. The Rev. Septimus Hodson, chaplain of the Asylum for Female Orphans in Lambeth, having praised the institution for its work in 'preserving a few souls safe and unpolluted from the torrent of dissipation and vice, which overflows the world', fathered a child on one of the inmates – aged thirteen. Among the clerical members of the Society for the Suppression of Vice, whose campaign against obscene literature will be described in a later chapter, were the Rev. Edward Robson, MA of Emmanuel College, Cambridge, non-resident vicar of Orston in Nottinghamshire, stipendiary minister at Trinity Chapel, Mile End and lecturer at St Mary's, Whitechapel, who seduced the daughter of the sexton at Whitechapel, the Rev. George Horridge, rector of Newton in Lancashire, and master of the school there, till convicted of raping one of his eleven-year-old female pupils, and the Rev. George Chisholm DD, rector of Ashmore in Dorset, and proprietor of a school in Hammersmith between 1790 and his death in 1825, who had five illegitimate children by a former maid-servant, whom he pretended was his niece.[21]

But perhaps the best illustration of the thesis that many of those most vocal and active in the campaign to relieve prostitution and to reform morals were mainly concerned with their self-image and prospects of self-promotion is provided by the career of the Rev. William Dodd, chaplain of the Magdalen Hospital at the time of its foundation, and indefatigable as a preacher in urging gratitude and good conduct on the unfortunate Magdalens: 'as nothing of severity will be shewn you, so nothing of unseemly and refractory conduct can be allowed, or will be permitted', he would tell them, and the affluent of the metropolis would flock to hear his mellifluous elocution and to watch his graceful postures and hand-movements. Along with his elegant writings and his fascinating eloquence his position as chaplain to the Magdalens was an important part of his stock in trade as one of the best-known younger ecclesiastical personalities in the capital, and no doubt many of his friends regretted almost as much as he did that he failed to obtain the clerical preferment that was worthy of his powers. His wife, whom he had married in 1751, was the cast-off mistress of the Earl of Sandwich and was as eager to get on as her husband. In January 1774 she offered the wife of the Lord Chancellor £3,000 down and an annuity of £500 in return for Dodd's being appointed to the most fashionable parish in London, St George's Hanover Square. As a result of this *faux pas* Dodd was dismissed from the list of royal chaplains and was given to understand that an appointment to a parish in the gift of the Crown was now out of the question. Three years later, overwhelmed by debts, he forged the Earl of Chesterfield's signature on a bill and was subsequently tried for forgery, convicted and hanged at Tyburn. It is possible that part of the eighteenth century's fascination with prostitutes, and the assumptions behind attempts to set up a practicable machinery for rescuing them, stemmed from a perception of the element of self-destructiveness, perhaps even of self-hatred, that might often be detected in the lives of the women who became streetwalkers: the fallen women embodied a rejection of all that the Enlightenment held as valuable and rational. At one level William Dodd had understood this very well, at another level it seems that even on the scaffold he never quite understood the dialectic of exploitation and being exploited which had been as central to his own life as to the lives of the unfortunate women whom he had lectured in the chapel at the Magdalen Hospital.[22]

6

The Deviant

It is characteristic of the social construction of reality in the eighteenth century that the first treatment of lesbianism in English literature, apart from a scurrilous poem and a piece of hack sensationalism dashed off by Henry Fielding to pad out the meagre details of a newspaper report, was an episode in a pornographic novel:

> She, who was never out of her way when any occasion of lewdness presented itself, turned to me, embraced and kiss'd me with great eagerness. This was new, this was odd; but imputing it to nothing but pure kindness, which, for aught I knew, it might be the London way to express in that manner, I was determin'd not to be behind-hand with her, and returned her the kiss and embrace, with all the fervour that perfect innocence knew.
>
> Encouraged by this, her hands became extremely free, and wander'd over my whole body, with touches, squeezes, pressures that either shock'd or alarm'd me.
>
> ... not contented with these outer posts, she now attempts the main spot, and began to — [1]

Lesbian sex has continued to feature in pornography and, even more strikingly, in erotic cinema during the twentieth century. Films like those in the *Emanuelle* series tend to suggest that the point about having two beautiful girls naked in bed together is that it provides the male customer with two sex objects for the price of one; yet in John Cleland's trail-blazing account of 1749, Fanny Hill's female lover is described unflatteringly as exhibiting 'the havoc which a long course of hackneyship and hot waters must have made of her constitution', with 'a pair of breasts that hung loosely down'. Perhaps the real attraction of lesbian sex for pornographers is that it can be presented as sex that isn't really sex, though containing the promise of the real thing with the reader: '"Oh! what a charming creature thou art!" ' exclaims Fanny Hill's unalluring bedmate, ' "What a happy man will he be that first makes a woman of you! ...

Oh! that I were a man for your sake!" ... now well assured that she had, by her touches, sufficiently inflamed me for her purpose, she roll'd down the bedclothes gently, and –' In a later work, which evidently borrows from this scene, a young West Indian-born girl spends a night being heavily petted by the niece of a brothel-keeper in Upper Brook Street – 'suffice it to assure our readers, that in the morning the innocent and ruddy Creole was but half a virgin' – as a prelude to being deflowered by a man who arrives by appointment the following day. There is also, in the pleasing fantasy that the novice partner in lesbian sex has no idea what is going on, an opportunity to present the young girl not as eager and enthusiastically compliant, as is generally the case in pornographer's sex, but as 'tame and passive', as in Fanny Hill's case:

> I lay then all tame and passive as she could wish, whilst her freedom raised no other emotions but those of a strange, and, till then, unfelt pleasure. Every part of me was open and exposed to the licentious courses of her hands ... the extension of my limbs, languid stretchings, sighs, short heavings, all conspired to assure that experienced wanton that I was more pleased than offended at her proceedings ...

Such passivity no doubt harmonised better with male fantasies about deflowering virgins than the somewhat aggressive sexuality of the standard heroines of pornography.[2]

Sex between women had been anathematised by St Thomas Aquinas, though some of his successors, such as St Antoninus (Antonio Pierozzi), Archbishop of Florence, in the fifteenth century and St Carlo Borromeo, Archbishop of Milan, in the sixteenth century did not count it, with sodomy, as a sin against nature but merely as a sin of lust. St Carlo Borromeo's penitential code meted out two years' penance for lesbian acts as compared to seven to fifteen years of penance for male homosexual acts.[3] The Councils of Paris (1212) and Rouen (1214) had forbidden nuns to share beds, and rumours of lesbian goings on in convents persisted in Britain even after the Reformation, being refreshed by anti-clerical pornography of continental origin which occasionally appeared in English translation, for example *Venus dans le cloître* (1683), probably by Jean Barrin, translated as *Venus in the Cloister: or, the Nun in her Smock* (*circa* 1692). Occasionally there were prosecutions: one woman was sentenced to death by drowning in Speier in 1477, and another at Geneva in 1568, and there was at least one case in

France, and two in Spain, in the sixteenth century of women being executed for using dildoes. Another woman was executed for lesbian offences at Halberstadt in 1721, but on the whole there seems to have been much less official preoccupation with lesbianism than with other forms of sexual irregularity: the first prosecution of lesbians in Amsterdam was not till 1792 and resulted only in a sentence of banishment from the city.[3]

In England lesbianism was never a legal offence, but in any case the possibility of sex between women seems to have been little appreciated. James Parsons, in *A Medical and Critical Enquiry into the Nature of Hermaphrodites* (1741), wrote of women with abnormally large clitorises who were said to practice tribadism with ordinary women but explained,

> they do not desire Women more than Men, from a natural Inclination, but because by a Gratification of this Nature there is not so much danger of being expos'd ... both find their account answer'd, without fear of that Accident [i.e. pregnancy], that is the necessary Consequence of dealing with Men.

According to contemporary folklore, wives who had dreams about making love to other women had nothing to worry about because, 'If a barren woman dreams she prostitutes herself with her own sex, shews she'll have a child; but to a fruitful woman much pain in bearing her children.' It seems that eighteenth-century men were simply not ready to grasp the point that some women might *prefer* other women to men. In *Fanny Hill* the author admits that Fanny's bedmate might have had 'one of those arbitrary tastes, for which there is no accounting' but goes on: 'Not that she hated men, or did not even prefer them to her own sex.' A pamphlet of 1771 which hints at the possibility of a fundamental emotional orientation towards women can hardly be said to do so in a sympathetic manner:

> Miss Sappho, who was the first young classic maid that bestowed her affections on her own sex ... was the first Tommy the world has upon record; but to do her justice, though there hath been many Tommies since, yet we never had but one Sappho.

Later in the 1770s Lady Eleanor Butler and Sarah Ponsonby, two young ladies of good family in Ireland, whose passionate friendship had been objected to by their relatives, ran off together to Wales, where they became internationally famous as the Ladies of Llangollen. Visitors to the area sought eagerly for introductions and the worst they had to suffer in the way of tittle-tattle were some paragraphs in the *St James's Chronicle* headed 'Extraordinary Female Affection', stating that while Sarah Ponsonby was 'effeminate, fair and beautiful', Lady Eleanor Butler 'is tall and masculine. She wears always a riding-habit. Hangs up her hat with the air of a sportsman in the hall; and appears in all respects as a young man, if we except the petticoats, which she still retains.' None of their scores of visitors ever seem to have supposed that unusual sexual practices were involved in their relationship, and given the climate of the times this should perhaps be put down to naïvety rather than to open-minded tolerance. It seems to have been assumed that because the Ladies of Llangollen did not want men, they did not want sex. This may indeed have been the case: but nowadays it would not be so easily taken for granted.[4]

The eighteenth century seems indeed to have been relatively sympathetic to female cross-dressers. A number achieved minor celebrity in England, notably Christian Davies (1667-1739), wounded in the head while serving as a dragoon in Marlborough's army at Ramillies in 1706, Phoebe Hessel (1713?-1821), wounded as an infantry private at Fontenoy in 1743 and commemorated by a street named after her in London's East End, in the neighbourhood where she was born, Hannah Snell (1723-1792), already a mother before she embarked on her career as soldier, marine and sailor, eventually married three times, Mary Anne Talbot (1778-1808), a drummer boy in the army which captured Valenciennes when she was fifteen and a powder-monkey on board *The Brunswick* at the Glorious First of June when she was sixteen, and 'William Brown', who rose to be captain of the fore-top on the 110-gun *Queen Charlotte* during the Napoleonic War despite the additional disadvantage of being black, and who concealed her sex on board a succession of overcrowded warships for eleven years. A girl who dresses as a man to join the army features in a ballad published around 1780 but still known today, 'Sweet Polly Oliver'. In the Netherlands 54 female cross-dressers have been traced between 1702 and 1783: curiously, the phenomenon seems to have become rarer around 1800. As in England, most of the Dutch cross-dressers served at one time or another as soldiers or sailors. It was sometimes suggested that they donned uniform in order to stay close to a male lover, but the life of much the best-documented cross-dresser, Dr James Miranda Barry, who served as a doctor in the army medical service between 1813 and 1859, indicates that in her case at least the chief motive was a determined preference for a man's career as opposed to that of a woman. One notes, incidentally, that a volume entitled *Lives of Most Remarkable Female Robbers*, extracted from Charles Johnson's *A General History of the Lives and Adventures of the Most Famous Highwaymen, Murderers, and Street-Robbers* and *A General History of Pyrates*, and including the story of the two cross-dressing but possibly mythical female pirates Anne Bonny and Mary Read, was published, in 1801, by a woman publisher, Ann Lemoine.[5]

In 1766 a prosecution for extortion brought to public attention the case of a female who had successfully passed herself off as a male for about four decades, having cohabited with another woman, as man and wife, for thirty-six years, been the licensee of the White Horse public house in Poplar, and served in all the offices of the parish save that of churchwarden, a post she was in line to take up when her secret came out as a result of her involvement with a gang who had discovered the truth and had been putting the squeeze on her. One of the extortioners was sentenced to stand in the pillory and to serve four years in gaol: the court seems to have been completely on the side of his victim. No comment seems to have been passed on the possible motives that had actuated the woman and her 'wife': it was rumoured that when they had first decided to live together they had drawn lots to decide who should be the husband. Nearly sixty years later a maid-servant in Scotland named Helen Oliver was reported to have assumed her brother's name and clothes after the ploughman who had been courting her turned out to be a cross-dressing woman: 'it is believed by Helen's relatives that it was the arguments of this personage which induced her to abandon the female dress and duties.' These arguments are unlikely to have been purely intellectual: Helen, *alias* John, Oliver went on to become engaged to a girl in Johnstone before a chance encounter with someone who knew her true identity led her to decamp. Another woman, on the run after taking a too active part in the Gordon Riots in London in 1780, passed herself off as a male pedlar for thirteen years: again one can't quite believe that that was the whole story.[6]

*

The possibility that lesbian sex might arise from being deprived of male company inevitably focused on the one institution in Protestant England where nubile middle-class females lived together in virtual seclusion from the world of men. Though female education in England lagged far behind the provision for males, boarding schools for girls had begun to be established in the early seventeenth century. In 1689 Henry Purcell's opera *Dido and Aeneas* had its première at Mr Josias Priest's school for young ladies in Chelsea, which indicates something of the scale and affluence of the largest of such institutions. By 1800 female education was a thriving industry, particularly concentrated in and around the London suburb of Hackney – it was no doubt the public outrage at the danger posed to the bevies of schoolgirls using the streets of this then respectable parish which led in 1805 to William Cooper, the so-called 'Hackney Monster', being sentenced to two years' imprisonment for flashing, instead of the more customary fine.[7]

Three girls' schools founded in the eighteenth century survive to this day (the Clergy Orphan Girls' School, founded 1749 – now St Margaret's, Bushey – the Godolphin School, opened for eight 'orphan gentlewomen' in 1784, and the Royal Cumberland Free Masons' School, opened, with fifteen pupils, in 1788 – now the Rickmansworth Masonic School), but generally speaking girls' schools, like a large number of eighteenth-century boys' schools, were underfinanced, badly managed speculative enterprises and the girls often seem to have been sent to boarding-schools because they were in the way at home, perhaps following the death of one parent and the remarriage of the other, or perhaps because the parents were not actually married, as was the case with Harriet Smith in Jane Austen's *Emma* and Eliza, the daughter of Colonel Brandon's beloved and seduced sister-in-law in *Sense and Sensibility*. No doubt the proprietors tried very hard, but somehow girls' boarding schools never quite managed to be respectable. Francis Foster, for example, claimed in 1779 that their influence on the girls was completely deleterious: 'they infallibly pollute their Minds, and initiate them in Vice.' The pages dealing with the disastrous effects of girls' boarding schools in the British Library's copy of *Serious Thoughts on the Miseries of Seduction and Prostitution, with a Full Account of the Evils that Produce Them* (1783) were torn out over a hundred years ago, but James Lackington's *Two Letters, on the Bad Consequences of Having Daughters educated at Boarding Schools* (1804) survive:

> the girls are often corrupted by the abandoned servant maids who now get into most houses ... If the school be large, it is ten to one but

some of the girls have overheard lewd hints, or discovered something
improper either in the servants, or their brothers, or books, which
they have communicated the first opportunity to their school fellows
... it is well known that many, very many, of those unhappy females
that are now sunk so deep in vice and infamy, and the worst degree
of misery, had their pure minds first tainted at *Boarding-Schools*.[8]

Nor was it simply a question of smutty talk. The author of a
pornographic novel published in 1749 seems to expect his readers
to understand immediately when he mentioned that 'As Miss had
been bred at a Boarding School, she had there learned vicious
Tricks'. Mary Wollstonecraft, who had run a boarding school at
Newington Green, remembered,

> what nasty indecent tricks do they also learn from each other, when
> a number of them pig together in the same bed-chamber, not to speak
> of the vices that render the body weak.

The vices referred to were masturbation, in its mutual and solitary
forms. It was of course *male* masturbation which the Bible had
seemed to condemn, in the story of Onan (Genesis ch. 38, v. 9), and
the vice was naturally seen as also being a problem at boys' schools;
Thomas Beddoes, a respected doctor, warned:

> even from *one*, it cannot fail to be communicated to a great number
> of school-fellows and to be kept up among succeeding races, like the
> eternal fire of Vesta.

Similarly H.T. Kitchener laid it down as a rule that:

> A single youth who has learnt this deplorable practice is capable of
> contaminating a whole school, as boys are always ready enough to
> catch at any thing that is novel to them ... a single impure is sufficient
> to infect a whole flock.

Nor was it a danger merely in boarding schools:

> if introduced into a school, it spreads with all the virulence of a
> contagious disease ... it is chiefly prevalent among youth of sedentary
> and studious habits. It is the imperious duty of every master of a
> school, or a manufactory, to guard against the introduction of this
> pernicious habit, for once introduced, extirpation is hardly within the
> scope of possibility.[9]

A real-life case of lesbianism at a girls' boarding school near Edinburgh, which became public property in 1811 when the alleged perpetrator sued her accuser for defamation, actually made much less stir than the question of masturbation, whether by boys or girls. Until the eighteenth century little importance seems to have been attached to masturbation. Falloppio in the sixteenth century even recommended it as a means of enlarging the penis when young. In 1669 it was still a topic which John Dryden could refer to humorously in the prologue of a play:

> As some raw Squire, by tender Mother bred,
> Till one and Twenty keeps his Maidenhead,
> (Pleas'd with some Sport that he alone does find,
> And thinks a secret to all Humane kind,)
> Till mightily in love, yet halfe afraid,
> He first attempts the gentle Dairy maid.

Alexander Robertson of Struan *circa* 1700 thought it no worse than recourse to a prostitute:

> Unless his full spermatick Sluice
>   Was ready to run o'er,
> Who'd spill a Drop of wholsom Juice
>   On such a stinking Whore?
>
> So to a House of Office streight
>   A School-Boy does repair,
> To ease his Postern of his Weight
>   And fr—— his P—— there.

As late as 1749, John Cleland refers to a girl masturbating in *Fanny Hill* almost as if it were a matter of course, and in the 1760s Robert Wallace, in his unpublished essay 'Of Venery' described the male teenager's discovery of masturbation as an 'agreeable experience'. But one should bear in mind that *Fanny Hill* was suppressed by the authorities, and that 'Of Venery' was only printed two centuries after the death of its author. A new orthodoxy had established itself in England, largely as a result of a bestselling, oft-revised work entitled *Onania; or the heinous sin of self-pollution, and all its frightful consequences in both sexes considered*, first printed in 1708.[10]

The hysterical tone of *Onania*, augmented by readers' letters and editorial responses that were published in subsequent editions, may suggest that the book circulated principally among the worse-educated classes, but in fact its views seem to have been enthusiastically espoused by the medical profession, and the reason why reprintings became rarer after the twenty-second edition of 1778 was probably that the same opinions had become available, in a more decorous and imposing format, in the publications of more respectable – or at least identifiable – authors (*Onania* was anonymous). A somewhat less populist work by the Swiss physician Samuel Auguste André David Tissot, originally published in Latin in 1758, came out in a French version at Lausanne in 1760 under the title *L'Onanisme; ou dissertation physique sur les maladies produites par la masturbation* and seems to have sustained interest in the problem on the continent: there were twenty-eight more French-language editions by 1842, eight more editions in the years 1870-1886, and the last commercial printing seems to have been in 1905: English editions appeared in 1766 and 1781 and a German translation in 1785. There was also a veritable flood of other publications on the topic in France after 1810, some of which were known in England.[11]

The author of *Onania* claimed that masturbation in males caused '*Stranguaries, priapisms ... Gonorrhoeas*, more difficult to be cured, than those contracted from women ... fainting fits and epilepsies ... consumptions ... nightly and excessive seminal emissions, a weakness in the *penis*, and a loss of erection, as if they had been castrated'; in women it caused '*barrenness*, by a venereal indifferency, and at length a total ineptitude to the act of generation itself'. According to Thomas Beddoes in 1802, 'Imagination and memory decay ... The ears incessantly ring; deafness ensues; and epileptic fits or atrophy'. Dr Alex P. Buchan, who claimed he had 'had an opportunity of listening to the confessions of a variety of victims to this pernicious practice', described the symptoms thus:

> Society is avoided, seclusion sought after, and this species of self-murderer at last assumes the appearance of a moving skeleton, enveloped in a leaden shroud. Hectic fever takes place, which finally terminates in an early death.

Few seem to have doubted that the practice was fatal: a clergyman, having described what happened in the Bible to Onan, with precise references to chapter and verse, asked

Who shall say the numbers which since his days have fallen into it? And who shall calculate the army which by Onanism have hastened the termination of a life of sin, and hurried themselves into eternity!

Admittedly one of the most distinguished medical writers of the day, John Hunter, stated:

I am clear in my own mind that the books on the subject have done more harm than good. I think I may affirm that this act in itself does less harm to the constitution than the natural.

And one or two other doctors were inclined to agree: but the consensus was that the practice was extraordinarily destructive to health.[12]

At least to begin with, the assumption may partly have been that masturbation must be unhealthy because it was sinful. John Armstrong, in his *The Oeconomy of Love*, wrote enthusiastically of spontaneous wet dreams:

> The boy may wrestle, when
> Night-working Fancy steals him to the arms
> Of Nymph oft wish'd awake, and, 'mid the rage
> Of the soft tumult, every turgid Cell
> Spontaneous disembogues its lucid store,
> Bland and of azure tinct.

But a few pages on he denounced masturbation:

> Banish from thy Shades
> Th'ungenerous, selfish, solitary Joy,
> Hold, Parricide, thy hand!

Edward Aven's notes to the 1771 edition of *The Oeconomy of Love* claimed of masturbation, that 'its Criminality is justly rank'd with the Vice of *Sodom*'. There was also the belief that all emissions of semen weakened the body. James Graham's *A Lecture on the Generation, Increase and Improvement of the Human Species* of 1780 proclaimed:

Thrice happy! supremely blessed! in my opinion, are those young men and women, who live, till they are at least twenty years of age, without ever once having had even one seminal emission in their whole life, asleep or awake, voluntarily or involuntarily!

But emissions caused by intercourse were thought less harmful than those resulting from masturbation or wet dreams. In the seventeenth century Sinibaldi had asked, 'Why do night-pollutions afford more pleasure, and do more debilitate than a man's spontaneous copulating with a woman?', and in 1799 the physician to the Saxon embassy in London claimed of masturbation: 'By this unnatural practice, a greater quantity of semen is evacuated, than by the natural commerce between the sexes.' Of course the suggestion that self-abuse might be more fun was unhelpful, and H.T. Kitchener asserted:

> every seminal ejaculation which is produced by manual or mental art, affords *less* pleasure, and at the same time enervates infinitely more than those which come unbidden, as it were, and are only the natural fruit of the pure sexual passion.

In defending masturbation John Hunter may have gone too far in the opposite direction:

> I think I may affirm that this act in itself does less harm to the constitution in general than the natural. That the natural with common women, or such as we are indifferent about, does less harm to the constitution than where it is not so selfish ... where the mind becomes interested it is worked up to a degree of enthusiasm, increasing the sensibility of the body and disposition for action; and when the complete action takes place it is with proportional violence; and in proportion to the violence is the degree of debility produced, or injury done to the constitution.

But since even Hunter admitted that any sexual emission weakened the body, he would have been obliged to admit the force of the argument put forward by the physician to the Saxon embassy:

> the circumstances, which render this hateful vice so destructive to both sexes, particularly at a tender age, are, that the opportunities of committing it are more frequent than those for the sexual intercourse.[13]

Part of the explanation of onanophobia may have been difficulty in diagnosing certain diseases. Contemporary accounts of the dire effects of masturbation seem nowadays so ludicrous that one tends to forget that young people diagnosed as suffering from the results of onanism sometimes really did die. Tissot, Beddoes, Buchan *et al.*

were respectable doctors who, though they may have made mistakes, knew a dead body when they saw one. One French text, *Des Égaremens secrets, ou de l'onanisme chez les personnes du sexe* (second edition 1830) has a double frontispiece showing the blooming Mlle A——— at fifteen years of age, and the same Mlle A——— thin, grey-faced and bed-ridden, in the *'dernier période de la maladie'* a year later. Perhaps the poor girl's real problem was leukaemia, a complaint not identified until the 1840s. Some of the patients who did not actually die may simply have had glandular fever (infectious mononucleosis). Nevertheless the main reason for the eighteenth century's terror of masturbation was clearly psychological. This is evident both in the scientific discussion of the weakening effect of sexual emissions and in the frequent connection made between masturbation and impotence. Alex P. Buchan gives an account of a youth 'whose athletic appearance offered the most satisfactory proof that his constitution had suffered no material injury from some improper habits acquired at school': his decline and end told one story for Buchan, perhaps another for us. On reading a copy of Tissot's *L'Onanisme* the unfortunate young man concluded 'he had for ever ruined his constitution' and, obsessed with his situation, 'he purchased every copy of Tissot he could lay his hands on' to distribute to his friends and acquaintances, both male and female. After a year of this he shot himself. A later generation would regard this man as a victim – yet another victim? – of Buchan's professional incompetence: but as far as Buchan was concerned he was simply yet another victim of the crime of self-abuse.[14]

*

But the horror of masturbation was as nothing compared to the horror of male homosexuality. 'Buggery com̃yttid with mankynde or beaste' had been made a capital offence in England in 1533, by 25 Hen. VIII c. 6. This statute was intended to be in force only until the last day of the subsequent parliament. The prohibition was made perpetual in 1540 by 32 Hen. VIII c. 3, and though repealed in 1547 by 1 Edw. VI was renewed with modifications in 1548 by 2 & 3 Edw. VI c. 29. This was cancelled by Queen Mary's Statute of Repeal (1 Mar. St. 1. c. 1. cl. 3) and the continuous history of sodomy as a capital offence really dates from 1562, when the statute 5 Eliz. c. 17 revived the Henrician legislation. According to the judgment in Rex *versus* Wiseman in 1718 and the subsequent judicial discussion, the law covered anal penetration of females as well as males, but few prosecutions seem to have been brought for buggering females: the practice was certainly known, however, for the Rev. William Dodd describes in his novel *The Sisters* how a prostitute is made to dance naked with red-hot pokers in the back room of a tavern till

> at length (gracious Heaven avert such horrid crimes from our guilty land!) at length demanding the perpetration of something too black to be named, too diabolical to be mentioned, which she, with just aversion utterly refusing, and resolutely denying, determined rather to die, they swore, unless she consented, they would burn her alive.

There is more evidence of prosecutions on account of sexual connection with animals, but nothing to compare with the situation in Sweden where between the 1630s and 1770s more than 600 men were beheaded and burnt for crimes involving cows, mares, ewes, sows and bitches. In New Haven, Connecticut, in 1647 one Thomas Hogg was accused of bestiality after a sow bore a deformed foetus which 'had a faire & white skinne & head, as Thomas Hoggs is'; an even more convincing circumstance was that when Hogg was taken to the sty and made to 'scratt' the sow the latter was immediately aroused whereas another sow, when fondled 'was not moved at all'. In spite of this evidence, and in spite of other minor charges, Hogg was still at liberty a year later. In England, in the early nineteenth century at least, men were executed for this offence, but perhaps partly because men accused of bestiality tended to be labourers rather than members of the affluent classes, little publicity was given to such cases. As far as most people were concerned, the legislation referred only to homosexual acts between men. (There was in fact no statute against homosexual practices not involving penetration, but it was a standard practice to prosecute lesser forms of statutory felonies as misdemeanours, and around 1800 this was to be the legal basis for an increasing number of non-capital prosecutions for homosexuality.)[15]

For the first two centuries during which sodomy was a capital offence, prosecutions seem to have been rare: one case at the Chelmsford Assizes between 1560 and 1680, two before the Somerset Quarter Sessions 1601-1660 and so on. A couple of trials achieved unusual notoriety, but only because of the social rank of the accused. On 14 May 1631 Mervyn, second Earl of Castlehaven and twelfth Lord Audley, was beheaded on Tower Hill, partly for assisting a friend to rape Lady Castlehaven and partly for sodomy with an employee, Laurence FitzPatrick, who was hanged for the latter offence at Tyburn on 6 July of the same year. Accounts of the Castlehaven trial were printed in 1642 and 1644 – no doubt the outbreak of civil war had whetted the bourgeoisie's appetite for details of aristocratic perversion – and there were five more printings of various versions of the trial between 1699 and 1719. On 5 December 1640 John Atherton, Bishop of Waterford since 1636 (but completely an Englishman, son of a canon of St Paul's and himself formerly a rector in Somersetshire) was hanged with his lover in Dublin: the sermon preached at his funeral by Nicholas Barnard, Dean of Ardagh, was reprinted as late as 1709 and provoked a pamphlet rebutting its alleged misrepresentations, entitled *The Case of John Atherton Bishop of Waterford in Ireland: Fairly Represented against a late Partial Edition of Dr Barnard's Relation, and Sermon at his Funeral*.[16]

The execution in 1726 of a milkman, an upholsterer and a woolcomber seems to have been the first instance when members of a homosexual coterie, as distinct from a pair of lovers, went to the gallows: a number of other men were arrested and questioned, and a woman known as Mother Clap, who ran the place of resort frequented by the convicted men, was sentenced to two years' gaol and to stand in the pillory. Nevertheless capital prosecutions remained rare throughout the eighteenth century. At this stage there was no provision for the compilation of penal statistics on a nationwide basis and figures for London and Middlesex go back only to 1749: they show one execution for sodomy in 1757, another in 1770, and a third in 1797. Pardons seem to have been as common as hangings; a publican convicted of sodomy received a pardon in 1761 and Robert Jones, a lieutenant in the Royal Artillery found guilty of sodomising a thirteen-year-old boy, was pardoned in 1777. Some verses in a contemporary newspaper which characterised Jones as

> A captain who employ'd his parts
> Upon male b—ms not female hearts

suggested that

> King George, in vengeance, let him live
> Like Cain, till conscience should forgive

but it seems more likely that Jones, author of a frequently reprinted treatise on fireworks and another on skating, had influential friends. It might even be possible to argue a degree of ambiguous official tolerance. When Thomas Cannon, who published a defence of homosexuality entitled *Ancient and Modern Pederasty Investigated and Exemplified* in 1749, was arrested on government orders for being the author of 'a certain Tract or Pamphlet, containing the most detestable Principles of Impurity', he was released on posting a bond for future good behaviour, and though sodomy was made a court-martial offence in the Royal Navy for the first time in the same year by 22 Geo. II c. 33 cl. 29, the enactment was merely a clause tacked onto a consolidation of the criminal laws pertaining to the Navy, intended to bring the Navy into line with practice in the civilian courts. Capital punishment for sodomy seemed old-fashioned to jurists and legislators influenced by the Enlightenment. The offence ceased to be capital in Austria in 1787, in France in 1791 and in Prussia in 1794. But in England the purge was just about to begin.[17]

*

In July 1804 sheriffs and chairmen of quarter sessions in the English counties were instructed by the government to remit calendars after every assize and quarter sessions listing the prisoners committed and the results of their trials, the object being 'to form an annual Criminal Register for the whole Kingdom, so far as extends to Felonious Offences, showing their nature and numbers, and their increase or diminution'. Statistics for the whole of England and Wales, deriving from these returns, are available from 1805 onward. In the first year of returns, there were no executions for sodomy. In the second year – 1806, evidently a slack year for murder – six men were hanged for sodomy as compared to only five for murder. Executions for sodomy averaged two a year thereafter till 1835. On 22 August of that year John Sparshott, aged nineteen, was hanged for sodomy, in company with a man convicted of burglary, at Horsham in Sussex, 'both exhibiting much fortitude and resignation ... The silly custom of passing the hands of the dead men over the necks of two or three females, as a supposed cure for glandular enlargements, was upon this occasion had recourse to.' Three months later John Smith and John Pratt were hanged for sodomy outside Newgate Gaol in London. 'The crowd was excessive but exceedingly decorous.' These seem to have been the last men to die in England because of their sexual preferences. Three other death sentences were commuted in 1835, as were others that were handed down in the years that followed. Sodomy ceased to be a hanging offence in 1861 by the terms of 24/25 Vict. c. 100 cl. 61, which made the crime punishable by penal servitude for life or for any term not less than ten years.[18]

The increase in capital prosecutions was paralleled by an increase of trials on the more easily proved charge of 'assault with intent to commit sodomy, and other unnatural Misdemeanours', there being 29 convictions on this count in England and Wales in 1810 and 22 in 1813.[19]

In this period there were only two prosecutions for sodomy in the High Court of Admiralty, which dealt with offences at sea not involving Royal Navy personnel, and the accused, an army recruit in 1807 and a merchant-navy captain in 1810, were both acquitted. In the Royal Navy there were no court-martials for sodomy from 1763 to 1796 inclusive, but from 1797 to 1800 there were seven death sentences handed down, one of those convicted being a ship's captain, Henry Allen, who was hanged on board *The Adventure* on 15 May 1797. After 1806 the court-martial records are poorly indexed and it is difficult to trace cases, though it appears that in a series of courts-martial in December 1815 and January 1816 four men were sentenced to death for sodomy in *The Africaine*.[20]

Soldiers stationed in Britain were subject to the civilian courts in the case of non-military offences, but there were a number of army courts-martial for sodomy in forces serving overseas. In 1811, in Lord Wellington's army in the Peninsula, four soldiers and a camp-follower were prosecuted: one soldier was hanged, another sentenced to one thousand lashes, the other three men being acquitted. Two years later two soldiers were sentenced to 800 lashes for 'Buggary' at Lisbon. Two soldiers tried in Guadaloupe in 1813 were acquitted, as were two others tried at Messina three months later, but a fifth soldier was hanged for sodomy at the Cape early in 1814. Rape prosecutions in the army overseas were, incidentally, not even half as numerous as sodomy prosecutions.[21]

*

One might suppose that in a culture generally hostile to male homosexuality, homosexual activity would sustain itself as a minority taste at a fairly constant level, but Alan Bray, author of *Homosexuality in Renaissance England*, has argued that, though there had been homosexual networks in larger towns, there had been no such thing as a homosexual social identity, perceived both by homosexuals themselves and by the heterosexual majority among whom they lived, till the end of the seventeenth century; the corollary of which would be that a significant proportion, perhaps the majority of homosexuals, would have remained isolated and unaware that there were other men like them for the whole of their lives. This possibility is not as startling as it might appear at first glance. Despite a tiresome emphasis on male virility, premarital sex was not the mandatory norm for most males in the sixteenth and seventeenth centuries, and, even in sub-groups where it was usual, devout religious beliefs enjoining chastity were not totally unknown. Consequently most men grew to maturity without being under any necessity of deciding how much they wanted to sleep with women. Equally men who were secretly drawn to their own sex, living in a moral climate where attraction did not necessarily involve the sequel of orgasm, would find it normal to repress and even deny their urges in the same way as other men did with regard to women.[22]

Perhaps the most celebrated homosexual scandal in England in the first half of the eighteenth century may be an illustration of the customary self-repression of the isolated homosexual. In January 1739 an undergraduate at Wadham College, Oxford named William French was summoned by a servant to the Warden's Lodgings. Later in the day he appeared ill at ease, later still he vomited, and began raving against the Warden, and he spent the following day weeping and complaining. George Baker, one of the younger resident graduates, guessed what was the matter, and after consultation with some of the college fellows the university vice-chancellor was informed. The Rev. John Swinton, Wadham's Sub-Warden, tried to persuade French to give evidence that nothing untoward had happened, but when the Warden, the Rev. Dr Robert Thistlethwayte, was arraigned before the Grand Jury other witnesses came forward. The college butler deposed that Thistlethwayte had once, five or six years previously, begun to act 'in a beastly Manner; endeavouring to kiss and tongue him, and to put his Hand in his Breeches'; thereafter he made a point of not being alone in a room with the Warden. A barber deposed that, eighteen months previously, he had been shaving Thistlethwayte when the latter groped his crutch, and on another occasion had said, 'How does thy Cock do, my dear Barber? Let me feel it.' The Grand Jury found a true bill against Thistlethwayte, but before the case could be tried he jumped bail and escaped to France, where he died towards the end of 1743. Meanwhile the indefatigable George Baker began to dig up evidence against Swinton, the Sub-Warden, who had been 'remarkably intimate' with Thistlethwayte since returning from Italy in the mid-1730s. Baker found a serving boy who seemed ready to give evidence against Swinton, but this witness appears to have been tampered with and Baker was eventually forced to make a public retraction of his allegations against the Sub-Warden. French graduated BA in 1740 but was deprived of his exhibition for failing to attend college examinations in the same year: nothing is known of his subsequent career, or of George Baker's. Swinton seems to have suffered no damage from his implication in the scandal: he became a prebendary of St Asaph's in 1743, migrated to Christ Church in 1745 and was appointed Keeper of the University Archives in 1767: in other words he was regarded favourably by the Crown, by Oxford's most prestigious college, and by the university fixers. At some point after 1743 he married, but had no children: which may or may not mean anything.[23]

Of course there were those who believed that the Thistlethwayte case was only the tip of the iceberg. There was for example an anonymous poem on the subject entitled *College-Wit Sharpen'd: or, the Head of a House, with a Sting in the Tail ... address'd to the Two Famous Universities of S-d-m and G-m-rr-h*. The text is headed 'The Wadhamites: a Burlesque Poem' but the clear implication of the title is that what had happened at Wadham was only a part of it. The scandal was still evidently being talked about in 1746 when young Tobias Smollett, in a poem entitled *The Advice*, denounced sodomy as

> A vice that 'spite of sense and nature reigns
> And poisons genial love, and manhood stains!

and hinted that there had been a cover-up:

> Let *Isis* wail in murmurs, as she runs,
> Her tempting fathers and her yielding sons;
> While Dullness screens the failings of the church,
> Nor leaves one sliding Rabbi in the lurch.

A footnote refers to 'the unnatural Orgies said to be solemnised on the banks of this river [i.e. the Isis, the name for the Thames at Oxford]; particularly in one place where a much greater sanctity of morals and taste might be expected'. But the successful later career of the Rev. John Swinton does make it difficult to believe that Smollett's – or George Baker's – view of what had been going on was widely accepted.[24]

We know nothing of Robert Thistlethwayte's successful sexual exploits with Swinton or with others: all we know is that, between the ages of forty-two and forty-eight he made advances to three younger men who repulsed him. We don't know if there had been earlier attempts, though it seems unlikely that Thistlethwayte had been grabbing at the crutches of undergraduates and college servants for twenty years without anybody hearing of it. The information we have suggests a man in middle-age who, as his grip on youth and on himself began to weaken, found himself occasionally giving in to urges which in earlier days he had either not recognised, or had succeeded in repressing.

Unfortunately for this theory, Thistlethwayte's earlier days coincide with the period in which his exact contemporary Dudley Ryder, later Lord Chief Justice, kept a diary. One of the entries, for 1 December 1715 relates a conversation with Samuel Powell, 'a very loose young man', then an undergraduate at Queen's:

> he has been told that among the chief men in some of the colleges sodomy is very usual and the master of one college has ruined several young handsome men that way, that it is dangerous sending a young man that is beautiful to Oxford.

As Thistlethwayte had only just been elected to a fellowship at Wadham he could not really be counted as one of 'the chief men' at Wadham: on the other hand in the small world of Oxford he must have known some of the men Powell was referring to. And there may also have been strange goings on at Cambridge. In 1730 Isaac Broderick was prosecuted for homosexual assaults on ten- and eleven-year-old boys only a few weeks after taking up an appointment as master at the Coopers' Company School in London. Broderick was only twenty-two but the number of his victims – though he was indicted on only two counts, a total of eight boys were named at his trial – makes it difficult to believe he was altogether without previous sexual experience: but he had spent the four years before his appointment as a sizar at Trinity College, Cambridge. Perhaps George Baker's suspicions were justified after all: come to that, one might wonder why a young, inexperienced BA like George Baker should jump to conclusions about homosexual goings on if homosexuality was something that was virtually unheard of.[25]

*

Perhaps the strongest argument against Alan Bray's claim that there was no conception of a homosexual social identity, even in London, till around 1700 is that there is plenty of evidence of homosexual groups being targeted by the authorities on the continent at an earlier date. Over forty men of the best families, including noblemen and clerics, were involved in a major investigation of the homosexual community in Venice in 1406 and 1407: sixteen or seventeen of the accused were condemned to death and burnt. Earlier, in 1354, a transvestite prostitute had been executed: it is difficult to believe that none of his clients had observed that he was not a woman. In Geneva between 1555 and 1569 there were fifteen sodomy trials, of which eight resulted in death sentences, and in 1590, after twenty years without sodomy prosecutions, six men were prosecuted, of whom five were sentenced to death. In 1610 there were twelve sodomy trials, resulting in four death sentences. In Seville 71 men were burnt for sodomy and bestiality between 1567 and 1616. In the Kingdom of Valencia, 37 men were executed for sodomy 1571-1630, including seventeen in the years 1621-25. Only in north-western Europe does there seem to have been a *increase* of official concern about homosexuality in the eighteenth century: in the province of Holland in what was then termed the United Provinces there were 96 convictions (mainly non-capital) for homosexual offences in 1730-31 alone, and Dutch prosecutions kept up a relatively high level – two or three a year, with peaks of twelve in 1764 and 1796, 22 in 1798 – throughout the remainder of the century. In Paris the police arrested 44 homosexuals in 1723, 146 in the two years 1737-38, 234 in 1749. In both Calvinist Geneva and Catholic Spain on the other hand the worst was over by 1700 – in Valencia there were more than 250 sodomy prosecutions between 1570 and 1700, fewer than 60 between 1701 and 1800.[26]

The falling off of prosecutions in Geneva and in Spain before 1700, taken together with the fact that Geneva had been dominated by strict Calvinists and Spain by strict Catholics, may suggest that the homosexuality that was prosecuted existed more in the phobia of the authoritarian bigots who controlled the government than in the sexual practices of those prosecuted. The period of maximum prosecution of homosexuals in Spain and Switzerland coincides with the peak of witchcraft prosecutions in other countries – particularly in Calvinist-dominated regions. The possibility that witches and homosexuals might provide alternative scapegoats for societies under pressure is not particularly supported by the fact that James I of England, who did so much to promote witch-phobia during his reigns in Scotland and England, was almost certainly homosexual: on the other hand the execution of fifteen homosexuals in Seville in April 1600 at the height of a plague epidemic does suggest that peaks of persecution coincided with crises in the community.[27]

The relation between the commission of an offence and its prosecution is not of course invariable, but depends both on the nature of the offence and on the culture of the society in which it was committed. Even murder has not always shown up on the statistics produced by some twentieth-century police states, though generally speaking murders tend to be reported much more completely than sex crimes. On the other hand, whereas only a minority of the witches burnt in the seventeenth century seem to have believed themselves capable of exercising malefic powers, the majority of convicted homosexuals seem to have done precisely what they were accused of, and since homosexuality was nowhere officially tolerated the waxing and waning of the incidence of prosecution is not easy to explain. This point will be returned to later.

*

In England in the seventeenth century, despite the execution of the Earl of Castlehaven, homosexuality was regarded as something of a joke. Potentially it might be a very damaging joke, as the enemies of William III no doubt hoped when they put it about that he was homosexual, as in a lampoon headed 'In Answer to one who said the REVOLUTION of 1688 resembled the Case of SATURN, who was dethroned by his Son JUPITER because he was old and good for nothing', which compared William to his father-in-law and predecessor James II:

Could WILLIAM have perform'd in ev'ry Grove,
In Imitation of the mighty JOVE,
And JAMES had grown less pow'rful than his Son,
The Revolution had been well begun:
But since nor Wife nor Daughter ever felt
WILL's manly Parts, but rather thought him gelt,
JAMES was but ill depos'd, whose fruitful Cods,
Scatter'd a generous Race of Demi-Gods,
While t'other unperforming puny Prig,
Could only with his Page retire and fr—.

But sexual relations between men was still something that might be referred to openly, even in the theatre. In Vanbrugh's play *The Relapse* the character named Coupler is portrayed as a randy old queen:

Coupler:	Ha! You young lascivious rogue, you: Let me put my hand in your bosom, sirrah.
Young Fashion:	Stand off, old Sodom.
Coupler:	Nay, pr'y thee now don't be so coy.
Young Fashion:	Keep your hands to yourself, you old dog, or I'll wring your nose off.
Coupler:	Hast thou then been a year in Italy, and brought home a fool at last?

And a little later:

Young Fashion:	Shew me but that, and my soul is thine.
Coupler:	Pox o' thy soul! give me thy warm body.

Later still Coupler kisses the younger man, who exclaims aside, 'Psha, the old letcher.'[28]

The first concerted action against homosexual coteries seems to have been organised by the Societies for Promoting a Reformation of Manners. In October 1707 eight men were tried before the Lord Mayor of London at the Guildhall for homosexual misdemeanours. One witness stated that Thomas Lane, a soldier, approached him on London Bridge and 'pulling out his Nakedness offer'd to put it into his Hand, and withal unbutton'd the Evidence's Breeches, and put his Hand in there'. The other prisoners were accused of similar behaviour. They may either have been homosexual prostitutes or layabouts indulging in drunken pranks: what suggests the involvement of the Societies for Promoting a Reformation of Manners is that one of the witnesses testified against three separate offenders, and three other witnesses each against two offenders.[29]

Eighteen months later an ex-guardsman named George Skelthorp, about to be hanged for two street robberies which he denied committing, confessed to having made 'a great deal of Money' from blackmailing homosexuals in the neighbourhood of one of their favourite resorts in Covent Garden: 'he went to stand in their Way, and when any of them would (as they often did) carry him to a By-place thereabouts to commit their foul Acts with him', he would threaten to expose them unless paid to keep quiet. One of them had retaliated by denouncing him as a foot-pad and he acknowledged 'that it was just with God thus to punish him, for having concealed and conniv'd at those foul Acts'. Some time later nine homosexuals were arrested in a brandy shop in St James's and the rumour was that Skelthorp had tipped off the authorities before his execution, though it was also claimed that the Duke of Ormonde's foot-boy, who was among those arrested, had been the informant. The role of the Societies for Promoting a Reformation of Manners in this incident is not clear, but they were certainly behind the trial and execution of three homosexuals in 1726 – though only a few months later Charles Hitchen, the Under City Marshal, a prominent member of the Societies, was convicted of attempted sodomy and sentenced to stand in the pillory, where he was nearly killed.[30]

By the mid-1720s there was evidently a flourishing homosexual sub-culture in London. In May 1726 the *London Journal* reported:

We hear that 20 Houses have been discovered which entertained Sodomitical Clubs; besides the Nocturnal Assemblies of great Numbers of these Monsters at what they call the Markets, which are, the Royal Exchange, Moorfields, Lincoln's-Inn Bog-Houses, the South Side of St James's Park, and the Piazza's of Covent-Garden, where they make their execrable Bargains, and then withdraw into some dark Corners to perpetrate their odious Wickedness.

Three years later an anonymous pamphlet repeated this list of picking-up places word for word, except that Moorfields was dropped and '*St Clement's Churchyard*' was added. More than eighty years later, during the peak years of prosecution in England, Robert Holloway's well-informed pamphlet *The Phoenix of Sodom*, though referring to 'many about town', could only specify four male brothels – one near the Strand, one in Blackman Street, Southwark, one near the Obelisk, St George's Fields, and one near Bishopsgate; and by this stage only St James's Park remained notorious as an outdoor picking-up spot – in 1808 the Home Secretary recommended that the gates of the park should be locked at night 'to prevent these scandalous practices'. Are we to deduce from this that there had actually been a *decline* in the number of places of homosexual resort? It may be unwise to take the assertions of pamphlets too seriously: among the places listed as 'Nocturnal Assemblies of great Numbers of these Monsters' in 1726 were the Piazzas at Covent Garden and the Royal Exchange, better known as resorts for *female* streetwalkers, and Moorfields, scene of a number of well-publicised sexual assaults on women: St Clement's Churchyard in the Strand, added to the list in 1729, was also notorious as a place for picking up women of easy virtue.[31]

In 1721 a pamphlet entitled *The Conspirators: or, the Case of Catiline* by 'Britannicus' – in fact Thomas Gordon – accused the Earl of Sunderland, then First Lord of the Treasury, of being a sodomite. This pamphlet went through at least ten editions inside a year, though an even more sensational publication two years later, *Love-Letters between a certain late Nobleman and the famous Mr Wilson*, which purportedly consisted of Sunderland's love letters to Edward 'Beau' Wilson, who had been killed in a sword fight in 1694, obtained far less attention. Sunderland had died in the meantime and the accusations made against him turned out little more than a nine-day wonder, but as the eighteenth century progressed rumours of homosexual activity among the ruling class seem to have become more numerous. The anonymous author of *A Ramble Through London: containing Observations on Men and Things* (1738) claimed to have entered into conversation with 'A *pale livid* looking baronet' on a bench in St James's Park, who 'complained grievously of the Lewdness of Women ... and inveigh'd bitterly against some harsh *Proceedings* of the *Law*, saying, if a speedy Stop was not put to them, there would be an end to *Fellowship* and *Society*'. In 1746 Tobias Smollett referred in a footnote to his poem *The Advice* to 'F--nt--n', 'Sh-lly' and 'C-pe' as 'Three courtly Knights, great admirers of that Taste which the Greeks stiled παιδεραστια' (i.e. pederasty). 'F--nt--n' was Sir Andrew Fountaine, Vice Chamberlain to Queen Caroline and Warden of the Mint, a noted connoisseur and collector, described by Pope in *The Dunciad* as

False as his Gems, and canker'd as his Coins.

'Sh-lly' was Sir John Shelley, MP for Lewes (actually a baronet rather than a knight, though the distinction is after all fairly technical): his predilections seem to have been well-known, for some months earlier Lady Petersham had announced at a dinner party,

> I have been at Hampstead this morning and I met Sir John Shelley, who had got a very shabby man with him, but the fellow was handsome: he looked so ashamed, that I fancy it was but just over.

'C-pe' was Sir John Cope KB, the general defeated the previous year by the Jacobites at Prestonpans. In his first major work, *The Adventures of Roderick Random*, published in 1748, Smollett introduced an earl who spoke in favour of the sexual tastes of Petronius Arbiter:

> I own that his taste in love is generally decried, and indeed condemned by our laws; but perhaps that may be more owing to prejudice and misapprehension, than to true reason and deliberation. The best man among the ancients is said to have entertained that passion; one of the wisest of their legislators has permitted the indulgence of it in his commonwealth; the most celebrated poets have not scrupled to avow it at this day; it prevails not only over all the east, but in most parts of Europe; in our own country it gains ground apace, and in all probability will become in a short time a more fashionable vice than simple fornication. Indeed there is something to be said in vindication of it, for notwithstanding the severity of the law against offenders in this way, it must be confessed that the practice of this passion is unattended with that curse and burthen upon society, which proceeds from a race of miserable deserted bastards, who are either murdered by their parents, deserted to the utmost want and wretchedness, or bred up to prey upon the commonwealth: And it likewise prevents the debauchery of many a young maiden, and the prostitution of honest men's wives; not to mention the consideration of health, which is much less liable to be impaired in the gratification of this appetite, than in the exercise of common venery, which by ruining the constitutions of our young men, has produced a puny progeny that degenerates from generation to generation: Nay, I have been told, that there is another motive perhaps more powerful than all these, that induces people to cultivate this inclination; namely, the exquisite pleasure attending its success.

It is fairly evident that Smollett had someone specifically in mind: in this instance the difference between an earl and a baronet is rather greater than that between a baronet and a knight: but they were equally, as far as people of Smollett's social background were concerned, members of the aristocracy.[32]

Despite the plebeian status of most of those prosecuted, homosexuality was generally referred to as specifically a vice of the upper classes, though Charles Churchill, in his poem *The Times*, suggested that

> Those who are mean high Paramours secure,
> And the rich guilty screen the guilty poor;
> The Sin too proud to feel from Reason awe,
> And Those, who practise it, too great for Law

It was also seen as a vice that had been imported from foreign parts, especially Italy, 'the *Mother* and *Nurse* of *Sodomy*'. Italy and its 'bugger'd boys' had been denounced by a British traveller as far back as 1632. George Baker of Wadham thought the Rev. John Swinton's sojourn in Italy terribly significant, while John Armstrong urged:

> Britons for shame! Be Male and Female still,
> Banish this foreign Vice; it grows not here.

The belief that homosexuality was essentially foreign also provided convenient support for the pretence that it was a *new* phenomenon: one anonymous pamphleteer claimed in 1749: 'Till of late Years, *Sodomy* was a *Sin*, in a manner unheard of in these Nations.' But by the middle years of the century various writers were convinced that homosexuality had become thoroughly naturalised in England. Having denounced upper-class incest and adultery, a pamphleteer of 1757 asserted: 'there's a reigning Sin yet more unnatural; more horrid than Hell, or any Fiend but Man, has Power to invent.' Charles Churchill claimed:

> Go where We will, at ev'ry time and place,
> SODOM confronts, and stares us in the face;
> They ply in public at our very doors
> And take the bread from much more honest Whores.

And as time passed the rumours of scandal became more specific as well as more frequent. The actor-dramatist Isaac Bickerstaffe fled to France in 1772 after attempting the virtue of a sentry outside the Savoy Barracks – he had himself been an officer in the army and continued to draw his half-pay till 1808. In December 1776 the dramatist Samuel Foote stood trial for having made a pass at his man-servant: a vitriolic attack on him by William Jackson entitled *Sodom and Onan: a Satire Inscrib'd to ——— Esq. alias, the Devil on two Sticks* also made pointed references to the unnatural tastes of Earl Tylney, Lord George Germain, one of the secretaries of state, and the Duke of Ancaster, Master of the Horse, and Lord Great Chamberlain at George III's coronation in 1761. Foote was acquitted but soon afterwards suffered a stroke and died in October 1777, surely as much a victim of his fellow-citizens' prejudice as if he had been hanged. In the 1780s rumours concerning the relationship of the fabulously wealthy William Beckford, MP for Wells, and the Hon. William Courtenay, afterwards Viscount Courtenay and Earl of Devon, led to the two men being ostracised by fashionable society. In 1811 Courtenay was forced to flee his ancestral home at Powderham Castle and take refuge abroad: Beckford, who remained in England, amused his increasingly melancholy solitude by making a scrap-book of newspaper reports referring to homosexual scandals. Sir William Meredith, third Baronet, MP for Liverpool 1761-1780 and Comptroller of the King's Household 1774-1777, who died at Lyons in 1790, James Ogilvy, seventh Earl of Findlater, who died at Dresden in 1811, and the Hon. Edward Onslow, MP for Aldeburgh 1780-1781, who died at Clermont-Ferrand in 1829, all settled abroad because of their sexual proclivities; the Earl of Leicester, later third Marquess Townshend, who was abandoned by his wife in 1808 on the grounds of his impotence, also chose to live abroad following a libel action against the *Morning Herald*, which had reported his relationship with a former waiter and other young men from the lower class. Lord Valentia was threatened with exposure by his wife's lover in 1796, but made no secret of his homosexuality while resident in Sicily in 1810.[33]

It was thought an indication of England's superiority to Italy that 'our *Beckfords & Bickerstaffes* ... run away at least from the original Theatre of their Crimes, & do not keep their Male Mistresses in Triumph like the Roman Priests & Princes', but of course homosexuals holding good positions did not run for cover till they absolutely had to. When the Right Rev. and Hon. Percy Jocelyn, Bishop of Ferns and Leighlin, was accused of an unnatural crime by his brother's coachman in 1811, he prosecuted him for bringing false charges and obtained a conviction, and it was not till 1822 (by which time he had become Bishop of Clogher) that he was caught red-handed buggering a guardsman in a public house and had to jump bail and flee to Ostend. (Later he moved to Scotland, the Act of Union between England and Scotland not having provided for extradition.) One anonymous commentator remarked of the Bishop of Clogher case,

> It familiarised the subject to the minds of all classes, and rendered that, which before was far thrown back from the imagination as something scarcely to be believed, the topic of ordinary discourse.

The scandal affected even the cabinet. The Marquess of Londonderry (better known by the courtesy title he had used in his father's lifetime, Viscount Castlereagh), Foreign Secretary, government spokesman in the House of Commons and the key man in the government, was undergoing a mental collapse and became obsessed with the idea that he too had been caught in the act of sodomy. No doubt this conviction related to urges hitherto pushed well down in his psyche, though it had no relation to anything that is known to have actually happened to him. Three and a half weeks after the Bishop of Clogher's arrest, Londonderry cut his throat. In 1825 a bishop's brother, Richard Heber, MP for Oxford University, escaped abroad just ahead of a warrant for his arrest on a charge of sodomitical practices. Fugitives like Heber – and Bickerstaffe, and Courtney, and the Bishop of Clogher – probably made a wise decision: Thomas Jephson, fellow of St John's College, Cambridge, was indicted for attempted sodomy in 1823 and after a seventeen-hour trial at the Old Bailey was acquitted, but instead of accepting the verdict of the court, the Senate of Cambridge University petitioned the Bishop of Ely to expel him from the university, and Jephson's colleagues at St John's banned him from residence in college. Evidently the maxim that one was innocent till proved guilty was ceasing to operate for homosexuals.[34]

*

When men were arrested as a result of being caught in the act of sodomy, it was generally difficult to ascertain whether they had been making a regular practice of such acts, to the point of becoming careless, or whether it was a first attempt, perpetrated on the spur of the moment without stopping to think of necessary precautions. In Valencia 43.8 per cent of accused homosexuals, after exhaustive questioning, admitted to only one act, and 19.2 per cent to fewer than five acts, but of course they had a motive for insisting on their inexperience. In England the normal judicial procedure gave little opportunity for disclosure of offences previous to the one in the indictment. As in the case of the Warden of Wadham, it might be unwise to read too much between the lines. On the night of Christmas Day 1805, for example, a forty-eight-year-old private of the 5th Regiment of Foot, named John Bourke, approached the bed of a recently enlisted thirteen-year-old drummer boy named Hawkes who was sleeping in the same room in the barracks at Subdeanry, 'took some Liberties with Hawkes, and at length perpetrated the Crime alleged ... on the Complaint of Hawkes, John Fivens, another Soldier in the same Regiment, and sleeping in the same Room, took him out of the Bed from Bourke'. Bearing in mind that it was Christmas it is not unlikely that Bourke was drunk, but from this account it is by no means clear that he made a habit of buggering thirteen-year-olds in barrack rooms occupied by other soldiers. On the other hand several prosecutions involving larger numbers of homosexuals evidently related to established homosexual coteries. For example, five of the six capital sentences imposed on homosexuals in 1806 were the result of the trial at Lancaster Assizes of a group from Warrington, of which the most prominent member, Isaac Hitchen, was said to be one of the richest men in the town, worth £60,000: it was shown in evidence 'that they regularly assembled at the house of Hitchen, on Monday and Friday evenings; and that they called one another brother'.[35]

In July 1810 twenty-three men were arrested at the Swan public house, Vere Street, Clare Market, in a carefully orchestrated raid involving three parties of patrolmen from Bow Street. Those arrested included the landlord, James Cook, who was apparently not homosexual at all but had taken the house as a commercial venture, a shop-keeper, five unemployed servants, three waiters, two servants with jobs, a tailor, a pedlar, a bricklayer, a corporal in the Guards and three guardsmen. Possibly as a result of information obtained from examining these men, further raids were carried out on premises in White Hart Yard, Drury Lane and at the Star and Crown, Broadway, Westminster: at the former place a bricklayer and a guardsman were caught in the act of making love, and at the latter a cobbler and a soldier were arrested. Other reports suggested that the Vere Street group included a coal merchant, a butcher, a blacksmith, a bargeman and a coal-heaver. Though one of those eventually hanged was an ensign in a West India regiment, this seems to have been a primarily lower-class group, but they had elaborate communal rituals – a chapel for mock weddings, at which a nonconformist preacher, the Rev. John Church, occasionally officiated (for Church see below), mock lyings-in, with a pair of bellows or a Cheshire cheese in lieu of a baby, and code names for one another such as Kitty Cambric, Black-eyed Leonora, Lady Godiva, and Duchess of Devonshire, these names obviously relating to a more complex self-image than the unpretentious pseudonyms, Susannah Haws, Lydia Gough, Moll Irons, or nicknames, Flying Horse Moll, and Pomegranate Molly, recorded as in use among male prostitutes in the 1720s. The involvement of guardsmen is noteworthy – the man the Bishop of Clogher was later caught with was also a guardsman, 'a fine soldierlike man and has not the air which those wretches usually have'. Over the next hundred and fifty years there were to be numerous reports that it was a standard practice in the Guards to supplement one's soldier's pay by male prostitution, without there being any particular stigma of homosexuality attached.[36]

In 1822 the Duke of Newcastle inadvertently opened a letter addressed to his valet and found it was a love-letter from John Doughty, a cabinet-maker of Grantham. Interrogation of the two men showed a third man, resident in London, to be involved: again it seems to have been a question of an established group.[37]

Other people, even when not necessarily involved in homosexual cliques, evidently made a habit of yielding to dangerous temptations. In June 1806 Patrick Colquhoun, of *Treatise on the Police of the Metropolis* fame, wrote, in his official capacity as a stipendiary magistrate at the Queen Square Office in London, to the mayor of Liverpool requesting him to keep a look-out for one James Samuel Oliver Massey, otherwise Miller or Milwood, charged with sodomy and possibly seeking a ship to take him to America. Massey 'had long been in the habit of seducing Drum boys belonging to the King's Guards' and was described as having 'something of the appearance of a decayed Gentleman: wears a silver mounted eye Glass suspended by a black Ribbon round his neck ... His greatest amusement is to attend Military parades, where he never fails to use his Glass in examining the appearance of the young men and Drum boys.'[38]

Even more conspicuous was the Rev. John Church, one of the most popular nonconformist preachers of his day. Born about 1780 and abandoned outside a church while still an infant, he was raised in the Foundling Hospital and later apprenticed to a gilder. By his own account he began dallying with the serving girls in his employer's household at the age of fifteen, and married when about twenty-one. His first homosexual experience was alleged to have been some months after his marriage. In 1808, when he was acting as a nonconformist minister at Banbury, he was accused of having attempted the virtue of several young men and had to decamp, abandoning his wife and children. In 1809 he began making a name for himself as a preacher in Southwark. A spell as a preacher in Colchester led to more accusations, and the father of a youth he had attempted to seduce followed him to London to exact vengeance:

> the father entered John Church's meeting-house, with two loaded pistols, one in each pocket; but, under the excess of agitation, he fainted away,and was carried out of the place.

In 1813 Church was tried for attempted sodomy but acquitted on the grounds that eleven years had elapsed since the alleged attempt; he also sued the *Weekly Despatch* for libel and was awarded damages. In 1816 he was again tried for attempted sodomy and this time convicted and sentenced to two years in gaol. Although frequently denounced in the press and in pamphlets he remained an extraordinary favourite with his congregations, especially the female members. When his first wife died, having been driven to alcoholism by the first reports of her husband's sexual activities, he quickly married a woman who ran a school for young ladies in Hammersmith. Clearly he liked women – but over a period of at least eight years he made little secret of the fact that he liked men even better.[39]

*

Whereas literature is an important source for attitudes – perhaps one should say, posturings – on the subject of seducing young girls, such was the public loathing of homosexuality that there are no allusions to it in what is conventionally termed literature between Churchill's unflattering references in his satire *The Times* in 1764 and an anonymous poem entitled *Don Leon* which began to be circulated surreptitiously in the 1830s. (Clumsy verse satires directed against Isaac Bickerstaffe in 1772 and Samuel Foote in 1776 and a passage in a lewd production of 1777 entitled *The Torpedo: a Poem to the Electrical Eel* scarcely merit inclusion in the category of literature.) Since it was not the convention to write with self-conscious frankness even about the sexual details of heterosexual relationships, homosexual authors did not even need to pose as sexually normal, as was arguably the case much later with Somerset Maugham, whose novels, shockingly honest by early twentieth-century standards in their treatment of love between man and woman, turn out on closer examination to have few female protagonists whom the male characters do not find physically or morally repellent. No doubt there is something in the suggestion that Thomas Gray's 'Elegy written in a country churchyard' was an expression of homosexual yearning, though a passage dealing with *femmes fatales* beginning

> Some rural Lais with all conquering charms,
> Perhaps now moulders in the grassy bourne,
> Some Helen, vain to set the field in arms ...

which would have balanced the allusions (in the earliest drafts) to 'a Village Cato', 'a mute inglorious Tully' and a 'Caesar, guiltless of his Country's Blood', was no doubt suppressed solely for structural and aesthetic reasons. It has also been argued that the relationship of Caleb Williams and his patron-persecutor Falkland in William Godwin's novel *Caleb Williams* was essentially homosexual, though, unlike Gray, Godwin gave no other indication of being homosexual. The fact that *Frankenstein*, by Godwin's daughter Mary Shelley, seems to parallel much of the narrative of *Caleb Williams*, with the same theme of a quasi-filial relationship that goes disastrously wrong and interferes with all other affective relationships, hardly supports a homosexual reading of Godwin's novel, but the sense of the isolation of the individual which underlies these as most, or all, other Gothic novels, and the implication that under the everyday exterior of social life lurk the most horrific secrets and guilts, may well have a basis in sexual neuroses of a type more prevalent in the later eighteenth century than at earlier periods. But to what extent these neuroses related specifically to homosexuality is likely to remain for ever unclear. It is certainly curious that this period, though after all a classic era of pornography, did not produce any homosexual pornography, or, apart from *Don Leon*, any clandestinely-circulated literary works defending homosexuality.[40]

This reticence is perhaps the more surprising in that two of the most celebrated writers of the early nineteenth century left manuscripts defending homosexuality that only became known after their death. Jeremy Bentham the philosopher scribbled voluminous notes, over a period of many years, on the subject of England's barbaric laws against sodomy: he seems to have regarded the subject as primarily interesting as the outstanding example of institutional sponsorship of absurd, ignorant, barbarous and destructive prejudices, but it is not totally impossible that he was himself homosexually inclined: this is certainly suggested by his remark: 'To other subjects it is expected that you sit down cool: but on this subject if you let it be seen that you have not sat down in a rage you have betrayed yourself at once.' Shelley the poet – definitely interested in women but inclined to present even sex in terms of the abstractest and most idealistic philosophy – drafted 'A Discourse on the Manners of the Antient Greeks Relative to Love' as an introduction to a translation he had prepared of Plato's *Symposium*. He did not seem particularly *au fait* with the homosexual underworld in England, choosing to emphasise the differences between contemporary European culture and the culture of classical Athens, and arguing that it was the degraded status of women in classical times that channelled emotion towards young men: 'beautiful persons of the male sex became the object of that sort of feelings, which are only cultivated at present as towards females.' He anticipated modern scholarship in suggesting that the youth of Athens did not consummate their love by anal penetration:

> We are not exactly aware – and the laws of modern composition scarcely permit a modest writer to investigate the subject with philosophical accuracy, – what the action was by which the Greeks expressed this passion. I am persuaded that it was totally different from the ridiculous and disgusting conception which the vulgar have formed on the subject.

And he made what should have been a telling point in stating that 'a person must be blinded by superstition to conceive of it as more horrible than the usual intercourse endured by almost every youth of England with a diseased and insensate prostitute'.[41]

*

For most people however homosexuality was a subject of the utmost repugnance. The standard form of indictment referred to 'that most horrid, detestable and sodomitical Crime (not among Christians to be named) called Buggery'. At Lancaster Assizes in 1806, the presiding judge, Sir Robert Graham, 'lamented that such a subject should come before the public as it must do, and above all that the untaught and unsuspecting minds of youth should be liable to be tainted by hearing such horrid facts' and 'very properly ordered that no notes should be taken on these trials, nor any young persons be allowed to be present at them'. A pamphlet entitled *Trial of David Robertson, of the Jerusalem Hotel, Charles-street, Covent-garden, late master of the Standard-Tavern, Leicester-fields, for an Unnatural Crime with George Foulton* was advertised in the 30 August 1806 issue of the *Lancaster Gazette*, in time to cash in on the interest aroused by the trial of the Warrington sodomites at Lancaster Assizes, but no copy of this publication seems to have survived and no other transcripts seem to have been published: *The whole trial of Col. Rob. Passingham and John Edwards, for a conspiracy against George Townshend Forrester, Esq.*, reporting a homosexual blackmail case in 1805, carefully edits out the scabrous details: 'He then related a very disgusting story of himself – of Mr Forrester coming to him in bed, and relating what is too disgusting to be repeated.'[42]

As with other varieties of sexual irregularity, there seems to have been a fear among the middle classes that homosexuality was contagious and addictive. When a labourer was tried in 1760 for 'an Attempt to commit Sodomy, on the Body of James Fassett', a schoolboy at Dulwich College, the crown counsel told the court:

> had he prevailed with this Lad, now Sixteen Years old, to commit this horrid and most detestable Crime, he would have infected all the others; and, as in Course of Years they grew big enough, they would leave the College to go into the World and spread this cursed Poison, while those left behind would be training the Children to the same vitious Practises.

But it was not merely the middle classes who were perturbed. At least three men who were exposed in the pillory for homosexual offences were stoned to death by the mob: Thomas Blair at Cheapside in 1743, Daniel Lobley at Bow in 1763, and Read, a coachman, at Southwark in 1780. After the arrests at Vere Street in June 1810 the suspects were taken in carriages from the watch-house at St Clement Danes to the magistrates' court at Bow Street to be committed, but a mob, mainly composed of women, was waiting at Bow Street and showered the suspects with mud. 'They were literally plaistered over from head to foot, as were the carriages, and even the horses.' When six of the Vere Street gang were sentenced to stand in the pillory in the Haymarket two hundred armed constables were needed to escort them from the Old Bailey, and even then all six were completely covered in mud by the time they reached the pillory. Not that exposure in the pillory was thought an adequate punishment:

> The monsters must be crushed, or the vengeance of Heaven will fall upon the land ... The present punishment cannot surely be deemed commensurate to an offence so abhorrent, and so shocking to human nature, besides, is it not dreadful to have female delicacy and manly feeling shocked and the infant mind perhaps polluted by such disgusting spectacles and the conversations to which they unavoidably give rise?

On another occasion constables escorting homosexuals from the Middlesex Sessions House to the nearby Cold Bath Fields Prison were confronted by a mob and told the prisoners to run to safety to the prison while they attempted to hold off the crowd – it was obvious to the prisoners that their only chance of safety was to reach the prison as quickly as possible.[43]

*

It is sometimes said that the overall increase in crime statistics in the early nineteenth century was the result of the activities of local vigilante groups which financed prosecution of every offence that came to their notice. There were no doubt many who would have agreed with a view proposed in 1802:

> That a great and general increase of moral corruption has taken place within a century, and, more particularly, within the last few years, is too obvious to need any proof ... Luxurious habits, dissipated manners, and shameless profligacy, are the characteristic of the age.

Yet the author of these words should not be taken as typical, for he also thought it 'incredible' that 'an attempt to pass a law to restrain the crying sin of adultery', by forbidding remarriage after divorce, had been thrown out by the House of Lords, and he was amazed that Mme de Staël, the leading European bluestocking of her day, was received in polite society when she came to London:

> A woman of the most infamous life is now received into the highest circles of fashion. The female in question, a foreigner, has lived publicly as the Mistress of Berthier, and of other French Republican Generals. With such a woman it seems that English ladies, of the highest rank, think it no disgrace to associate!!!

It should also be noted that the Associations for the Prosecution of Felons established in many localities from the mid-eighteenth century onwards generally only prosecuted on behalf of subscribing members, and the two organisations which operated on a more general basis focused their attention on two specific areas of delinquency. The branches of the Association for Preserving Liberty and Property against Republicans and Levellers maintained a campaign against political subversives during the 1790s; the more durable Society for the Suppression of Vice concentrated much of its effort against obscene books. A lot of people suffered in the magistrates' courts as a result of the attentions of these two organisations, but they had no part in any increase in the prosecution of serious crime. In fact, bearing in mind the substantial increase of population during this period, it is rather curious that sodomy was, with forgery and the uttering of forged instruments, the only crime which showed a significant increase in the number of capital sentences.[44]

Another possible explanation for the increase of sodomy prosecutions in the early nineteenth century is that, separate from overall trends in criminality and policing, official activity against homosexuals seems in the past to have gone in waves. It might be that a period of apparent relaxation would lead to homosexuals becoming more visible, till they provoked a sudden onset of persecution, causing them to retreat underground for a period, till a falling off of prosecutions heralded a new phase of relaxation. One might hypothesise a period of relaxation in the 1690s, when Vanbrugh could show a homosexual character in one of his plays kissing a young man on stage, a minor purge 1707-9, and the trials and executions of 1726, and then seventy years of rough and ready tolerance, bolstered by the apparent open-mindedness of the so-called Enlightenment, until in the 1790s the French Revolution and its ideas seemed suddenly to threaten the entire fabric of civilisation and provoked a general mood of political and social paranoia.

This argument gains apparent support from the most famous of homosexuality cases, the trial of Oscar Wilde. Before Wilde's disgrace in 1895 there seems little doubt that the discussion of homosexuality was becoming more open – love between young men even became the theme, in the chastest possible way, of respectable novels like A.C. Benson's *Memoirs of Arthur Hamilton, BA* of 1886 and Howard Sturgis' *Tim* of 1891. At the same time certain men were becoming less cautious about flaunting a homosexual life style. Then, when Oscar Wilde lost his libel action against the Marquess of Queensberry and was arrested and charged with having committed unnatural acts, scores of prominent homosexuals are alleged to have fled abroad, though at the same time, according to the Director of Public Prosecutions, 'there was, for about eighteen months ... a perfect outburst of that offence all through the country'. This picture of the general moral climate is not entirely corroborated by police statistics.

	annual average 1888-92	1893	1894	1895	1896	1897
1. 'unnatural offences' reported to the police	84	73	66	70	148	44
2. ditto, tried in court	32	36	24	33	92	21
3. *attempts* to commit 'unnatural offences' reported to the police	58	130	126	162	56	120
4. ditto, tried in court	101	117	111	137	64	126
5. total offences reported (1 + 3)	142	203	192	232	204	164
6. total offences tried (2 + 4)	133	153	135	170	156	147

Oscar Wilde was convicted of homosexual offences in May 1895. Neither the complaints to the police nor the number of prosecutions are much above previous norms during the period of the Oscar Wilde trials or for several months thereafter. The first substantial change is that in the following year complaints to the police involve fewer 'attempts' than in previous years, and more actual 'commissions', though this is presumably the result of a change in the way the

police handled complaints: one notes that the increase in 'commissions' is also visible in the prosecutions actually undertaken by the
police, whereas before 1892 many 'commissions' reported to the
police were, after investigation, tried simply as 'attempts'. The total
number of complaints, and of trials, in the two categories combined
hardly changes, and the figures for 1897 are fairly close to those of
1894. Of course the moral climate at any given period is difficult to
assess, and the theory of successive waves of tolerance and repression may well be valid for certain aspects of, for example, public
debate: but it really doesn't seem to work for prosecutions.[45]

An American scholar, A.N. Gilbert, has attempted to link prosecutions within the Royal Navy during the Napoleonic War with a
general climate of war-induced angst, referring to the Freudian link
between anality and death. In fact one of the remarkable things
about these twenty-two years of war is how *little* most people seemed
to have worried about it, and how psychologically distant it remained:

> In this career of revolution, war has unfolded all its splendid and
> terrible forms, in such a crowded succession of enterprises and
> battles, with every imaginable circumstance of valour, skill, and
> destruction, that its grandest exhibitions are become familiar to us,
> almost to insipidity. We read or talk, over our wine or our coffee, of
> some great battle that has recently decided the state of a kingdom,
> with an emotion nearly as transient as of an old bridge carried away
> in our neighbourhood by a flood, or a tree overthrown by the wind or
> struck with lightning. It is, even after every allowance for the natural
> effect of iteration and familiarity, perfectly astonishing to observe
> what a degree of indifference has come to prevail in the general mind,
> at the view of events the most awful in their immediate exhibition,
> and the most portentous as to their consequences.

In the Navy itself death from war-related injuries remained much
less frequent than death from illnesses that also affected civilians:

Mortality in the Royal Navy 1793-1815

As a result of battle	6,663
As a result of ships being wrecked or burnt	13,621
Disease or 'ordinary accidents on board'	72,102

A more plausible explanation of the number of wartime courts-martial for buggery is that the Royal Navy in wartime was very much

larger than in peacetime, and depended on the pressing of merchant seamen for much of the additional manpower. Naval vessels were generally much larger than merchant vessels (only the East India Company had vessels larger than Royal Navy frigates, which within the Navy were regarded as too small for service in the line of battle: a Royal Navy sloop would be regarded as a big ship by civilian standards) and because of their military function they carried disproportionately large crews for their tonnage. The iron discipline maintained on board such vessels involved close and unceasing supervision by petty officers. The likelihood of a randy homosexual volunteering to serve under such conditions in peacetime seems remote. In the merchant service, smaller crews under the orders of captains who had themselves been ordinary seamen involved a totally different atmosphere. Crews would be largely drawn from the same community and individuals may have been friends since childhood: the captain, chiefly concerned with keeping up crew numbers, sailing on schedule and returning a profit, would have every incentive to avoid wasting time by reporting untoward behaviour to the magistrates of the ports where he made landfalls. Homosexuality may have been not uncommon on such ships: but the press-gang never asked seamen if they were homosexual when they shanghaied them into service in the very different conditions of the Royal Navy.[46]

The situation in the Royal Navy may also be read as part of a general culture of moral panic: but it may be too facile to argue, as some scholars have done, in terms of a moral panic in Britain specifically resulting from a reaction to the events of the French Revolution. The Proclamation Society, forerunner of the Society for the Suppression of Vice, originated in a Royal Proclamation issued against obscene literature, drunkenness, blasphemy, etc. issued in 1787, two years before the storming of the Bastille, and much of the conservative propaganda disseminated in the 1790s also derives from the 1780s. A case can be made for supposing that throughout the 1790s the English upper classes' notion of what precisely was involved in mob-rule derived, not from news reports from Paris, but from personal memories of the Gordon Riots which had devastated London in 1780. Come to that, a case can be made for seeing the French Revolution as merely one part of a continent-wide crisis of government which had been affecting English politics, as well as those of other countries, at least since the 1760s. Of course events in France helped raise the temperature of the debate, but they were not the only contributory factor. For example the increase in crim. con. prosecutions in the 1790s must have had some other cause or causes, and Lord Chief Justice Kenyon's denunciations of upper-class immorality, which became a regular feature of crim. con. trials in the ten years before his death in 1802, can probably best be explained by his own personal hang-ups, since his successors showed themselves markedly more moderate in their language.[47]

The point here is not to deny that there was something peculiar and distinctive about the moral climate in England *circa* 1800, but to suggest that it may have had longer-term roots than horror at events in France.

*

Specifically on the subject of homosexuality, one notes that women featured prominently in the mobs attacking homosexuals at the pillory, and in the crowds attending hangings. No doubt some of these women were streetwalkers, though not necessarily motivated by the same economic discontents as the brothel madam in *A Ramble Through London* (see above, p. 134), who denounced the *'pale livid* looking Baronet' who talked of love between men, 'saying it was along of such Villains as he, that she was so reduced in the World'. Women as much as men may have clung to the doctrine expressed by the anonymous author of *Satan's Harvest Home* in 1749: 'each sex should maintain its peculiar Character.' It may be that the hysteria about homosexuality was part of a process of hardening sexual stereotypes: they had been hard enough previously of course, but one of the key characteristics of better-class males, the readiness to resort to physical violence, and the routine carrying of weapons, went out of fashion in the eighteenth century, and may have required some compensatory assertion of masculinity. Despite religious sanctions and, for the majority of social groups, communal disapproval of extra-marital sex, active virility was emphasised. Sylvester Douglas, a minor political figure *circa* 1800, recorded in his diary an example of the kind of manly, role-reinforcing conversation which took place over the port at upper-class dinner parties after the women had retired:

Storer says that Selwyn professed never to have had connection with a woman but seven times in the whole of his life, and that the last was with a maid at the Inn at Andover, when he was 29 ... When at

Eton, Eden would lock Conway up for hours with Polly Jones but nothing ever happened between them. In all the familiar and libertine parties and conversations in which he used to be engaged in their younger days, living with some of the cleverest but most profligate persons of his time, Conway was never known to mention his having any connection with a woman ... Storer says that all Thomas Grenville's acquaintance have the same belief concerning him.

When Thomas Grenville's cousin William Pitt became Prime Minister in 1784 the fact that he was only twenty-four was regarded as less remarkable than his total lack of interest in women. Epigrams were circulated on the subject:

> 'Tis true, indeed, we oft abuse him,
>   Because he bends to man;
> But Slander's self dares not accuse him
>   Of stiffness to a woman.

and

> 'No! no! for my virginity,
> 'When I lose that,' quoth Pitt, 'I'll die';
> Cries Wilberforce, 'If not till then,
> 'By G—d you must outlive all men.'

and

> *Puer loquitur*
> Though big with mathematic pride,
> By me this axiom is denied,
> I can't conceive, upon my soul,
> My parts are equal to the *whole.*

In the present century Pitt's chastity and preference for the company of admiring young men has led to the assumption that he was homosexual, but this seems never to have been suggested during his lifetime. He may have had a lucky escape: 'Damn the fellow! now I think of it, I never remember his having a girl at college!' remarked an acquaintance of a man who had brought a charge of malicious prosecution against a soldier who had accused him of attempting an unnatural crime.[48]

(Pitt's courtship in 1796 of the Hon. Eleanor Eden – daughter of the man who used to lock up the Hon. Henry Conway with Polly

Jones at Eton – though broken off apparently because of his personal indebtedness, gave rise to a novella depicting him as the archetypal heartless seducer, but this seems to have been written by an exile in Germany who was not *au fait* with social and political gossip in London.)[49]

The English ecclesiastical courts did not give the same encouragement as those in Roman Catholic countries for suits for divorce on the grounds of the husband's impotence: there were only a couple of such cases in England in the eighteenth century, both of which failed. Nevertheless a number of doctors found a remunerative practice among men who feared for their virility: 'The idea of being incapable of sexual intercourse preys upon their minds, and too frequently leads them to think they are unfit to live.' One such doctor was accustomed to recommend marriage as a remedy, though he recorded,

> on one occasion a gentleman waited on me the morning after marriage, with distraction in his looks, and a loaded pistol in each pocket, threatening instant destruction to me or himself, as having induced him to impose upon an amiable woman, and ruined his peace of mind for ever.

The poor man was persuaded to go back to his bride and try again, and eventually fathered three children. It will be recalled that 'a weakness in the *penis*, and a loss of erection, as if they had been castrated' had been among the consequences of masturbation specified in *Onania*: no doubt this aspect of masturbation contributed greatly to its dread reputation throughout the eighteenth century.[50]

Hardening gender stereotypes would not only have affected men who were primarily, though diffidently, heterosexual. Mock weddings, make-pretend pregnancies and lyings-in – reported as far back as 1709 – and the use of girls' names at places of homosexual resort were not the necessary and inevitable concomitants of homosexual sex: the stereotype of the camp queer which survives today is to a large extent an eighteenth-century creation, relating to specific aspects of eighteenth-century homosexual sub-culture rather than to the nature of homosexuality generally. It may have been precisely the emphasis on marriage and childbirth and sexual normality in this period which helped establish effeminacy and pseudo-feminine activities like make-pretend child-bearing as part of a secret homosexual counter-culture.[51]

But the hardening of sexual stereotypes could also have affected homosexuals by making non-homosexuals more disposed to spy on, investigate, report and prosecute homosexual activity. It may have been that in earlier periods homosexuality was less noticed because non-homosexuals were less ready to draw conclusions about their neighbours that would later seem obvious and irresistible. Thus the increase of prosecutions of homosexuals may be seen as an index of a shift in a whole complex of attitudes in society as a whole. This may include types of attitude which we do not as yet even know how to identify, let alone understand. Nearly two centuries after the period in question, unisex fashions and Gay Liberation coincided, in conditions of general reaction to the radical enthusiasms of 1968, though it is far from clear that the coincidence was merely chronological. The emphasis on the line of the buttocks, evident both in unisex and in the earlier exclusively female mini-skirt fashion, is also to be found in the women's fashions of the 1790s and 1800s. Around 1800 men's bottoms were being defended by the full rigour of the law just as women's bottoms were becoming more in evidence – a complete inversion of what happened 170 years later. There must have been a connection at *some* level, but the psychological processes involved need much more study by social scientists before it will be safe for a mere historian to offer a cut-and-dried theory.

7

Separating the Spheres

It has become fashionable to argue that changes in the early nineteenth century with regard to the complementary roles of women and men involved not the *subordination* of women as such but rather their mobilisation in separate spheres of activity and influence. Of course 'the beloved rights and privileges which the fair sex claim, as mothers, daughters, wives, sisters' represented a somewhat constricted sphere, and it cannot have been entirely fortuitous that the idea that subordination involves benefits and privileges which are denied to those placed in superior positions was applied in this period not only to the role of women but also to the divisions between economic classes, and was one of the favourite themes of the right-wing discourse with which the Georgian establishment sought to defend its monopoly of political power in the face of growing protest from the lower orders; but perhaps the best argument against the theory that there was a constructive realignment of the role of women in the 1790s and 1800s is the mainly negative terms in which Mary Wollstonecraft's pioneer feminist tract, *A Vindication of the Rights of Women*, was criticised on its appearance in 1792.[1]

A Vindication of the Rights of Women was one of those books that were more attacked than read – there were only four editions in Britain and Ireland in the 1790s as compared to three in America, where, with a much smaller population, there was evidently a relatively larger appetite for progressive doctrines. Almost no one seemed to be prepared to acknowledge that Wollstonecraft might have had even a glimmering of a point in any of her remarks about the subjugation and degradation of women: even her condemnation, in her fifth chapter, of the views of Rousseau and the cynical Earl of Chesterfield brought her no credit with the numerous other, more conservative, writers of the 1790s who denounced Rousseau and Chesterfield. A rather better-selling work, whose opinion was quoted approvingly in the *Gentleman's Magazine*, suggested:

Surely parents and guardians should, with the utmost affectionate
earnestness, for the sake of their country, of themselves, of their
dearest hopes, and of every institution, divine or human, warn and
caution young female readers against such writings as Mrs Wollstonecraft Godwin's, if they perceive an inclination in them to peruse
her works.

Other critics resorted to parody, as in Thomas Taylor's *A Vindication of the Rights of Brutes* (1792), *A Sketch of the Rights of Boys
and Girls by Launcelot Light and Laetitia Lookabout* (1792) and a
poem entitled 'Maternal Despotism: or, the Rights of Infants', published in a volume entitled *Senilities* in 1801.

> Unhand me nurse! thou saucy quean!
> What does this female tyrant mean? ...
>   Have I not right to kick and sprawl,
> To laugh or cry, to squeak or squall! –
> Has ever by my act and deed,
> Thy *right* to rule me been decreed?

Richard Polwhele's *The Unsex'd Females: a Poem* (1798) attacked
not only Wollstonecraft but also her friend the novelist and essayist
Mary Hays, denouncing the latter as a 'Wollstonecraftian'. There
were also at least two novels published around 1800 in which
seducers made use of *A Vindication of the Rights of Women* to
overcome the scruples of their victims, Charles Lucas' *The Infernal
Quixote* and George Walker's *The Vagabond*.[2]
   Most if not all those who wrote against Wollstonecraft – or
Woolstoncraft or Wolstonecroft as they sometimes called her – were
men, and male writers were also very insistent that their womenfolk, whatever they might do to extend their separate sphere, should
keep their distance from other members of the female sex who had
failed to measure up to middle-class standards:

> that native modesty; that extreme delicacy, bashfulness, and reserve;
> which are peculiar to the female sex ... are indispensably necessary
> to keep within bounds those passions, which, if unrestrained, would,
> by their violence and impetuosity, drive us upon the fatal rocks of
> sensuality and licentiousness.

It would be quite wrong, therefore, to allow one's wives and daughters to mix freely with fallen women:

> Honour, especially in women, can admit of no compromise with dishonour; no approaches from one to the other must be suffered; the boundary between them must be considered as impassable; the line by which they are divided is the RUBICON of female virtue.

In fact the honour of a honourable woman was so precious it justified cruelty to women who had been dishonoured:

> The principal, and, indeed, only satisfactory reason given for the extreme severity with which females, who have fallen from the path of virtue, are treated in this country, is the necessity of separating them entirely from the virtuous, in order to prevent contamination.

Or, to put it shortly, *'The infamy of Vice is the last bulwark of Virtue'*. There was of course a general prejudice against women being too active outside the home (William Wilberforce even objected to Female Anti-Slavery Associations on the grounds that 'for ladies to meet, to publish, to go from house to house stirring up petitions – these appear to me proceedings unsuited to the female character as delineated in Scripture'), but the participation of virtuous women in the running of refuges for penitent prostitutes was especially dangerous:

> Not content with endeavouring to bring back lost women across the line themselves, they take virtuous women to the other side of it for this purpose: dangerous experiment! ... Can it be possible that any set of men could have been so infatuated, so bigoted, so blind, as to place their mothers, wives, sisters, daughters, or female acquaintances, in a situation to hear the tales of two hundred of the most depraved wretches, of the off-scourings of the earth, of the sweepings of the streets ...?[3]

If even the reminiscences of illiterate streetwalkers were likely to tempt one's mother to stray from the path of chastity, carefully-written novels by internationally famous authors represented a fearsome menace. The corrupting effect of reading fiction had been a subject of complaint since the earliest days of the genre: in Charles Gildon's *The Post-boy rob'd of His Mail* of 1692 a libertine advises the maid-servant who is assisting him to seduce her mistress, 'After her Mind has been employ'd in Romances, Plays and Novels, then nought but sweet Ideas fill her Soul, and Love can't be denied admittance, those having so well prepar'd its way.' The Rev. Edward Barry MD provided a helpful explanation of the processes at work:

Among the many incentives to seduction, that of Novel reading most assuredly ranks as one ... the main drift of such writing is to interest, to agitate, and convulse the passions, and is but too prone, by a sympathy of sentiment to lead the mind astray; if such reading does not disgust and tire by its usual bombast and inanity, it effects on the juvenile reader, what the hot-bed does to the tender plant: and gives a dangerous precocity of sentiment: the notes once taught, a desire to play on the instrument will naturally succeed.

The very mummery of a tale, which *swindled* tears from the eyes, and transport from the heart, which gave sensations it could not relieve, has left a train of gunpowder in the mind, and in such a manner, that one chance spark of fire might be sufficient to blow up reputation; and make a bankrupt of virtue.

In 1797 a school-mistress suggested:

young ladies cannot be too careful in their selection of books; and if by chance they meet with one at which delicacy recoils, it is their duty to shut it with as much contempt as they would turn from a person who had insulted them with improper language.

But a couple of years later a cleric was complaining that 'the ravings of *Werter*' and 'the impudently profane lessons of the *Monk*' are 'now devoured by *Miss in her teens*' while the works of Joseph Addison and Samuel Johnson were scarcely known. Philosophical works were regarded as equally dangerous: in Smollett's *The Adventures of Roderick Random* the downfall of Miss Williams begins with her fondness for reading 'Shaftesbury, Tindal, Hobbs, and all the books that are remarkable for their deviation from the old way of thinking': later 'the voluptuous pages' of Rousseau and 'the fashionable Hume', and above all Wollstonecraft's *A Vindication of the Rights of Women* headed the list. In *The Infernal Quixote* Charles Marauder lays siege to Emily Bellaires by means of books, 'particular passages of which he often marked, and sometimes pointedly read. Among the first was Mrs Wollstonecraft's *Rights of Women*.'[4]

Some novelists attempted to use their pens to combat the tide of moral subversion. 'To check the rapid growth of Vice, and in order to facilitate the advancement of Virtue, has been the chief design in the following letters', claimed James Bacon in the preface to *The Libertine*, an epistolary novel about a stereotypical seducer. Jane West announced at the end of her *A Tale of the Times*:

as the most fashionable, and perhaps the most successful, way of vending pernicious sentiments has been through the medium of books of entertainment, she conceives it not only allowable but necessary, to repel the enemy's insidious attacks with similar weapons.

Among those who followed her example were Elizabeth Hamilton, in *Memoirs of Modern Philosophers* (1800), Robert Charles Dallas, in *Percival, or Nature Vindicated* (1801) and the anonymous author of *Dorothea; or, the Ray of New Light* (1801). Alternatively, women might be given improving books to read so that they would not need to look at dirty ones: the Rev. James Fordyce's *Sermons to Young Women* went through fourteen editions between 1766 and 1814 as compared to the same author's *Addresses to Young Men* which achieved only five editions between 1777 and 1816, and the Rev. Thomas Gisborne's earnest but challenging *An Enquiry into the Duties of Men in the Higher and Middle Class of Society in Great Britain* went through seven editions 1794-1824 whereas its companion volume *An Enquiry into the Duties of the Female Sex* – a comparatively insipid work, no doubt reflecting the comparatively insipid reality of middle-class women's lives – sold twice as well, with thirteen editions 1797-1823. But the most important and appealing technique of counter-attack against corrupting books was prosecution in the law courts.[5]

*

On 1 June 1787 King George III had issued a proclamation urging judges and magistrates to 'suppress all loose and licentious prints, books, and publications, dispersing poison to the minds of the young and unwary', and also to proceed against 'excessive drinking, blasphemy, swearing, lewdness, profanation of the Lord's Day', etc. A Society for carrying into effect His Majesty's Proclamation against Vice and Immorality – generally known as the Proclamation Society – was formed to encourage this good work. It was felt in some quarters to be insufficiently energetic and in 1802 a new organisation, initially conceived as working for the same objectives as the Proclamation Society but with a wider membership, was launched under the denomination 'Society for the Suppression of Vice, and the Encouragement of Religion and Virtue'. Its primary objects, besides the suppressing of obscene books, were 'the Prevention of the Profanation of the Lord's Day', 'the Protection of Female Innocence, by the Punishment of Procurers and Seducers', the discouragement of cruelty to animals and the insuring of lottery tickets, the detection of false weights, and the prevention of breaches of the peace generally. One writer on prostitution complained:

> Had those persons, who have arrogated to themselves the title of 'the Society for the Suppression of Vice', devoted their attention to the suppression of this vice, they might have made themselves of real service to their country, they would have deserved well of society, and they might, probably, have gained that popularity and fame which they will never obtain by nibbling at the petty vices of the lower orders, and depriving them of the few comforts and enjoyments they have left, under pretence of reforming their morals.

But in practice grinding the faces of the poor was only incidental to what the Society saw as its chief priority, the hunting down of purveyors of obscene literature. Back in 1708 James Read, convicted of publishing *The Fifteen Plagues of a Maiden-Head*, had escaped punishment because the Lord Chief Justice decided that obscenity was only prosecutable in the ecclesiastical courts, and though Edmund Curll was fined in 1727 for publishing *Venus in the Cloister* and Meibom's *A Treatise on the Use of Flogging in Venereal Affairs*, the authorities seem generally to have been deterred by expense, and perhaps by the unpredictability of juries, from making a habit of prosecuting obscene literature: for example when the secretaries of state suppressed John Cleland's *Memoirs of a Woman of Pleasure* and Thomas Cannon's *Ancient and Modern Pederasty Investigated and Exemplified* in 1749, nobody was actually brought into court. The Society for the Suppression of Vice decided to put an end to the virtual immunity enjoyed by dealers in pornography and later claimed:

> The list of prosecutions of this class of offenders, which the Society has instituted, and the success that has attended its exertions, would alone establish its title to the gratitude and the liberal support of all friends of public morals: – of all, more especially, who wish to preserve from contamination the purity and decency of the rising generation.

In fact the thirty or forty successful prosecutions of obscene books claimed for the period 1802-1817, though vastly more costly in expenditure of time and energy than the shopping of 39 fortune-tellers and 56 persons involved in illegal lotteries whom the Society had had arrested on vagrancy charges, averages out as fewer than three a year, and much of the information given by the Secretary of the Society to a parliamentary enquiry in 1817 was already contained in the original 'Proposal for Establishing a Society for the Suppression of Vice, and the Encouragement of Religion and Virtue', which had been circulated in 1802. The Society also made the interesting discovery that in certain circumstances the objective of suppressing vice might be in conflict with the desire to encourage religion and virtue. Alexander Hogg, for example, was able to deflect prosecution as a publisher of lewd books by reminding the Proclamation Society that he also published *The Family Bible*, *The Life of Christ*, Foxe's *Book of Martyrs*, *The Whole Duty of Man* and *The Christian Magazine*. Shortly afterwards the Solicitor-General, the notoriously strait-laced and philoprogenitive Hon. Spencer Perceval, received the following letter:

Sir,
    Enclosed you will receive proposals for an obscene work, containing Representations of scenes in Prints highly dangerous to the morals of the rising Generation. I trust you will take such notice of the Work as you may think expedient, in doing of which you will render an important service to the Fathers of Families who look to the welfare of their Children.
                        I am yours
                        a friend
                        to Youth

The proposed book was *A New and Complete Collection of the Most Remarkable Trials for Adultery, &c* by R. Gill – to be sold by J. Gill (actually Alexander Hogg – and actually only the second volume, the first having come out in 1799). The notice which the government thought expedient to take was the prosecution of Hogg for publishing 'in a certain lewd and obscene book ... diverse wicked lewd impious impure bawdy and obscene Prints representing and exhibiting Men and women in the Act of Carnal Copulation and in various other most indecent lewd and obscene Attitudes and postures to the great displeasure of Almighty God to the Scandal and Reproach of Christian Religion in Contempt of our said Lord the King, etc., etc.' Hogg's defence, that the Proclamation Society had already decided against prosecuting him on account of his religious publications, seems to have fallen somewhat flat; incidentally, the three plates in volume two of *A New Collection of Trials for Adultery*, while slightly more explicit than the four in volume one, which had not been prosecuted on publication in 1799, were by no means as shocking as the indictment suggested: the only couple depicted actually making love were shown covered by a blanket save for their heads and one of the woman's arms.[6]

The defenders of purity may also have been slightly disingenuous in suggesting that the trade in obscene books was dominated by foreigners. In 1802, during the short-lived Peace of Amiens with France, it was announced:

> It is a fact, but recently discovered, that there exists in this country, a society established for the sole purpose of circulating obscene books and prints, among the rising generation; that they employ, for this diabolical purpose, a great number of emissaries, who find the means of introducing them into places of education for young females, and into private families ... We are, in all probability, indebted for the existence of this society to the *great nation* [i.e. France] which all description of persons seem now so fond of visiting.

The 'emissaries' or travelling salesmen who touted obscene books around the country were said to be mainly Italian; 'indecent snuff-boxes' and other lewd bric-à-brac were said to be mainly imported and for this reason were less in evidence during the war with Napoleon, 'though the advantages of obstructed intercourse in this respect were in some degree counteracted by the great quantities manufactured at the prisons for prisoners of war'. A correspondent of the Society for the Suppression of Vice writing from Bristol in December 1808 had found, on visiting the prisoner of war camp at Stapledon, 'a variety of devices in bone, and indeed of the most obscene kind, particularly those representing (sodomy), a crime which ought not to be named among Christians, which they termed *"the new fashion"* '.[7]

In the course of the Society for the Suppression of Vice's investigation of travelling porn-merchants it was discovered that

> the principal vent for their commodities were schools, and those chiefly for females, into which they would contrive to introduce these articles by means of servants. Women were also employed as agents in this trade, who would gain admission into schools for females, under the pretence of purchasing cast-off clothes from servants.

In practice only two of the thirty or forty successful prosecutions by the society up to May 1817 involved people selling to girls' boarding schools, but from the emphasis these institutions received in the Society's statements it is difficult to avoid the impression that the protection of female ignorance was regarded by the Society's members as having a unique importance.[8]

*

Improper goings on goings-on at girls' schools were a constant preoccupation with middle-class parents. It was not merely a question of masturbation (as detailed in the last chapter) or the circulation of lewd books or the dangers of employing young doctors to attend the girls when sick, though one connoisseur of schoolgirls noted,

> Many have been ingenuous enough to acknowledge that they had often feigned illness to procure the pleasure of being visited by the doctors, who used to go to their bedroom, unaccompanied by the Governess; and love has often proved the consequence of the imprudence of all the parties.

Perhaps the main objection was that formation of an independent character which, in the twentieth century, came to be cited as the greatest advantage of a boarding-school education:

> Girls educated in schools ... not only adopt sentiments of their own, before they have any right to do so, but they hesitate not to pronounce and defend their opinions in earnest and bitter altercations with their parents, and extend this conduct to the most important affair of life — to the choice of a husband. 'We have a right to chuse and judge for ourselves,' say they, with a degree of pertness, arrogance, and determination, which, among our good Ancestors ... a female of thirty would never have dared to assume, towards the venerable Heads of her family.

Bearing in mind that — as far as one can judge in the complete absence of statistics — only a minority of girls from better-off households were sent away to school and that boarding schools for boys were both more numerous and, in the case of the great Public Schools, considerably larger, it seems likely that girls' schools were merely the scapegoat for an uneasiness and dissatisfaction on the subject of daughters that was disseminated fairly generally throughout the affluent classes. One notes that in Jane Austen's novels none of the protagonists have been at girls' schools (though secondary characters like Harriet Smith may have been), but that the social attitudes acquired by young ladies in the course of their upbringing are a constant preoccupation, virtually the central theme of *Emma*, and given major emphasis in the case of such characters as Marianne Dashwood, Mary Crawford and Isabella Thorpe. There is some indication that, in the evolving middle-class household, fathers were paying more attention to their womenfolk while at the same time giving them less to do: it seems that middle-class women were less occupied with domestic chores than hitherto, though the whole area of household management is difficult to quantify. At any rate it appears that fathers of families, who had always had enough to worry about in their sons, were now worrying even more about their daughters.[9]

Among the obvious advantages of keeping a girl away from companions of her own age was that she would not hear about sexual intercourse until her parents were ready to tell her. Henry Thomas Kitchener, in his *Letters on Marriage*, advised:

> I would keep girls entirely ignorant of these subjects till the age of puberty, and perhaps for a few years afterwards; but as soon as a judicious mother perceived that she could impart the information with safety, she should, I think, make the communication as full and unreserved as possible. This would induce them to think of a man, which would mature their passions, and occasion their breasts to grow to their proper size, without which, they are never likely to be healthy mothers or good nurses.

What maturing the emotions consisted of may be deduced from a passage a little earlier in the same text:

> A gentleman eminent for his literary attainments married to a sensible good-tempered woman, and blessed with a large family of children, assured me, that during the whole time that he lived with his wife he never could have any intercourse of this kind with her without many previous entreaties on his part, and seldom without tears on hers. The ideas of filthiness and indelicacy were so united in her mind with the idea of the act, that she could not separate them, and this prevented her from receiving any the least animal gratification from that species of intercourse. Now, had this woman been properly informed by her mother as to the nature of the sexes, and been told some years before her marriage what exquisite delight that act is calculated to impart,

she would probably have received much pleasure from the anticipation; which would have matured her passions, and made her quite a different being.

(At the same time, Kitchener denounced the notion that women were naturally libidinous as a falsehood circulated by libertines, so perhaps the best part of the exquisite delight in question was to be experienced by the husband.) Even with boys a degree of circumspectness was required when divulging the dread secret of human generation. Dr Thomas Beddoes suggested that information regarding the function of the male organ should be delayed till 'An accident, in which this tender part should receive a blow, would furnish a fair occasion for taking up the subject'. Above all it was desirable to avoid the risk to social decorum involved in telling the facts of life to children too young to appreciate their true import: Kitchener related an instance of what might happen if parents were foolish enough to reveal too much too soon:

> A large party of genteel people, of both sexes, were set down to an early dinner, and the heads of the family, who have too much goodness of character ever to sacrifice the interests of their children to the modish manners of the world, had the young folks all around them; when, in consequence of something which had been said, one of the younger children, who had been deemed too young to be admitted into the class with its elder brethren, simply asked its mother, 'how children were made?' Had such a thing happened elsewhere, a prudent mother would have found no difficulty in giving the child such a reply as would have prevented any repetition of the question. But here, her brother did not wait for the reply of the mother, but began to describe the whole process of procreation with the perspicuity of an anatomist, to the utter consternation of his father and mother, and the whole party then assembled. Little master was proud of the information which he had in his power to convey; and he took the company so by surprise, that nobody seemed to have any ability to interfere, and he was enabled to finish his descriptive detail, with little or no interruption.[10]

*

The increasing decorousness – or prudery – of the age extended even to the penal code. Before 1790 women convicted of petty treason (which covered coining and the murder of husbands or employers) were burnt at the stake. Sir Benjamin Hammet, who in May 1790 moved in the House of Commons for this form of punishment to be abolished, thought it was 'the savage remains of Norman policy'. Earlier William Blackstone, the eighteenth century's great legal commentator, claimed it derived from 'the laws of the antient Druids'. It seems, however, that burning at the stake had developed simply as a traditional alternative to the statutory mutilation of the bodies of traitors: as Blackstone pointed out, 'the natural modesty of the sex forbids the exposing and publicly mangling their bodies'. (Such matters were important in the era of public execution: in 1752 Mary Blandy, about to be hanged in the normal way for poisoning her father, said on the scaffold, 'Gentlemen, don't hang me high for the sake of decency', and after she was cut down it was noted with disapproval that to get to the coffin waiting in a nearby house her body was 'carried thro' the crowd upon the shoulders of a man with her legs exposed very indecently'.) In moving for the law to be changed Hammet told his colleagues that 'he had no doubt but that the House would go with him in the cause of humanity'.[11]

In 1652 the husband-murderer Prudence Lee was deliberately burnt alive, but subsequently the practice was to strangle the condemned woman before lighting the pyre. The last woman to be burnt alive at the stake in England was Katherine Hayes, at Tyburn on 3 November 1726. She had been found guilty of instigating two men to murder and dismember her husband: for some reason the executioner ignited the pyre before garrotting his victim, and was driven off by the flames before he could put her out of her agony. The later practice was to stand the condemned women on a stool, with a noose fixed to a post at her back, to remove the stool, and to begin piling faggots around the post after she appeared to be dead:

Phoebe Harris, the female convict, was led by two officers to a stake, about eleven feet high, fixed in the ground, near the top of which was an inverted curve made of iron, to which one end of an halter was tied. The prisoner stood on a low stool, which, after the Ordinary had prayed with her a short time, was taken away, and she hung suspended by her neck, her feet being scarcely more than twelve or fourteen inches from the pavement. Soon after the signs of life had ceased, two cartloads of faggots were placed round her, and set on fire; the flames soon burning the halter. She then sunk a few inches, but was supported by an iron chain passed over her chest, and affixed to the stake. It was more than three hours before the fire was extinguished, and then some scattered remains were observable among the ashes. She was a well-made little woman, of a pale complexion, and rather handsome features. When brought to the stake, she trembled much, and appeared to be struck with horror at the punishment she was to undergo. She never spoke, but found [? seemed] absorbed in agony of mind.

The last such execution, that of Christian Murphy alias Bowman, on 18 March 1789, involved only minor variations on this procedure:

the woman, in a white dress, was brought out of Newgate alone; and after some time spent in devotion, was hung on the projecting arm of a low gibbet, fixed at a little distance from the scaffold. After the lapse of a sufficient time to extinguish life, faggots were piled around her, and over her head, so that her person was completely covered: fire was then set to the pile, and the woman was consumed to ashes.[12]

As there was no centralised compilation of penal statistics till the 1800s it would be difficult to say how many women were executed in this fashion before the change in the law in 1790. There were at least four such executions in the 1780s, and a fifth woman was convicted of coining and sentenced to be burnt in 1790 but was not executed in this manner because of the alteration of the law. Sir Benjamin Hammet, MP for Taunton, a banker and stock-jobber, had been one of the sheriffs of London in 1789 and had been obliged to attend the execution of Christian Murphy; he had been encouraged to move for a change in the law by the sheriff detailed to supervise the burning of the female coiner sentenced in 1790.[13]

Most of the women burnt were probably coiners, though Mary Saunders was burnt at Monmouth in March 1764 for killing her mistress, and Rebecca Downing, at Ringswell, outside Exeter in August 1782, for killing her master. In the popular imagination, however, burning at the stake was thought to be specifically reserved for husband-murderers: a man whose Hackney carriage passed over the pile of smouldering ashes where Christian Murphy had just been burnt for coining was told by the coachman, 'Oh, sir, they have been burning a woman for murdering her husband.'[14]

Another modification of the criminal code, this time in 1817, was the abolition of the public flogging of women, following a newspaper report that:

a woman, young and beautiful, had been whipped in the public streets ... she was in a state of intoxication, seemed quite lost to every sense of her situation, and shortly returned to her old courses.

As Lieutenant-General William Thornton, MP for New Woodstock, pointed out when raising the matter in the House of Commons, 'Spectacles such as this were not likely to improve the public morals.'[15]

*

It is obviously more than a mere coincidence that the abolition of public rituals of judicial violence specially reserved for women occurred in the same period as the elaboration of the doctrine of female asexuality, but such developments ought not to be seen as part of a process relating exclusively to women.

Fear of women's sexuality, for example, may be difficult to distinguish from fear of sexuality generally. Age-old theories about the weakening effect of sexual intercourse were still being trotted out by doctors:

> The emission of semen enfeebles the body more than the loss of twenty times the same quantity of blood, more than violent cathartics, emetics, &c. ... even libidinous thoughts, without any loss of semen, are debilitating, though in a less degree, by occasioning a propulsion of blood to the genitals.

But it was not simply a question of the conservatism of the medical profession: James Graham, perhaps the most successful quack practitioner of his day, commended those who 'never fail to spring up the moment after each amorous embrace, to lave and immerse the whole male apparatus, and the female apartment of pleasure in very cold water', and condemned 'that odious, most indelicate and most hurtful custom of man and wife continually *pigging* together in one and the same bed'. Of the latter custom he wrote:

> Nothing is more unwise, – nothing more indecent, – nothing more unnatural, than for a man or woman to sleep, to snore, and steam, and do every thing else that's indelicate together, three hundred and sixty-five times – every year!

Graham himself had an eye for a pretty girl – in the 'Temple of Health' he established at the Adelphi in 1780 he employed a fifteen-year-old named Emma Lyon, later famous as Nelson's Lady Hamilton, to pose as the Goddess of Health – but he clearly had some sort of psychological block about natural bodily functions; yet he evidently also had a shrewd sense of what his customers wanted to hear and his success as a quack inevitably suggests that the people who flocked to consult him were in the grip of a combination of fears and longings little different from his own.[16]

In many cases, no doubt, men projected their personal sexual anxiety on to women; but the issue of female sexuality was only a secondary and incidental feature of *Onania* (which was after all, second only to *Aristotle's Master-piece* as the eighteenth century's bestselling text on a sexual topic) and was completely absent and divorced from the intensifying campaign against male homosexuals. In fact one could claim that sexuality, which was something that men and women had been perceived to share and have in common before the 1700s, became increasingly a male territory thereafter. The separate sphere that was evolving for women allowed them only defloration and child-birth – nothing before, after, or in-between, unless they happened to belong to that other separate female sphere, inhabited by the fallen women who had given themselves over to licentiousness, depravity and, if physiologically possible, perhaps even lust.

Of course changing attitudes to sex, and changing notions of the role of women in society were part of a much larger and more general process of change. The class element in standard perceptions of seduction, rape and prostitution has already been indicated. Sexual morality was among the areas in which, during the eighteenth century, the middle class flexed its muscles and explored its own identity. But even the threefold division of society into upper class, middle class and lower class is merely an analytic tool applicable to a certain phase of the evolution of the world's economic and socio-political structure. The emergence of the idea of the individual, whether simply a phase in the evolution of bourgeois culture or a principle underlying all political and economic progress, is obviously closely bound up with the history of attitudes to sex and gender: Lovelace and other eighteenth-century seducers are in some respects prototypes of the twentieth century's existential individual, committed to subordinating the world to his own determinations, while their victims, isolated by an error that was scarcely their fault, illustrate the predicament of the individual trapped in a hopeless struggle against the collective; and Mary Wollstonecraft, in some ways the archetype of the strong-willed female hunted from pillar to post by the inexorable logic of social institutions designed to serve males – even down to her death in childbed, when she might have been saved by a more advanced obstetric science — was the forerunner of all those twentieth-century women who longed to have, like their men, 'a room of their own'. But social class and the emergence of individualism are not part of the history of sex, they are part of the larger history of our species within which the history of sex is merely one (or several?) of the strands. A great deal more work — including histories of sex in other European and extra-European countries — needs to be done before we will be ready to put the strands together.

I shall leave the other countries and the other centuries, and the assembling of the whole story, to other scholars: at the moment I can only offer this short volume as a loose end.

Notes

All books cited were published in London unless otherwise stated.

Introduction

1. Lorenzo da Ponte's libretto for *Don Giovanni* (1787), Act 1, Scene 5; Lawrence Stone, *The Family, Sex and Marriage in England 1500-1800* (1977), pp. 572-99.

The three field marshals among Augustus the Strong's progeny were Maurice de Saxe in the French army – one of the outstanding military commanders of the eighteenth century – and Johann Georg Chevalier de Saxe and Friedrich August Graf von Rutowski in the Saxon army. The last-named, incidentally, had a Turkish mother, suggesting that Don Giovanni was not unique in the national distribution of his favours.

2. Stone, *Family, Sex and Marriage*, pp. 622-3, 643. For the present author's discussion of organised religion *c.* 1800 see A.D. Harvey, *Britain in the Early Nineteenth Century* (1978), pp. 64-78.

3. Jeannette Parisot, *Johnny Come Lately: a short history of the condom* (1987), pp. 8-9; Daniel Turner, *Syphilis: a Practical Dissertation on the Venereal Disease* (1717), p. 74; Angus McClaren, *Reproductive Rituals: the perception of fertility in England from the sixteenth century to the nineteenth century* (1984), pp. 82-6 for condoms; ibid., pp. 70-2 for the rhythm method, which however was based on the belief that women were at their most fertile directly after menstruation; ibid., pp. 75-8 for coitus interruptus; ibid., pp. 73-5 for contraceptive potions, which seem by the eighteenth century to have lost such reputation for efficacy as they may have had earlier.

4. E.A. Wrigley and R.S. Schofield, *The Population History of England 1641-1871: a reconstruction* (Cambridge 1989 edit.), p. 255; Peter Laslett, *Family Life and Illicit Love in Earlier Generations* (Cambridge 1977), pp. 215, 232; for Harriette Wilson see her *Memoirs* (4 vols, 1825) which have one of the classic opening sentences of literature: 'I shall not say why and how I became, at the age of fifteen, the mistress of the Earl of Craven'; *The Confessions of the Countess of Strathmore, written by Herself* (1793), pp. 55-6; Richard De Courcy, *Seduction: or, the Cause of Injured Innocence Pleaded* (1782), p. v; *Calumny: being an Answer to a Pamphlet and Poem entitled Seduction* (1782), p. 3 – 'Otaheite' is of course Tahiti, already famed for its uninhibited women, 'Parya' seems to be an unusual spelling of pariah; Wrigley and Schofield, *Population History of England*, pp. 266, 254 n 94. Wrigley and Schofield's book incorporates much of the work of the Cambridge Group for the Study of Population and Social Structure, of which Wrigley is a co-founder.

5. McClaren, *Reproductive Rituals*, pp. 89-112 deals with ideas on and the practice of abortion, which seems generally to have been discussed as something done by other people; ibid., pp. 135-42 for the legislation making it a criminal offence in 1803; *The Confessions of the Countess of Strathmore, written by Herself,*

p. 89; John Armstrong, *The Oeconomy of Love: a Poetical Esseay* (1736), p. 5, lines 58-60; Edwards Shorter, *A History of Women's Bodies* (1983), p. 261; *The Whore's Rhetorick, Calculated to the Meridian of London; and conformed to the Rules of Art* (1683), p. 185.

6. Michel Foucault, *The History of Sexuality*, vol. 1 (1981) pp. 115, 121.

There are of course a large number of other scholars working in this general area: the pages of *The Journal of the History of Sexuality*, published by the University of Chicago Press, give some idea of the kind of work being done, especially in America.

7. John Armstrong, *The Oeconomy of Love*, p. 18, lines 244-8, 251-2; ibid., pp. 14-15 and p. 26, lines 358-61; Thomas Campbell, *Specimens of the British Poets; with Biographical and Critical Notices* (7 vols, 1819), vol. 6, p. 342; Thomas Middleton Rayser, ed., *Samuel Taylor Coleridge: Shakespeare Criticism* (2 vols, 1960), vol. 2, p. 35; John Cannon, ed., *The Letters of Junius* (Oxford 1978), p. 454 (poem 'Harry & Nan', first printed in John Almon's *Political Register*, June 1768); *Edinburgh Review*, vol. 53 (1831), p. 547 (review of Thomas Moore's *Letters and Journals of Lord Byron*).

1. Women's Bodies – and How Men Looked at Them

1. J. Gautier d'Agoty the Elder's *Anatomie des Parts de la Génération de l'Homme et de la Femme* of 1773, one of the first anatomical treatises to have colour illustrations, may well have been the first publication to show a woman with sepia-coloured nipples and areoles.

The National Gallery, London, has a painting of 'A Blonde Woman' by Palma Vecchio, *c.* 1520, which shows a natural-sized pink areole, but the subject and format suggest a private commission: no doubt there are other exceptions to the rule that areoles were not generally shown, but they remain exceptions.

2. For the iconography of Christ on the Cross see Leo Steinberg, *The Sexuality of Christ in Renaissance Art and in Modern Oblivion* (1984), pp. 8-9.

3. For classical sculptures see Kenneth Clark, *The Nude* (1950), pp. 72-3, 78, 81-2.

4. John Hall-Stevenson, 'Antony's Tale: or the Boarding-School Tale' in *Crazy Tales* (1762) – quoting from *Works of John Hall-Stevenson* (3 vols, 1795), vol. 3, p. 17; ibid., vol. 3, p. 20; *Venus in the Cloister: or, the Nun in her Smock* (1725 – English version of a seventeenth-century French original), p. 134 and cf. p. 137; John Cleland, *Fanny Hill* (first published as *Memoirs of a Woman of Pleasure* 1749, second edition, abbreviated and expurgated, as *Memoirs of Fanny Hill*, published, but suppressed by the authorities, in 1750: citations from 1970 Mayflower paperback edit.), p. 41; ibid., p. 148; *The Genuine and Remarkable Amours of the Celebrated Author Peter Aretin* [? 1776 – imprint gives MDCCLXCVI], p. 11; *Rare Verities. The Cabinet of Venus Unlocked and Her Secrets laid open. Being a Translation of part of Sinibaldus his Geneanthropeia* (1658 – actually 1657), p. 28.

5. Jacques Boileau, *A Just and Seasonable Reprehension of Naked Breasts and Shoulders* (1678), p. 133 (LVI); Samuel Richardson, *Clarissa Harlowe* (1747-8), vol. 4, letter 45; 'Lemuel Gulliver', *The Pleasures and Felicity of Marriage, Display'd in Ten Books* (1745), p. 2; G.B. Hill and L.F. Powell, eds, *Boswell's Life of Johnson* (6 vols, Oxford 1934-64), vol. 1, p. 201.

6. *The Fruit-Shop, a Tale* (2 vols, 1765), vol. 2, pp. 146-51; Gulliver, *Pleasures and Felicity of Marriage*, p. 2; *The Fifteen Plagues of a Maiden-Head* (1707), p. 3; *Works of John Hall-Stevenson*, vol. 3, p. 17; William Woty, 'Epistle to Doctor Graham' in *Fugitive and Original Poems* (Derby 1786), at p. 46.

7. Samuel Croxall, *The Fair Circassian* (1720), stanza VII, lines 13-14, and cf. at an earlier date Robert Herrick's 'Upon the Nipples of *Julia*'s Breast', *Hesperides* (1648), p. 190; Cleland, *Fanny Hill*, p. 41; [Bernard Mandeville], *The Virgin Unmask'd: or, Female Dialogues Betwixt an Elderly Maiden Lady and her Niece* (1709), p. 4; *Spectator*, no. 145, 16 August 1711 – vol. 1, p. 439 of 4-vol. Everyman edition, edited by Gregory Smith, 1907; Richardson, *Clarissa*, vol. 40, letter 50, and cf. Henry Fielding, *Tom Jones* (1749), book IV, chap. 2; *The Mirror of the Graces: or the English Lady's Costume* (1811), p. 101; Jean Marishall, *The History of Miss Clarinda Cathcart and Miss Fanny Renton* (2 vols, 1766), vol. 1, p. 39; [John Cleland?], *Genuine Adventures of the Celebrated Miss Maria Brown* (2 vols, 1766), vol. 1, p. 63.

8. Louis Reau, *Houdon: sa vie et son oeuvre* (2 vols, Paris 1964), vol. 1, p. 227, cf. plates IV and V.

9. Fuseli did an Eve for Du Roveray's edition of *Paradise Lost* in 1802 and another for an edition of the Works of the British Poets in 1805. William Hamilton also provided illustrations of Eve for the Du Roveray *Paradise Lost*. For Etty's letters asking to be remembered to Fuseli, see Dennis Farr, *William Etty* (1958), pp. 120, 122, Etty to Sir Thomas Lawrence, 26 March 1823 (from Venice) and 14 Nov. 1823 (from Paris); for Delacroix's odalisque see Aaron Scharf, *Art and Photography* (1968), pp. 93-4; for early nude photography see Jorge Lewinski, *The Naked and the Nude: a history of nude photography* (1987), esp. p. 26, Vallou de Villeneuve's 'Nude on a Couch', *c.* 1853; Sir Astley Paston Cooper, *On the Anatomy of the Breast* (1840), p. 2.

The redness of women's nipples was celebrated by seventeenth-century poets such as Joshua Sylvester, the translator of Du Bartas (1611), Herrick (see note 7 above) and Thomas Shipman, in 'Beauties Periphrasis' (1674), but was rarely alluded to after Croxall's time: see however *An Essay on Woman. A Poem* (1763 – not the famous poem by John Wilkes but another piece in blank verse), p. 18.

10. *The Art-Journal*, vol. 11 (1849), pp. 39-40.

11. Figures for lithographic printers in London are from Michael Twyman, *A Directory of London Lithographic Printers 1800-1876* (1976), pp. 4, 9; Alois Senefelder, *A Complete Course of Lithography: containing Clear and Explicit Instructions in all the Different Branches and Manners of that Art: to which is prefixed A History of Lithography* (1819, translation of German edition of 1818), pp. 371-3; Charles Blunt, *An Essay on Mechanical Drawing* (1811), p. 1.

12. T. Cogan, *The Works of the Late Professor Camper on the Connexion between the Science of Anatomy and the Arts of Drawing, Painting, Statuary, &c* (1794), pp. iv-v – Petrus Camper had been professor of medicine at Groningen.

13. There are four surviving versions of 'Venus and the Organ-player'. Besides the painting referred to in the text the Prado also has an earlier version with Cupid and no dog, the Staatliche Museum, Berlin has a 'Venus, Cupid, Organ-player and Little Dog' and the Uffizi a 'Venus, Cupid and Little Dog' – but no organ-player. Together with the two versions of 'Venus and the Lute-player' this multiplicity of versions testifies to the popularity of the theme in Titian's lifetime. These paintings are discussed in Erwin Panofsky, *Problems in Titian: mainly iconographic* (1969), pp. 122-5. His suggestion is that the theme (except in the Uffizi version) is the choice between the delights of sound (music) and those of vision. This is, of course, compatible with the interpretation put forward here.

The Kunstmuseum Basel has a 'Reclining Nude and Piano-player' *c.* 1799-1800 by Fuseli (see Plate 9). Though the piano-player is a woman, and is leaning sideways merely in order to have a better look at her music, the composition is an adaptation of the Titian paintings discussed here. It is not clear why Fuseli painted it: on the back of the same canvas is a painting of three courtesans.

14. Oliver Lawson Dick, ed., *Aubrey's Brief Lives* (1960), pp. 255-6; Pierre de Bourdeille (Seigneur de Brantôme), *The Lives of Gallant Ladies* (1965 paperback edit.), p. 174 (the first French edition was in 1665 but the text was probably written before 1600); Cleland, *Fanny Hill* (1970 Mayflower paperback edit.), pp. 52-3; ibid., pp. 55-6; ibid., p. 215; Charles Walker, *Authentick memoirs of the Life Intrigues and Adventures of the Celebrated Sally Salisbury with the Characters of her most Considerable Gallants* (1723), p. 47; *The History of the Human Heart; or the Adventures of a Young Gentleman* (1749 but citing 1886 edit.), p. 157 – see Peter Naumann, *Keyhole and Candle: John Clelands «Memoirs of a Woman of Pleasure» und die Entstehung des pornographischen Romans in England* (Heidelberg 1976), p. 430, n. 52 for the authenticity of this novel, now known only from a nineteenth-century reprint.

15. Cleland, *Fanny Hill* (1970 edit.), p. 58; ibid., p. 168; ibid, p.147.

16. John MacLaurin, *The Keekiad* (1760 but citing 1824 edit.), p. 16; ibid., p. 17; *The History of the Human Heart*, p. 158.

Gazing at vaginas also features in the clandestinely circulated *The Genuine and Remarkable Amours of the Celebrated Author Peter Aretin* [? 1776], pp. 79-80.

17. M.G. Lewis, *The Monk: a Romance* (1796 but citing World's Classics paperback edit. 1980), p. 271 (the pose of the Medici Venus is left hand over crutch and right hand over left breast); John Keats, *The Eve of St Agnes* (written winter 1818-19, published 1820), stanza XXVI; Cleland, *Fanny Hill*, p. 141.

For the relationship between landscape painting and literary descriptions of landscape in the eighteenth century see A.D. Harvey, *English Poetry in a Changing Society 1780-1825* (1980), pp. 23-4. For the legal proceedings against *Fanny Hill* see William H. Epstein, *John Cleland: images of a life* (New York 1974), pp. 75-80.

18. David Lodge, *How Far Can You Go* (1980), p. 39; Nicolas Venette, *Conjugal Love Reveal'd* (1720), p. 129; *Rare Verities. The Cabinet of Venus Unlocked and Her Secrets laid open. Being a Translation of part of Sinibaldus his Geneanthropeia* (1658 – actually 1657), p. 64; Venette, *Conjugal Love Reveal'd*, pp. 127-8.

See also Douglas Hall, *In Miserable Slavery: Thomas Thistlewood in Jamaica 1750–86* (1989), pp. 87, 88, 122, for the position adopted by at least one Englishman when having sex with slave women.

19. For Dr Fell and the fellows of All Souls see David Foxon, *Libertine Literature in England 1600-1745* (1964), pp. 6-7; *The Whore's Rhetorick, Calculated to the Meridian of London; and conformed to the Rules of Art* (1683), p. 171 – based on a work by Ferrante Pallavicino, though in Pallavicino's original text of 1642 the whores of the title are plural: *La retorica delle Putane*.

20. Lynne Lawner, *I Modi: the Sixteen Pleasures: an erotic album of the Italian Renaissance* (1988), pp. 9, 17; *The Genuine and Remarkable Amours of the Celebrated Author Pietro Aretin* [? 1776], p. 69.

The position in *L'Aretin Francois* which most closely corresponds to a surviving design in the original Aretine series also appears in a collection of erotic prints entitled *L'Aretin d'Auguste Carrache*, but this, despite the pretence that it is by Agostino Carracci, dates only from the later 1790s. The not very interesting text of *L'Aretin Francois* is attributed to the miscellaneous writer, poet and dramatist François-Felix Nogaret (1740-1831).

21. Venette, *Conjugal Love Reveal'd*, p. 127; *The Life and Amours of Lady Ann F-l-y developing the Whole of Her Intrigues* etc. (1785), p. 8; *The Trial of Lady Ann Foley* [1785], p. 52; *Life and Amours of Lady Ann F-l-y*, p. 18.

22. *The Mirror of the Graces; or, the English Lady's Costume* (1811), p. 95; ibid., pp. 92-3; *Gentleman's Magazine*, vol. 74 (1804), p. 428.

23. John Bowles, *Reflections on the Political and Moral State of Society at the close of the Eighteenth Century* (1800), p. 138.

24. Adam Sibbit, *Thoughts on the Frequency of Divorce in Modern Times and on the Necessity of Legislative Action, to Prevent their Increasing Prevalence* (1800), p. 19 (Sibbit was rector of Clarendon, in Jamaica); Charles Lucas, *The Infernal Quixote: a Tale of the Day* (4 vols, 1801), vol. 2, pp. 155-6; John Bowles, *Remarks on Modern Female Manners, as Distinguished by Indifference to Character, and Indecency of Dress: extracted from 'Reflections Political and Moral at the Conclusion of the War'* (1802), p. 8: the passage also appears in the fourth edition of Bowles' *Reflections*, but not in previous editions; Thomas Beddoes, *Hygëia: or Essays Moral and Medical on the Causes affecting the personal state of our Middling and Affluent Classes* (3 vols, Bristol 1802-3), vol. 1, Essay Third, p. 75. In the British Library's copy of *Hygëia* the passage where Beddoes refers to 'a practice of *damping* the cobweb garments, which otherwise would hang about the limbs too loosely', has been annotated in the margin, perhaps by James Woodhouse, the book's original owner, 'astonishing madness, cursed vanity'.

25. [Richard Graves], *Senilities: or, Solitary Amusements: in Prose and Verse: with a Cursory Disquisition on the Future of the Sexes* (1801), pp. 230-1 ('On the Present Loose Drapery of the Fair Sex'); Walter Sickel, ed., *The Glenbervie Journals* (1910), p. 153, 21 Oct. 1811.

26. Jane Richardson and A.L. Kroeber, 'Three Centuries of Women's Dress Fashions: a Quantitative Analysis', *Anthropological Records*, vol. 5, no. 2 (1940), pp. 111-53; see esp. pp. 129 and 149.

27. Paul Poiret, *My First Fifty Years* (1931), p. 73.

28. Abel Boyer, *The Political State of Great Britain*, vol. 30 (1725), p. 514. For Meibom see Ian Gibson, *The English Vice: beating, sex and shame in Victorian England and after* (1978), pp. 1-5. He really was named Meibom – it means Maypole in Low German. The last English language edition of his treatise was in 1898, the last French language edition in 1909.

29. Thomas Shadwell, *The Virtuoso. A Comedy. Acted at the Duke's Theatre* (1676), p. 46 (Act III). In Act IV (p. 64) Hazard says of Mrs Figgup, Snarl's mistress, 'she keeps a very virtuous School, for the disciplining of hopeful towardly old Gentlemen': see also Gordon Williams, *A Dictionary of Sexual Language and Imagery in Shakespearean and Stuart Literature* (3 vols, 1994), vol. 1, pp. 515-16, *sub* 'flogging school'; John Armstrong, *The Oeconomy of Love: a Poetical Essay* (1736), p. 37, lines 528-30; Cleland, *Fanny Hill* (1970 edit.), pp. 176-80; Henry Ashbee, *Index Librorum Prohibitorum: being Notes Bio-Biblio-Ikonographical and Critical on Curious and Uncommon Books* (privately printed 1877), p. 246; ibid., pp. lxiii-lxv; ibid., p. xlii; *The Cherub: or Guardian of Female Innocence* (1792), p. 17; William Bagwell, *A Plain Statement of Facts, relative to Sir Eyre Coote* (1816) – Colonel Bagwell was Coote's brother-in-law.

30. Cleland, *Fanny Hill* (1970 edit.), pp. 144-6.

Ruth Perry, 'Colonising the Breast: Sexuality and Maternity in Eighteenth-Century England', *Journal of the History of Sexuality*, vol. 2 (1991), pp. 204-34 suggests that an increasing emphasis on the value of maternal breast-feeding generated the increased interest on the part of men in women's breasts. There is no need to insist on monocausal explanations of course, but Ms Perry's analysis is difficult to reconcile with the argument suggested here, that women's breasts were being seen in a different way as part of a process of seeing women's bodies as a whole in a different way.

2. The Waning of Female Lust

1. D.M. Frame, ed., *The Complete Works of Montaigne* (Stanford 1957), p. 650; J.H. Osborn, ed., *The Autobiography of Thomas Whythorne* (1962), p. 15; *Rare Verities. The Cabinet of Venus Unlocked and Her Secrets laid open. Being a Translation of part of Sinibaldus his Geneanthropeia* (1657), p. 16. The imprint states the date of publication incorrectly as 1658; the more usual form of the name Caelius Rodiginus is Coelius Richerius Rhodiginus, actually Ludovico Ricchieri (1469-1525), a noted Italian humanist; Nicolas Venette, *Conjugal Love Reveal'd; on the nightly pleasures of the marriage bed, and the advantages of that state* (7th edit. 1720), p. 161; ibid., p. 126.

2. For Tomás Sánchez see Pierre Darmon, *Trial by Impotence: virility and marriage in pre-Revolutionary France* (1985), p. 4; Angus McClaren, *Reproductive Rituals: the perception of fertility in England from the sixteenth century to the nineteenth century* (1984), p. 26; Venette, *Conjugal Love Reveal'd*, pp. 20-1; Bernard Mandeville, *A Modest Defence of Publick Stews: or, an Essay upon Whoring, as it is now practis'd in these Kingdoms* (1724), p. 21.

3. Venette, *Conjugal Love Reveal'd*, pp. 118-19.

4. *The Ladies Physical Directory* first appeared in 1716 as *A Rational Account of the natural weaknesses of women, and of the several distempers peculiarly incident to them*. The third edition of 1727, *The Ladies Physical Directory: or, a treatise of all the weaknesses, indispositions, and diseases peculiar to the female sex, from eleven years of age to fifty or upwards*, does not contain the passages quoted here: the seventh edition of 1739 may be the first with the additional material cited: it is on p. 70 of the British Library's copy of the 1742 edition.

The phrasing on the title page hardly suggests that the 'gentlewoman' at the Two Blue Posts was the author, though she may have supervised the contents. A case may be made for suggesting that, as medical practitioners became more numerous, some of them began to make a speciality of female ailments and developed more confidential relations with women patients than hitherto, and therefore became more inclined to put forward the woman's rather than the man's view when they wrote about sex, but the tone of the *Ladies Physical Directory* does not altogether indicate that it was an example of such a process.

5. Wallace's essay has been printed in the present century, in Norah Smith, 'Robert Wallace's "Of Venery"', *Texas Studies in Literature and Language*, vol. 15 (1973), pp. 429-44, the quotation being from pp. 434-5.

6. [Robert Couper], *Speculation on the Mode and Appearances of Impregnation in the Human Female* (Edinburgh 1789), pp. 42-3, cf. 1797 edit., p. 72. (This passage appears almost word for word in Ebenezer Sibly, *The Medical Mirror: or Treatise on the Impregnation of the Human Female* (1794 – 6th edit. 1814), p. 22: 'To many women the embraces of the male are extremely, if not completely, indifferent; and to some they are absolutely disagreeable.' This must be one of the more blatant plagiarisms of the period.) Henry Thomas Kitchener, *Letters on Marriage, on the Causes of Matrimonial Infidelity, and on the Reciprocal Relations of the Sexes* (2 vols, 1812), vol. 2, p. 74; E.L. Griggs, ed., *The Collected Letters of Samuel Taylor Coleridge* (6 vols, Oxford 1956-71), vol. 4, pp. 905-6, Coleridge to unknown 8 Jan. 1819; *Westminster Review*, vol. 53 (1850), p. 457.

7. *The Whore's Rhetorick Calculated to the Meridian of London: and conformed to the Rules of Art* (1683), pp. 43-4; *A New Atlantis for the Year One thousand seven hundred and Fifty-eight* (1758), p. 52; Cleland, *Fanny Hill* (1970 edit.), p. 170; *The Genuine and Remarkable Amours of the Celebrated Author Peter Aretin* [? 1776], pp. 51, 78; Couper, *Speculation on the Mode and Appearances of Impregnation* (1789 edit.), p. 43, and cf. Sibly, *Medical Mirror*, p. 23.

The use of 'critical minute' in *The Genuine and Remarkable Amours of the Celebrated Author Peter Aretin* to refer to orgasm may be ironical: the phrase – first recorded, according to the *Oxford English Dictionary*, in 1673 – normally signified the moment when a woman capitulated to her lover's persuasions. See e.g. *The History of the Human Heart: or, the Adventures of a Young Gentleman* (1749, but citing 1886 edit.), p. 81 and [Richard Griffith], *The Triumvirate: or, the Authentic Memoirs of A. B. and C.* (2 vols, 1764), vol. 2, p. 106.

8. John Astruc, *A Treatise on all the Diseases Incident to Women* (1743), p. 155 – note that this is a translation of notes taken from lectures and that there is no antecedent published French text; Jean Astruc, *A Treatise on the Diseases of Women* (2 vols, 1762), vol. 1, p. 346; [William Cullen], *Synopsis Nosologiae Methodicae* (Edinburgh 1769), p. 67; J.D.T. Bienville, *Nymphomania, or, a Dissertation concerning the Furor Uterinus* (1775), pp. ii-iii – cf. Amsterdam 1778 French-language edition, p. viii: Astruc's chapter on *furor uterinus* is in fact at the end of his first book, i.e. at the end of vol. 2 of the 4-volume 1761 French edition and at the end of vol. 1 of the 2-volume 1762 English edition. The Latin text appears in English in the 1762 English edition, and the whole book appears in Latin in an edition published at Venice 1763-7; Bienville, *Nymphomania* (1775), pp. 31, 36 and cf. Astruc, *Treatise* (1762), vol. 1, pp. 342-3: cf. also Astruc's discussion of classical authorities, vol. 1, pp. 344-5, and Bienville's virtually identical survey, pp. 40-3; Alex P. Buchan, *Venus Sine Concubitu* (1818), p. 33; *Critical Review*, vol. 39 (1775), p. 252: this review also states of nymphomania that 'many physicians have been led to question its existence'; Bienville, *Nymphomania*, p. 40, cf. Astruc, *Treatise* (1762), vol. 1, p. 344.

Astruc's *metromania* (womb-madness) is from the Greek μητρα, womb, and is quite distinct from William Gifford's 1794 coinage *metromania* (verse-madness, mania for writing poetry) which is given in the *Oxford English Dictionary* and which derives from μετρον, measure – Astruc's text, incidentally, printed the word in Greek characters but it appears transliterated in Cullen.

9. The quotation is from Eliza Haywood, *Love in Excess: or the Fatal Enquiry* (1719), p. 49; Samuel Richardson, *Pamela, or Virtue Rewarded* (2 vols, 1741 – actually 1740), vol. 2, pp. 38, 40.

10. Shakespeare, *The Rape of Lucrece* (1594), line 1654.

11. Shakespeare, *Measure for Measure* (1604 ? – first printed 1623), Act II, Scene 4, lines 100-4, 106-8, 180-5 and Act III, Scene 1, lines 194-6. Charlotte Lennox, *Shakespeare Illustrated* (3 vols, 1753-4), vol. 3, p. 133.

12. Milton, *Comus* (1634), lines 446-9.

13. *Hell Upon Earth, or the Town in an Uproar* (1729), p. 9; Samuel Richardson, *Clarissa* (7 vols, 1747-8), vol. 4, letter 43; John Wilkes, *An Essay on Woman* (1763), lines 87-90; *The Fair Concubine: or, the Secret History of the Fair Vanella* (1732), p. 27 (this is a highly coloured account of the Hon. Anne Vane, mistress of Frederick, Prince of Wales); Eliza Haywood, *The British Recluse: or, the Secret History of Cleomira, Suppos'd Dead* (1722), pp. 46-7; Eliza Haywood, *Idalia: or, the Unfortunate Mistress* (1722), p. 22.

14. Venette, *Conjugal Love Reveal'd*, pp. 82-100 (ch. IV: 'If there be any Signs of a Maiden head'); Daniel Defoe, *Moll Flanders* (1722, but quoting Oxford University Press's 1971 edit.), p. 29; Richardson, *Pamela* (2 vols, 1740), vol. 1, p. 254 (Journal, 37th Day of Imprisonment, answer to B.'s proposals, article 5); *Anti-Pamela: or, Feign'd Innocence Detected, in a Series of Syrena's Adventures* (1741 – possibly by Eliza Haywood), p. 34; Cleland, *Fanny Hill* (1970 edit.), p. 53, cf. John

Fletcher *The Faithful Shepherdess* (c. 1610) Act 1, scene 1; [R. Lewis?], *The Adventures of a Rake* (2 vols, 1759), vol. 1, p. 91; *Fanny Hill*, p. 53; *The History of the Human Heart: or, the Adventures of a Young Gentleman* (1749 but citing 1886 edit.), p. 38; Eliza Haywood, *Cleomelia: or, the Generous Mistress* (1727), p. 89; *Dreams and Moles, with the Interpretation and Signification* (first published c. 1750 but citing Hull edition c. 1815), Francis Grose, *A Classical Dictionary of the Vulgar Tongue.*

15. M.G. Lewis, *The Monk* (1796, but quoting World's Classics paperback edit. 1980), p. 384.

16. Cleland, *Fanny Hill* (1970 edit.), pp. 119-36; Henry Ashbee, *Index Librorum Prohibitorum: being Notes Bio-Biblio-Ikonographical and Critical on Curious and Uncommon Books* (privately printed 1877), p. 148.

17. Venette, *Conjugal Love Reveal'd*, p. 87; *Dreams and Moles*, p. 22; *The Times*, 7 March 1804, p. 3d.

A potion that will show 'whether a woman be a maid or not' is mentioned in *The Changeling*, by Thomas Middleton and William Rowley (first acted 1623), Act Four, Scene One, lines 41 foll.: 'A merry, slight but true experiment, the author Antonius Mizaldus' – i.e. Antoine Mizauld, French doctor and astrologer (1520-78).

3. Seduction

1. [Philip Thicknesse], *Man-Midwifery Analysed: and the Tendency of that Practice Detected and Exposed* (1764), p. 21 (Thicknesse, incidentally, was a patron of Gainsborough and the first man to erect a memorial to Chatterton); John Blunt, *Man-Midwifery Dissected: or, the obstetric Family Instructor* (1793), p. 218; Thicknesse, *Man-Midwifery Analysed*, pp. 16-17; [Francis Foster], *Thoughts on the Times, but chiefly on the Profligacy of our women, and its Causes* (1779), pp. 12-13; Thicknesse, *Man-Midwifery Analysed*, pp. 7, 9; Foster, *Thoughts on the Times*, pp. 160-1. See also Roy Porter, 'A Touch of Danger: the man-midwife as sexual predator' in G.S. Rousseau and Roy Porter, eds, *Sexual Underworlds of the Enlightenment* (Manchester 1987), pp. 206-32.

2. Foster, *Thoughts on the Times*, pp. 191-2; Blunt, *Man-Midwifery Dissected*, p. 89, cf. *The Tryal between J.G. Biker, Plaintiff; and M. Morley, Doctor of Physic, Defendant* (1741) and Jean Donnison, *Midwives and Medical Men* (1988), p. 42; Foster, *Thoughts on the Times*, p. 162; Blunt, *Man-Midwifery Dissected*, p. 88; Foster, *Thoughts on the Times*, pp. 196-8.

3. Foster, *Thoughts on the Times* p. 24; Blunt, *Man-Midwifery Dissected*, p. xx; [Lewis Melville, ed.], *Windham Papers* (2 vols, 1913), vol. 2, pp. 2-3, Windham to Edmund Burke 17 Jan. 1796: for the assumed connection between revolutionary doctrine and sexual licence see also A.D. Harvey, 'George Walker and the Anti-Revolutionary Novel', *Review of English Studies*, vol. 28 (1978), pp. 290-300, at pp. 292, 296-7; Thomas Ewell, *Letters to Ladies, Detailing Important Information Concerning Themselves and Infants* (Philadelphia 1817), p. 26, quoted in Jane B. Donegan, *Women & Men Midwives: Medicine, Morality and Misogyny in Early America* (Greenwood, Conn. 1978), p. 177.

4. *The Life and Amours of Lady Ann F-l-y* [Foley] *developing the Whole of Her intrigues* etc. (1785), p. 27; Foster, *Thoughts on the Times*, p. 6; J. Haggard, *Reports in Cases argued and determined in the Ecclesiastical Courts at Doctors' Commons, and in the High Court of Delegates* (3 vols, 1829-32), vol. 1, p. 752, opinion of Sir John Nicholls 1825.

Crim. con. is discussed in detail in Lawrence Stone's *Road to Divorce: England 1530-1987* (1990), pp. 231-300. Tables 9.1 and 9.2 on p. 430 show:

	crim. con. prosecutions	divorces by private act	of which followed on crim. con. trials
1770-9	36	34	25
1780-9	37	12	11
1790-9	73	43	39
1800-9	52	23	22

5. Robert Elliott, *The Gretna Green Memoirs* (1842), pp. 3, 19, 35; Stone, *Road to Divorce*, p. 276.

The Earl of Westmorland and his bride went through a second marriage service in England less than three weeks after their Gretna Green wedding. Lord Erskine on the other hand tried to obtain a divorce from his second wife in 1820 but found that the Gretna Green marriage was valid in Scots law. He and Lady Erskine separated in 1821.

6. *Aristotle's Master-piece, or the Secrets of generation displayed in all the parts thereof* (1684), p. 6; *Aristotle's Master-piece: or, the Secrets of generation display'd in all the parts thereof* (1690), p. 2; *Aristotle's Compleat Master-piece, in three parts* (1728), p. 30.

7. *Rambler*, no. 107 (26 March 1751) (2 vols, 1753 edit., vol. 2, p. 638) and *Gentleman's Magazine*, vol. 21 (1758), p. 128; Oliver Goldsmith, *The Vicar of Wakefield* (World's Classics 1959 edit.), p. 138; Mary Wollstonecraft, *Posthumous Works of the Author of a Vindication of the Rights of Women* (4 vols, 1798), vol. 1, p. 99; *Annual Register* 1823, Chronicle p. *132.

8. Susan Staves, 'British Seduced Maidens', *Eighteenth-Century Studies*, vol. 14 (1980), pp. 109-34; Edward Relfe, *An Essay on the Seduction of Women* (Lewes [1780]), p. v; Hannah Cowley, *The Scottish Village: or Pitcairne Green* (1786), pp. 7-8; *Pretty Doings in a Protestant Nation. Being a View of the Present State of Fornication, Whorecraft and Adultery in Great Britain, and the Territories and Dependencies thereunto belonging* (1734), p. 4 – according to the title page this pamphlet is translated from the French of Father Poussin, but it is fairly evident that the English text is the original; *Some Authentic Memoirs of the Life of Colonel Ch———s Rape-Master-General of Great Britain* (1730), pp. 10, 15 – in British Library *sub* Charteris; Septimus Hodson, *Sermons on the Present State of Religion in this Country, and on Other Subjects* (1792), p. 194; *Annual Register* 1807, p. 432. See also *The Bawd: a Poem* [? 1782], p. 12 for procuresses recruiting country girls, and *The Whore: a Poem Written by a Whore of Quality* [? 1782], pp. 18-21 where the narrator claims to have been an innocent country girl seduced by a heartless lover.

9. Edward Barry, *Essays, on the Following Subjects: Celibacy, Wedlock, Seduction, Pride ... Excess, Death* (Reading 1806), p. 49; William Mackenzie, *The Sorrows of Seduction* (1805), Delineation IV, lines 89-92; *The Fair Concubine: or, the Secret History of the Beautiful Vanella* (1732), pp. vii-viii; Hugh Kelly, *Memoirs of a Magdalen: or, the History of Louisa Mildmay* (2 vols, 1767), vol. 1, pp. 68, 71; *Gentleman's Magazine*, vol. 21 (1751), p. 164; J.M. [John Moncreiff], *The Scale: or, Woman weighed with Man: a Poem* (1752), pp. 16-17, 19 (Canto 2, lines 34-9, 104-7); Relfe, *Essay on the Seduction of Women*, p. 5; Charles Horne, *Serious Thoughts on the Miseries of Seduction and Prostitution with a Full Account of the Evils that Produce Them* (1783), signature b2; Charles Wickstead, *Ethelston the Suicide: with Other Poems* (1803), p. 100, from stanza XIX of 'The Old Man and his Ruined

Daughter' – the allusion is to the Upas Tree made famous by Erasmus Darwin in *The Loves of the Plants* (1789); Eliza Parsons, *The Errors of Education* (3 vols, 1791), vol. 1, p. 135.

10. Anon., *The Sorrows of Love* (Edinburgh 1801), Book II, lines 656-8; *The Evils of Adultery and Prostitution: with an Inquiry into the Causes of their Present Alarming Increase, and some means recommended for Checking their Progress* (1792), p. 21; Robert Merry, *The Pains of Memory* (1796), p. 12; Relfe, *Essay on the Seduction of Women*, p. 4; Thomas Holcroft, *Seduction* (1787), Act II, Scene 1; *Gentleman's Magazine* (1804), p. 1012, letter signed 'Ernulphus'. For the widespread belief that the Freemasons and the Illuminati brought about the French Revolution see J.M. Roberts, *The Mythology of the Secret Societies* (1972), pp. 168-202.

One of the all-time classics of seduction literature, P.A.F. Choderlos de Laclos' *Les Liaisons Dangereuses*, belongs to this period: first published in 1782, it appeared in English translation as *Dangerous Connections* in 1784 but seems to have been circulated in Britain mainly in the original French version.

11. *Gentleman's Magazine*, vol. 80 (1810), pt. 1, p. 25; Mary Wollstonecraft, *A Vindication of the Rights of Women: with Strictures on Political and Moral Subjects* (1792), p. 155; *The Evils of Adultery and Prostitution*, p. 21; *The Cherub: or, Guardian of Female Innocence* (1792), p. 8; Relfe, *Essay on the Seduction of Women*, p. 3.

12. *The Evils of Adultery and Prostitution*, pp. 23-4; Samuel Johnson in *Rambler*, no. 107, 26 March 1751; John Hunter, *Treatise on the Venereal Disease* (1786), p. 203; William Wordsworth, *The Excursion* (1814), Book 6, lines 845-8.

13. *The Evils of Adultery and Prostitution*, pp. 21-2; *Thoughts on Means of Alleviating the Miseries attendant upon Common Prostitution* [1799], p. 5; Moncreiff, *Scale*, p. 17 (Canto 2, lines 50-5); J.B., *Laura; or, the Fall of Innocence: a Poem* (1787), p. 22; Samuel Richardson, *Clarissa* (7 vols, 1747-8), vol. 5, letter 30 (enclosure); ibid., vol. 5, letter 37; Parsons, *Errors of Education*, vol. 2, p. 137; Kelly, *Memoirs of a Magdalen*, vol. 1, p. 72, Sir Robert Harold to his friend Charles Melmoth; M.G. Lewis, *The Monk* (1796 but citing 1980 World's Classics paperback edit.), p. 392; Robert Bage, *Mount Henneth* (1781 but citing 2nd edit. 1788), vol. 1, p. 221; Barry, *Essays*, p. 53; Miss [S.] Hatfield, *Letters on the Importance of the Female Sex: with Observations on their manners, and on Education* (1803), p. 51; Jane Austen, *Pride and Prejudice* (1813 but citing 1972 Penguin paperback edit.), p. 305.

14. Barry, *Essays*, pp. 53-4; *The Suicide Prostitute: a Poem* (Cambridge 1805), p. 2; Moncreiff, *Scale*, p. 17 (Canto 2, lines 59-61); William Hale, *Considerations on the Causes and Prevalence of Female Prostitution: and on the Most Practicable and Efficient Means of Abating and Preventing That, and All Other Crimes, against the Virtue and Safety of the Community* (1812), p. 9; William Hale, *A Reply to the Pamphlets Lately Published in Defence of the London Female Penitentiary: with Further Remarks upon the Dangerous Tendency of that Institution* (1809), p. 47, cf. Hale, *Considerations on the Causes and Prevalence of Female Prostitution*, pp. 10-11; W.H. Poulett, *Adversity: or the Miseries of the Seduced: a Poem: interspersed with Narratives* (Bristol 1805), p. 69; S.T., *Address to the Guardian Society* (1817), p. 17.

15. Patrick Colquhoun, *A Treatise on the Police of the Metropolis: containing a detail of the Various Crimes and Misdemeanours by which Public and Private Property and Security are, at Present, injured and endangered; and suggesting Remedies for their Prevention* (6th edit. 1800), p. 339; *Female Sensibility: or, the History of Emma Pomfret. A Novel Founded on Facts* (1783), p. 69; *The Loiterer*, no. 57 (27 Feb. 1790), pp. 5-7; Gordon S. Haight, *George Eliot: a biography* (New

York 1968), p. 249 and n 1 and *Nottingham Journal*, 20 March 1802 for the true life episode, involving one of George Eliot's aunts, which may have provided a model for the role of Dinah Morris in *Adam Bede*; 'The Bashful Maid', a broadsheet, British Library shelfmark 11621 k5 (5); *Rambler*, no. 170 (2 Nov. 1751); *Gentleman's Magazine* (1768), vol. 58, p. 491; S.T., *Address to the Guardian Society*, p. 23.

16. *Memoirs of Harriette Wilson* (4 vols, 1825), vol. 1, p. 5; *Confessions of Julia Johnstone: written by herself* [1825], p. 12; *The Woman of the Town: or, Authentic Memoirs of Phebe Phillips: otherwise Maria Maitland; well known in the vicinity of Covent Garden. Written by herself* (1801), p. 9; [William Giles], *The Victim, in Five Letters to Adolphus* (1800), pp. 77-8, cf. [A.A. Giles], *Aegidiana* (privately printed, 1910) p. 140: cf. the lines, 'For the Grave of a Prostitute, written by Herself in her last Illness,' *Annual Register* 1805, pp. 968-9, actually written by Samuel Jackson Pratt; Mary Cockle, *Important Studies, for the Female Sex, in Reference to Modern Manners; addressed to a Young Lady of Distinction* (1890), which has 14 pages 'On the Duties of a Wife' and 82 pages 'On Seduction', of which however 70 are a novella. Jane Austen also deals with the seduction of a married woman in chapter 31 of *Sense and Sensibility* (1811); S.T., *Address to the Guardian Society*, p. 19.

4. Rape

1. Joseph Gurney, *The Whole Proceedings on the King's Commission of the Peace, Oyer and Terminer and Gaol Delivery ... held at Justice Hall in the Old Bailey, on Wednesday the 4th of December, 1776, and the following Days*, pp. 361, 376; E. Hodgson, *The Whole Proceedings on the King's Commission ... held at Justice Hall in the Old Bailey, on Wednesday the 10th of December, 1783, and the following Days*, p. 358; E. Hodgson, *The Whole Proceedings ... etc. ...on Wednesday the 10th of December, 1788, and the following Days*, p. 809; *Parliamentary Papers* 1819 XVII, pp. 302-3; Home Office, *Criminal Statistics: England and Wales 1991* [Command Papers 1992-3 Cm 2134], pp. 46-7, Table 2.5.

It may be misleading to compare the number of crimes recorded by the police today with the number of criminals convicted in the early nineteenth century, but the recording of crimes by the police means that the police at least are satisfied that a crime has been committed whereas before the establishment of an organised police force the only crimes officially recorded as having occurred are the ones for which someone was convicted: it was up to private individuals to bring prosecutions, and failure to obtain a conviction, especially in the case of rape, could be interpreted as official doubt that the crime charged had actually been committed. Nowadays, incidentally, most homicide convictions are for manslaughter rather than murder but many of these manslaughter cases would have been judged murder in the 1800s.

2. Home Office, *Criminal Statistics: England and Wales 1997* [Command Papers 1998-9 Cm 4162] p. 33 Table 2.1 and p. 73 Table 4.1: see also Dane Archer and Rosemary Gartner, *Violence and Crime in Cross National Perspective* (New Haven 1984), pp. 32-3, 35, 39; *Parliamentary Papers* 1819 XVII, pp. 306-12 – 'serious crimes', in this instance, are those tabulated in these national statistics and exclude offences dealt with summarily by magistrates; *Select Trials at the Sessions-House in the Old Bailey, for Murder, Robberies, Rapes, Sodomy, Coining, Frauds, Bigamy and Other Offences ... From the Year 1720, to this Time* (4 vols, 1742), vol. 3, pp. 95-6, case heard October 1728; *Parliamentary Papers* 1819 XVII, pp. 306-12.

3. *Annual Register* 1763, p. 96; William Oldnall Russell and Edward Ryan, *Crown Cases reserved for Consideration; and decided by the Twelve Judges of England, from the Year 1799 to the year 1824* (1825), pp. 211-12: the ruling upheld the judge's decision, in Rex *v.* Hodgson at the Yorkshire summer assizes in 1811, to allow an objection to questioning a rape victim on the subject of her former sexual connections, and to bringing one of her former lovers as a defence witness: cf. Job Sibly, *The Whole Proceedings on the King's Commission of the Peace for the City of London ... in the Old Bailey ... 30 November 1810, and following days* (1810), no. 831 for a case where a man offered as his defence in a rape trial six witnesses who swore to his good character, with the result that he was recommended for pardon when convicted; *The Trial of Henry St Geo. Tucker Esq. for an Assault with Intent to Commit a Rape, on the Person of Mrs Dorothea Simpson, held in the Supreme Court of Judicature, at Fort William, in Bengal* (1810), p. 194.

4. Clive Emsley, *Crime and Society in England 1750-1900* (1987), pp. 139-40 and *Annual Register* 1817, pp. 196-203.

5. Antony E. Simpson, 'Vulnerability and the Age of Female Consent: Legal Innovation and its Effect in Prosecutions for Rape in Eighteenth-century London', in G.S. Rousseau and Roy Porter, eds, *Sexual Underworlds of the Enlightenment* (Manchester 1987) pp. 181-205 at p.188, Table I; broadsheet entitled *The Last Awful Moments of John Caffin, a Black, who was executed at the Old Bailey on Monday last. August 25, 1817, For committing a Rape On a Child, Seven Years Old*; *Parliamentary Papers* 1819 XVII, pp. 213-30, 250; *The Times* 12 Sept. 1789 p. 2b, and cf. ibid, 3 Sept. 1789, p. 3c, 10 Sept. 1789, p. 3b, 12 Sept. 1789, p. 3b, 14 Sept. 1789, p. 4a, 20 Nov. 1789, p. 3c, 14 Dec. 1789, p. 4a: see also Anna Clark, *Women's Silence Men's Violence: sexual assault in England 1770-1845* (1987), pp. 48-9; Randolph Trumbach, *Sex and the Gender Revolution* (Chicago 1998–), vol. 1 pp. 211-18, and Simpson, 'Vulnerability and the Age of Female Consent', pp. 193-5; Job Sibly, *The Whole Proceedings on the King's Commission of the Peace for the City of London ... in the Old Bailey ... 30 November 1804, and following days* (1804), nos 145, 146. See *Select Trials etc.* (1742), vol. 1, p. 370, for an instance of a young rape victim not being admitted as a witness because she did not seem to know the meaning of an oath.

Sex with girls under the age of twelve had been made a crime by Edward I's first Statute of Westminster 3 Ed. I c. 13 (1275); sex with girls under ten had been made a felony without benefit of clergy by 18 Eliz. c. 7 (1586).

6. *The Rape: a Poem* (2nd edit. 1768), p. 6; Thomas Holcroft, *Anna St Ives: a Novel* (7 vols, 1792), vol. 7, p. 119; Amelia Opie, *Adeline Mowbray, or the Mother and Daughter: a Tale* (3 vols, 1805), vol. 1, ch. 9, p. 169 of 1805 edit.

The role of furniture in eighteenth-century sex is a topic that deserves further research. In Henry Brooke's *Juliet Grenville: or, the History of the Human Heart* (3 vols, 1774) Letty Turney is startled by being grabbed suddenly from behind by a man whom she does not recognise as her long lost husband: 'I screamed, and made a violent effort to get from him; and giving him a push at the same time, he fell backward over a chair, and throwing his hand behind him to save himself, he dislocated his right shoulder.'

7. See A.D. Harvey, *Literature into History* (Basingstoke 1988), pp. 31-2; *Gentleman's Magazine*, vol. 38 (1768), pp. 180-6; A.D. Harvey, *Britain in the Early Nineteenth Century* (1978), pp. 99-101.

Peter Wagner, 'The Pornographer in the courtroom: trial reports about cases of sexual crimes and delinquencies as a genre of eighteenth-century erotica' in Paul Gabriel Boucé, ed., *Sexuality in Eighteenth-Century Britain* (Manchester 1982), pp. 120-40, discusses the interest in reports of crim. con. cases, whereas J.N. Adams and G. Averley, *A Bibliography of Eighteenth-Century Legal Literature* (Newcastle 1982) list transcripts of only five rape trials 1780-1800, of which three occurred in Ireland. On the other hand, if rape was combined with murder, the public curiosity was insatiable, as for example in the Mary Ashford case in 1817. At least four separate transcripts of Rhynwick Williams' trial were published, in addition to *An Appeal to the Public, by Rhynwick Williams, containing Observations and Reflections on Facts relative to his very Extraordinary and Melancholy Case* and Theophilus Swift's *Vindication of Renwick Williams, commonly called The Monster.*

8. Anna Clark, *Women's Silence Men's Violence,* p. 137, Appendix I, Table 4; *The Cherub: or, Guardian of Female Innocence* (1792), p. vi; Francis Bickley, ed., *The Diaries of Sylvester Douglas (Lord Glenbervie)* (2 vols, 1928), vol. 1, p. 6, 7 Dec. 1793; Alfred Spencer, ed., *Memoirs of William Hickey* (4 vols, 1913-25), vol. 1, p. 47: this edition is slightly toned down: the word 'luscious' is supplied by Peter Quennell's one-volume edition of 1975, p. 27; Anna Clark, *Women's Silence Men's Violence,* p. 139, Appendix II, Table 6; *The Trial of Andrew Robinson Bowes, Esq. for Adultery and Cruelty* (1789), pp. 24-5, 27-8.

9. *The Trial of Andrew Robinson Bowes,* pp. 1-5.

10. *A Letter from Montague Burgoyne, Esq. ... giving a summary account, of the Prosecution, Conviction and Deprivation of the Rev. Dr. Edward Drax Free* (1830), p. 11-13. See also R.B. Outhwaite, *Scandal in the Church: Dr. Edward Drax Free, 1784-1843* (1997).

11. Eliza Parsons, *The History of Miss Meredith: a Novel* (2 vols, 1790), vol. 1, p. 31; J.M. [John Moncreiff], *The Scale; or Woman weighed with Man: a Poem* (1752), p. 22 (Canto 2, lines 170-5); *Parslow, Sykes & Kindillan ... Trial of R. Kindillan Esq. for a Rape on the Body of Miss E. Egan* (1789); Jonathan Swift, 'The Story of the Injured Lady', written 1707, published 1746, citing Jonathan Swift, *Irish Tracts 1720-1723 and Sermons,* ed. Louis Landa (Oxford 1948 – vol. 9 of 16-vol. edit. of Swift's prose works 1939-74), p. 5; Eliza Parsons, *The Errors of Education* (3 vols, 1791), vol. 2, pp. 135-6; Jane Austen, *Pride and Prejudice* (1813 but citing 1972 Penguin paperback edit.), p. 297; Germaine Greer, 'Seduction is a four-letter word', originally published in *Playboy* January 1973 and reprinted in Greer's volume *The Madwoman's Underclothes: essays and occasional writings 1968-85* (1986); Thomas Otway, *Venice Preserved* (1682), Act III, Scene 2; *Satan's Harvest Home: or the Present State of Whorecraft, Adultery, Fornication, Procuring, Pimping, Sodomy and the Game of Flatts* (1749), p. 9; *Fanny; or, the Deserted Daughter. A Novel. Being the First Literary Attempt of a Young Lady* (2 vols, 1792), vol. 1, p. 142; [Samuel Jackson Pratt], *The Pupil of Pleasure: or, the New System Illustrated ... by Courtney Melmoth* (2 vols, 1776), vol. 2, p. 145.

12. Samuel Richardson, *Clarissa* (7 vols, 1747-8), vol. 7, letter 10; Edward Gibbon, *Decline and Fall of the Roman Empire,* vol. 3 (1781), p. 238, ch. 31; Jane Porter, *The Scottish Chiefs: a Romance* (5 vols, 1810), vol. 3, p. 68; Edward Relfe, *An Essay on the Seduction of Women* (Lewes [1780]), p. 5.

5. The Desperate

1. *Parliamentary History,* vol. 35, col. 234-5, 2 April 1800; Frederick A. Pottle, *Boswell's London Journal 1762-3* (1982 Futura paperback edit.) p. 91, 14 Dec. 1762; ibid., p. 248, 31 March 1763; ibid., p. 301, 18 June 1763; 'Peter Pindar' John Wolcot, *Lord Auckland's Triumph: or the Death of Crim. Con.* (1800), pp. i-ii; *Boswell's London Journal,* pp. 283-4, 19 May 1763; ibid., p. 258, 13 April 1763; ibid., p. 281, 17 May 1763.

2. *The Woman of the Town: or, Authentic Memoirs of Phebe Phillips, etc.* (1801), p. 27; *The Six and Twentieth Account of the Progress made in the Cities of London & Westminster, and Places Adjacent, By the Societies for the Promoting a Reformation of Manners* [1720]; *Parliamentary Papers* 1857-8 LVII, pp. 429, 436; *Parliamentary Papers* 1817 VII, p. 533; William Tait, *Magdalenism: an Inquiry into the*

Extent, Causes, and Consequences of Prostitution in Edinburgh (Edinburgh 1840), p. 22; *Parliamentary Papers* 1817 VII, p. 459.

3. *The Town and Country Magazine*, vol. 8 (1776), p. 345; ibid., vol. 15 (1783), p. 9; the names of over 280 upper-class men and their kept mistresses who were featured in *The Town and Country Magazine* in the 1770s and 1780s are given by Horace Bleackley in *Notes and Queries*, series 10, vol. 4, pp. 242, 342-4, 462-4, 522. A. Aspinall, ed., *Mrs Jordan and Her Family: being the Unpublished Correspondence of Mrs Jordan and the Duke of Clarence, later William IV* (1951), esp. pp. 177-9, 207-15; perhaps William IV deserved congratulations for only making one of his illegitimate sons an earl: both Charles II and James II made their illegitimate sons dukes.

4. *Fund of Mercy; or An Institution for the Relief and Employment of Destitute and Forlorn Females* (1813), p. 3; Patrick Colquhoun, *A Treatise on the Police of the Metropolis: containing a detail of the Various Crimes and Misdemeanours by which Public and Private Property and Security are, at Present, injured and endangered; and suggesting Remedies for their Prevention* (6th edit. 1800), p. 340; Patrick Colquhoun, *A Treatise on Indigence; exhibiting a General View of the National Resources for Productive Labour ... etc.* (1806), p. 40; *Fund of Mercy*, p. 6.

The idea of 1,666 men dying each year from venereal diseases contracted in London is sheer fantasy. Both syphilis and gonorrhoea may cause abscesses or ulceration which might occasionally lead to death through septicaemia, but in this period doctors were not yet aware of the connection between syphilis and syphilis-related degenerative disorders manifesting themselves ten years or more after initial infection, such as General Paralysis of the Insane, nor of the very rare instances in which gonorrhoea causes inflammation of the kidneys, and consequent renal failure, or pericarditis. The Bills of Mortality for the metropolitan area gave a figure of 11 deaths from 'French pox' in 1813 and 86 in 1817; in 1818, when the disorder was reclassified in the statistics as 'venereal disease' the figure was 19, and only 14 in 1819 (*Annual Register* 1813, p. 322; ibid. 1817, p. 237; ibid. 1818, p. 363; ibid. 1819, p. 305). The variation in the official figures from one year to another indicates the difficulty of attributing a cause of death in cases of venereal infection, but of course even the high figure of 86 within the area of the Bills of Mortality in 1817 hardly suggests an overall figure of 1,666.

5. S.T., *Address to the Guardian Society* [1817], p. 13.

6. Michael Ryan, *Prostitution in London, with a Comparative View of that of Paris and New York* (1839), pp. 169-70, cf. Colquhoun, *Treatise on the Police of the Metropolis* (6th edit.), p. 339; *Parliamentary Papers* 1843 XXVI, p. 173; *An Account of the Institution of the Lock-Asylum, for the Reception of Penitent Female Patients, when discharged from the Lock Hospital* (1796), p. 3; Colquhoun, *Treatise on the Police of the Metropolis* (6th edit.), pp. 334-5.

7. Colquhoun, *Treatise on Indigence*, pp. 7-8; Saunders Welch, *A Proposal to render effectual a Plan to remove the Nuisance of Common Prostitutes from The Streets of this Metropolis* (1758), p. 48, quoting his letter in *London Chronicle* 1758.

8. Samuel Johnson in *Rambler*, no. 107, 26 March 1751, reprinted in *Gentleman's Magazine*, vol. 21 (1751), p. 128; William Dodd, *The Sisters; or the History of Lucy and Caroline Sanson, Entrusted to a false Friend* (2 vols, 1754), vol. 2, p. 163; *Parliamentary Papers* 1817 VII, p. 459; Michael Ryan, *Prostitution in London*, p. 170; Tait, *Magdalenism*, p. 24; *Parliamentary Papers* 1817 VII, p. 459.

9. Colquhoun, *Treatise on the Police of the Metropolis* (6th edit.), p. 335 n; *An account of the Institution of the Lock-Asylum*, pp. 3-4.

10. *An Account of the Institution of the Lock-Asylum*, p. 4.

11. *Boswell's London Journal*, p. 357, 3 Aug. 1763; ibid., p. 244, 25 March 1763; William Dodd, *An Account of the Rise, Progress, and Present State of the Magdalen Hospital, for the Reception of Penitent Prostitutes* (1761), p. 1; Welch, *Proposal*, p. 19; W. Buchan, *Observations concerning the Prevention and Cure of the Venereal Disease* (1796), p. 29; *Memoirs of Sir Finical Whimsy and his Lady* (1752), p. i; Mary Wollstonecraft, *A Vindication of the Rights of Women* (1792), p. 315.

12. Edward J. Bristow, *Vice and Vigilance: Purity Movements in Britain since 1700* (Dublin 1977), pp. 16-18; ibid., p. 21; ibid., pp. 29-30; *Six and Twentieth Account* – and subsequent accounts – *of the Progress made in the Cities of London & Westminster, and Places Adjacent, By the Societies for Promoting a Reformation of Manners*: there is a bound volume of these reports in the British Library, shelf mark 694 k 11; Bristow, *Vice and Vigilance*, p. 31; ibid., p. 55 and *The Works of the Rev. John Wesley, MA* (32 vols, Bristol 1771-4), vol. 4, pp. 87, 92-3.

13. *Report of the Provisional Committee of the Guardian Society* (1816), p. 9; ibid., p. 12; *Report of the Committee of the Guardian Society for the Preservation of Public Morals* (1817), p. 27; ibid., p. 35; *Parliamentary Papers* 1824 XIX, pp. 279-80; ibid., pp. 217, 221, 258.

The so-called Vagrant Act was 7 James I c. 4, modified by 17 Geo II c. 5, which was replaced by 3 Geo IV c. 40, which in turn was renewed, with modifications, by 5 Geo IV c. 83. The parliamentary returns cited here were printed at the time the latter act was being discussed as a bill in Parliament.

14. Welch, *Proposal*, p. 17 n; Randolph Trumbach, 'Sex, Gender, and Sexual Identity in Modern Culture: Male Sodomy and Female Prostitution in Enlightenment London', *Journal of the History of Sexuality*, vol. 2 (1991), pp. 186-203, at pp. 202-3.

The four lying-in hospitals were the British Lying-In Hospital (1745), the City of London Lying-In Hospital (1750), the Queen's Lying-In Hospital (1752), and the Westminster New Lying-In Hospital (1765).

15. Septimus Hodson, *Sermons on the Present State of Religion in this Country, and on Other Subjects* (1792), p. 200.

16. *An Account of the Nature and Intention of the Lock-Hospital, near Hyde Park Corner* [1802], p. 16, cf. p. 10; *An Address to the Benevolent Public on Behalf of the London Female Penitentiary* (1807), p. 11 and n; *The Fourth Annual Report of the Committee of the London Female Penitentiary* (1811), p. 13; *Refuge for the Destitute, Hackney Road and Hoxton. Instituted 1805* – leaflet in British Library, shelf mark 1865 c. 13 (11), published 1820; *Eighth Report of the Committee of the Guardian Society for the Preservation of Public Morals* (1827), p. 12; *Fund of Mercy; or An Institution for the Relief and Employment of Destitute and Forlorn Females* (1813), p. 4; Hodson, *Sermons on the Present State of Religion*, p. 201.

17. *Fourth Annual Report of the Committee of the London Female Penitentiary*, p. 13; *General State of the Magdalen-Hospital, for the Reception of Penitent Prostitutes ... Published by Order of the General Court, 26th April, 1786*, p. 4; *Address to the Benevolent Public on Behalf of the London Female Penitentiary*, p. 11 and n; *Second Annual Report of the Committee of the London Female Penitentiary* (1809), p. 23.

18. *The Plan of the Magdalen House for the Reception of Penitent Prostitutes* (1758), p. 18, cf. *The Rules Orders and Regulations, of the Magdalen House, for the Reception of Penitent Prostitutes* (1759), p. 21, same wording, and *The Rules and Regulations of the Magdalen Charity* (4th edit. 1769), p. 31; William Dodd, *Advice to the Magdalens* (1760), p. 2; Trumbach, 'Sex, Gender and Sexual Identity', pp. 198-201; *Address to the Benevolent Public on Behalf of the London Female Penitentiary* (1817), p. 16; John Thomas, *An Appeal to the Public; or a Vindication of the*

Character of Mr William Hale, from the Calumnious Aspersions of the Reviewer in the Evangelical Magazine (1809), p. 49; William Hale, *An Address to the Public Upon the Dangerous Tendency of the London Female Penitentiary* (1809), p. 18; Thomas, *Appeal to the Public*, p. 44; William Hale, *Considerations on the Causes and Prevalence of Female Prostitution; and on the Most Practicable and Efficient Means of Abating and Preventing That, and All Other Crimes, against the Virtue and Safety of the Community* (1812), pp. 7, 12; Tait, *Magdalenism*, p. 84.

19. *A Plan of the Magdalen House*, p. 17, cf. *By-Laws and Regulations of the Magdalen Hospital* (1816), p. 28.

20. *Eighth Report of the Committee of the Guardian Society* (1827), pp. 12, 15; *Woman of the Town: or, Authentic Memoirs of Phebe Phillips*, p. 25; *Report of the Committee of the Guardian Society ... 30th October 1817*, pp. 11-13; John Butler, *A Sermon Preached in the Chapel of the Magdalen Hospital ... on Thursday, May 11, 1786*, p. 16.

21. Hodson, *Sermons on the State of Religion*, p. 21; *Rules and Regulations of the Magdalen Charity* (4th edit. 1769), p. ii; William Hale, *Address to the Public*, p. 7; *European Magazine*, vol. 55 (1809), p. 47, cf. *Evangelical Magazine*, vol. 17 (1809), pp. 118-22, 161-4, 352, 384-8, 423-5, 471-3, 513-15 and vol. 18 (1810), pp. 168-70; S.T., *Address to the Guardian Society* (1817), p. 3; Joseph Gurney, *The Whole Proceedings on the King's Commission of the Peace, Oyer and Terminer and Gaol Delivery held at Justice Hall in the Old Bailey, on Wednesday the 4th of December 1776, and the following Days*, pp. 375-6; Russen, a former chair-maker and Dissenting teacher, who had been ordained in the Church of England in the expectation of his departure to Florida as a missionary, was acquitted of raping the older pupil but convicted of raping one of the younger girls and hanged: see *Annual Register* 1777, p. 207; [William Benbow], *The Crimes of the Clergy; or the Pillars of Priest-Craft Shaken* (1823), p. 27; ibid., pp. 77-8; ibid., p. 63 and cf. Thomas Faulkner, *The History and Antiquities of the Parish of Hammersmith* (1839), p. 308.

The pamphlets attacking William Hale are, in alphabetical order of authors:

(1) William Blair, *Prostitutes Reclaimed and Penitents Protected*.

(2) id., *A Letter to Mr Hodson, on the Inadequacy of the Poor Laws for Employing, Protecting & Reclaiming Unfortunate Females Destitute of Work; in Answer to Mr Hale's Reply*.

(3) James Clarke, *The London Female Penitentiary Defended*.

(4) Robert Hawker, *A Letter to William Hale*.

(5) George Hodson, *The Remonstrant: a Letter to Mr W. Hale, in Reply to his Address to the Public, upon the Injurious Tendency of the London Female Penitentiary*.

(6) id., *Strictures on Mr Hale's Reply to the Pamphlets in Defence of the London Female Penitentiary*.

(7) id., *A Vindication of the London Female Penitentiary, in Reply to the Rev. Mr Thomas's Objection to that Institution, contained in his late Appeal to the Public* – apparently the last pamphlet in the controversy, published in 1810.

(8) 'Juvenis', *Cursory Remarks on a Recent Publication Addressed to the Public, upon the dangerous tendency of the London Female Penitentiary* – apparently the earliest reply to Hale.

(9) W. Shrubsole, *A Defence of the London Female Penitentiary; being a Letter to Mr W. Hale, in vindication of the London Female Penitentiary*.

22. William Dodd's career is very well documented, but see especially John Money, 'The Masonic movement, or, ritual, replica, and credit: John Wilkes, the Macaroni parson, and the making of the middle-class mind'; *Journal of British*

Studies, vol. 32 (1993), pp. 358-95, esp. pp. 367-70, 376-82; for Dodd's disgrace in 1774 see John Fortescue, *The Correspondence of King George the Third from 1760 to December 1781* (6 vols, 1927-8), vol. 3, p. 54, no. 1375, Earl of Hertford to George III 28 Jan. 1774.

6. The Deviant

1. John Cleland, *Fanny Hill* (1749 but citing 1970 Mayflower paperback edit.), pp. 19-20. A pamphlet also printed in 1749, *Satan's Harvest Home: or the Present State of Whorecraft, Adultery, Fornication, Procuring, Pimping, Sodomy and the Game of Flatts*, refers, in the phrase 'game of flatts', to lesbian sex and claims, p. 18, that it is 'practis'd frequently in *Turkey*, as well as at *Twickenham*'; the scurrilous poem was William King's *The Toast* (Dublin 1732); for Henry Fielding's *The Female Husband: or, the Surprising History of Mrs Mary, alias M' George Hamilton* (1746), which was based on reports in the *Bath Journal* 22 Sept. 1746 and the *Daily Advertiser* 7 Nov. 1746, see S. Baker, 'Henry Fielding's *The Female Husband*: Fact and Fiction', *PMLA*, vol. 74 (1959), pp. 213-24. It should be noted that the offence for which Mary Hamilton was prosecuted was not lesbianism but fraud. There was a similar case in 1777, reported in the *Annual Register* 1777, pp. 191-2.

2. Cleland, *Fanny Hill*, pp. 19-20; ibid., p. 21; *The Cherub: or, Guardian of Female Innocence* (1792), p. 21; Cleland, *Fanny Hill*, pp. 20-1.

3. Judith C. Brown, 'Lesbian Sexuality in Medieval and Early Modern Europe', in Martin Duberman, Martha Vicinus and George Chauncey, eds, *Hidden from History: Reclaiming the Gay and Lesbian Past* (1991), pp. 67-75 at pp. 68-9; ibid., p. 72; Louis Crompton, 'The Myth of Lesbian Impunity: Capital Laws from 1270 to 1791', in Salvatore J. Licata and Robert P. Petersen, *The Gay Past: a Collection of Historical Essays* (New York 1985 – originally *Journal of Homosexuality*, vol. 6, nos 1 and 2, 1980), pp. 11-25 at p. 17; Brigitte Eriksson, 'A Lesbian Execution in Germany, 1721: the Trial Records', in Licata and Petersen, *Gay Past*, pp. 27-40; E. William Monter, 'La sodomie à l'époque moderne en Suisse romande', *Annales*, vol. 19 (1974), pp. 1023-33, at p. 1029; Theo van der Meer, 'Tribades on Trial: Female Same-Sex Offenders in Late Eighteenth-Century Amsterdam', *Journal of the History of Sexuality*, vol. 1 (1991), pp. 424-45, at p. 429.

4. James Parsons, *A Medical and Critical Enquiry into the Nature of Hermaphrodites* (1741), p. 22; *Dreams and Moles, with the Interpretation and Signification* [Hull 1815 ?], p. 5 – a very popular chap-book, frequently reprinted by provincial presses *c.* 1750-1840; Cleland, *Fanny Hill*, p. 21; *Sapphick Epistle from Jack Cavendish* (1771), p. 6 n; *St James's Chronicle* 17-20 July 1790, p. 4b – there was a shorter version of the same article in the *London Chronicle*, vol. 68, p. 77a, 20-22 July 1790. The two ladies wrote to Edmund Burke for advice regarding possible legal redress: see T.W. Copland et al., ed., *The Correspondence of Edmund Burke* (10 vols, Cambridge 1958-78), vol. 6, pp. 131-2.

5. Rudolf M. Decker and Lotte C. van de Pol, *The Tradition of Female Transvestism in Early Modern Europe* (Basingstoke 1989), pp. 104-12 for a list of 119 cross-dressers in the Netherlands 1550-1839, including 54 1702-83; ibid., p. 9: of 93 cross-dressing Dutch women whose profession is known, 83 served in the army or navy; *Annual Register* 1761, p. 144, 1769, p. 148, 1813, Chronicle p. 3 gives instances of women joining up in the hope of being reunited with their husbands, though 'William Brown' (*Annual Register* 1815, Chronicle p. 64) claimed that it was quarrelling with her husband which induced her to join the Royal Navy. June Rose, *The Perfect Gentleman: the Remarkable Life of Dr James Miranda Barry, the Woman Who Served as an Officer in the British Army from 1813 to 1859* (1977).

See also *The Life and Extraordinary Adventures of Susanna Cope: the British Female Soldier* (Banbury c. 1810), *The Interesting Life and Wonderful Adventures of that Extraordinary Woman Anne Jane Thornton, the Female Soldier; Disclosing Important Secrets, Unknown to the Public* (1835) and *Notes and Queries*, series 10, vol. 1, p. 406. Curiously, the most famous cross-dresser of the period, the Chevalier d'Éon, who had been French minister plenipotentiary in London in 1763 but who spent the last twenty-five years of his life in England dressed as a woman, turned out in the end to be a man after all.

6. *Annual Register* 1766, pp. 116, 144 and *The Gentleman's Magazine* 1766, pp. 339, 359-60, 492-3: see also Emma Donoghue, *Passions between Women: British Lesbian Culture 1668-1801* (1993), pp. 64-73; *Annual Register* 1822, Chronicle pp. 72-3; *Annual Register* 1793, Chronicle p. 19: cf. Helena Whitbread ed. *No Priest but Love: Excerpts from the Diaries of Anne Lister, 1824-1826* (Otley 1992) and Jill Liddington ed. *Presenting the Past: Anne Lister of Halifax 1791-1840* (Hebden Bridge 1994) for the secret diaries of a lesbian in the 1820s.

7. For the 'Hackney Monster', see William Robinson, *The History and Anti-quities of the Parish of Hackney in the County of Middlesex* (2 vols, 1843), vol. 1, p. 237, and cf. the broadsheet *Sentence and Committal to Newgate of Henry Bishop, Pin-Maker in Redcliff-Street, Bristol, For Indelicate exposure of his Person, which took place at Guildhall, on Monday Jan. 31 1813*, from which it appears that Bishop got off with three months' gaol and a £20 fine.

8. [Francis Foster], *Thoughts on the Times, but chiefly on the Profligacy of our Women, and its Causes* (1779), p. 17; *The Confessions of J. Lackington ... to which are added Two Letters, on the Bad Consequences of Having Daughters educated at Boarding Schools* (1804), p. 210.

Some idea of the pretensions of the better schools is given by M.E. Grimshaw's booklet *Pre-Victorian Silver School Medals awarded to Girls in Great Britain* (Cambridge 1985).

9. *The History of the Human Heart; or, the Adventures of a Young Gentleman* (1749 but citing 1886 edit.), p. 35; Mary Wollstonecraft, *A Vindication of the Rights of Women; with Strictures on Political and Moral Subjects* (1792), p. 379; Thomas Beddoes, *Hygëia: or Essays Moral and Medical on the Causes affecting the personal state of Our Middling and Affluent Classes* (3 vols, Bristol 1802-3), vol. 1, Essay Fourth, p. 44; Henry Thomas Kitchener, *Letters on Marriage, on the Causes of Matrimonial Infidelities and on the Reciprocal Relations of the Sexes* (2 vols, 1812), vol. 1, p. 22; Alex P. Buchan, *Venus sine Concubitu* (1818), p. 26 – the Latin title of this last work means 'Venus without lying together'.

10. For the defamation case in the Court of Session in 1811, see *Miss Marianne Woods and Miss Jane Pirie against Dame Helen Cumming Gordon* (New York 1975). Lilian Hellman's play *The Children's Hour* (1934) is loosely based on this case. J.H. Plumb, 'The New World of Children in Eighteenth-Century England', *Past and Present*, no. 67 (1975), pp. 64-95, at p. 92; John Dryden, 'Prologue to the Wild Gallant Reviv'd, (written ? 1667, printed 1669); Alexander Robertson, *Poems on Various Subjects and Occasions*, Edinburgh [1750], pp 82-3; Cleland, *Fanny Hill*, pp. 132-3; Norah Smith, 'Robert Wallace's "Of Venery" ', *Texas Studies in Literature and Language*, vol. 15 (1973), pp. 429-44, at pp. 436-7; Robert H. MacDonald, 'The Frightful Consequences of Onanism: notes on the history of a Delusion', *Journal of the History of Ideas* vol. 28 (1967), pp. 423-31, at p. 424 n 4 where it is argued fairly conclusively that *Onania* was first published in 1708, not in 1710 as supposed hitherto. *Onania* may even have been responsible for attrib-uting masturbation to Onan: the account in Genesis actually suggests *coitus interruptus*. An attempt to share Onan's credit for inventing masturbation with

his brother Er seems to have been rather a flop: only two editions are known of a short imitation of *Onania* published in 1724 under the title *Eronania, On the Crimes of those two Unhappy Brothers Er and Onan*. See also Karl-Felix Jacobs, *Die Entstehung der Onanie-Literatur im 17. und 18. Jahrundert* (Munich 1963).

Diogenes Laertius (*Lives and Opinions of Eminent Philosophers* VI.6) mentions masturbation as one of the anti-social habits practised by Diogenes, the philosopher who lived in a barrel, cf. Kitchener, *Letters on Marriage*, vol. 1, p. 24 n.

11. Lawrence Stone, *The Family, Sex and Marriage: in England 1500-1800* (1977), p. 515, suggests that propaganda against masturbation in France peaked between 1810 and 1850, whereas Isabel V. Hull, *Sexuality, State, and Civil Society in Germany 1700-1815* (Ithaca 1996), pp 260-1 indicates that the Germans were most concerned in the 1780s.

Since masturbation is traditionally referred to as 'the solitary vice' it is interesting to note that Tissot was also the biographer of Johann Georg Zimmerman whose *Von der Einsamheit* ('Of solitude') was an international bestseller.

12. *Onania* (20th edit.), pp. 22-3; ibid., p. 25; Beddoes, *Hygëia*, vol. 1 Essay Fourth, p. 43; Buchan, *Venus sine Concubitu*, pp. 29-30, cf. p. 43; Robert Hawker, *The Poor Man's Concordance and Dictionary to the Sacred Scriptures* (1812 but citing text in *The Works of the Rev. Robert Hawker DD*, 10 vols, 1831, vol. 6), pp. 628-9; John Hunter, *A Treatise on the Venereal Disease* (1786), p. 200; and see also Michael Ryan, *Prostitution in London, with a Comparative View of that of Paris and New York* (1839), p. 13.

13. John Armstrong, *The Oeconomy of Love: a Poetical Essay* (1736), p. 4, lines 40-5; ibid., p. 8, lines 105-7. (A parricide is someone who murders anyone in his own family, in this case hypothetical offspring: murdering one's father is patricide); Edward Aven's edition of John Armstrong, *The Oeconomy of Love: a Poetical Essay* (1771, p. 7 n; James Graham, *A Lecture on the Generation, Increase and Improvement of the Human Species* [1780], p. 25; *Rare Verities. The Cabinet of Venus Unlocked and Her Secrets laid open. Being a Translation of part of Sinibaldus his Geneanthropeia* (1657), p. 61; A.F.M. Willich, *Lectures on Diet and Regimen: being a Systematic Inquiry into the most Rational Means of Preserving Health and Prolonging Life* (1799), p. 499: the second, enlarged edition, also 1799, alters 'this unnatural practice' to 'this execrable practice'; Kitchener, *Letters on Marriage*, vol. 1, p. 27; Hunter, *Treatise on the Venereal Disease*, p. 200; Willich, *Lectures on Diet and Regimen*, p. 499.

14. Buchan, *Venus sine Concubitu*, pp. 67-8. *Des Égarements secrets, ou l'onanisme chez les personnes du sexe* is by J.L. Doussin-Dubreuil.

George L. Mosse, *Nationalism and Sexuality: Respectability and Abnormal Sexuality in Modern Europe* (New York 1985), illus. 1 opposite p. 96, prints an earlier illustration of a woman dying of masturbation, from R.L. Rosier, *Des Habitudes Secrets ou de l'onanisme chez les femmes* (1822) and discusses, pp. 11-12, J.F. Bertrand's waxworks museum in Paris which, from 1775 till the 1800s, seems mostly to have depicted cases of masturbation. It seems to have been a French discovery that the effects of masturbation lent themselves especially to *visual* portrayal.

15. For Rex *v.* Wiseman, see John, Lord Fortescue, *Reports of select cases in all the courts of Westminster-Hall* (1748), pp. 91-3; William Dodd, *The Sisters: or the History of Lucy and Caroline Sanson, Entrusted to a false Friend* (2 vols, 1754), vol. 1, p. 204; Jonas Liliequist, 'Peasants against Nature: Crossing the Boundaries between Man and Animal in Seventeenth- and Eighteenth-Century Sweden', *Journal of the History of Sexuality*, vol. 1 (1990-91), pp. 393-423, at p. 394; Robert F. Oaks, '"Things Fearful to Name": Sodomy and Buggery in Seventeenth-Century

New England', *Journal of Social History*, vol. 12 (1978-9), pp. 268-81, at p. 276:
Polly Morris, 'Sodomy and Male Honor: the Case of Somerset 1740-1850', in Kent
Gerard and Gert Hekma, eds, *The Pursuit of Sodomy: Male Homosexuality in
Renaissance and Enlightenment Europe* (New York 1989), pp. 383-406, at p. 389,
Table I and cf. broadsheet *An Account of the Last Awful Moments of Robert Chilcott,
who was executed at Ilchester, on Wednesday last, September 4, 1822, for commit-
ting a detestable Crime on a Sow*. Chilcott, incidentally, was seventy-one at the
time of his execution.

Minor forms of homosexuality were made a statutory offence by 24/25 Vict. c.
100 cl. 62 but the basis for most prosecutions from the 1880s onwards, including
Oscar Wilde's, was 48/49 Vict. c. 69 cl. 11. In 1817 one Samuel Jacobs was
pardoned after conviction for forcing his penis into the mouth of a seven-year-
old boy and ejaculating: the judges decided that this did not constitute sodomy:
William Oldnall Russell and Edward Ryan, *Crown Cases reserved for Consideration; and decided by the Twelve Judges of England, from the Year 1799 to
the year 1824* (1825), pp. 331-2. For other instances of fellatio in the eighteenth
and early ninetenth century see Rictor Norton, *Mother Clap's Molly House: the
Gay Subculture in England 1700-1830* (1992), pp. 107-8. The slang term for fellatio
seems to have been 'fluting', though the word 'flute' was also used for the penis
without implying any unusual sexual practice.

16. For Assize and Quarter Sessions records, see Alan Bray, *Homosexuality in
Renaissance England* (1982), p. 71.

17. Edward J. Bristow, *Vice and Vigilance: Purity Movements in Britain since
1700* (Dublin 1977), pp. 29-30; *Parliamentary Papers* 1818 XVI, pp. 184-7;
Laurence Senelick, 'Mollies or Men of Mode? Sodomy and the Eighteenth-Century
London Stage', *Journal of the History of Sexuality*, vol. 1 (1990), pp. 33-67, at p. 63
and p. 63 n 77, and cf. cutting from an unidentifiable source in a volume of cuttings
and pamphlets labelled 'Tracts' in the British Museum, shelf mark Cup 363 gg 31;
William H. Epstein, *John Cleland: Images of a Life* (New York 1974), p. 62 and cf.
Notes and Queries series 2, vol. 8, pp. 65-6.

18. Public Record Office HO 42/79; *The Times* 25 Aug. 1835, p. 7a; ibid. 28 Nov.
1835, p. 3f.

19. *Parliamentary Papers* 1819 XVII, pp. 308-11.

20. Public Record Office HCA 1/61/394-5 (26 June 1807) and HCA 1/61/438-41
(27 July 1810); the defendant in the last case was also acquitted of assault with
attempt to commit sodomy: HCA 1/61/444-6 (22 Jan. 1811); Public Record Office
Adm. 12/26; ibid. Adm. 51/1298; ibid. Adm. 12/27F.

21. Public Record Office WO 90/1, Judge Advocate General's Office Register,
General Courts-Martial: Abroad 1796-1825 f 75 v, 76, 85, 86 v, 87, 89 v, cf. f 71, 83,
87 v, 92.

When the French Army sacked Lübeck in November 1806 even the inmates of
a hospital for the female insane were raped: Oscar von Lettow-Vorbeck, *Der Krieg
von 1806 und 1807* (4 vols, Berlin 1891-6) vol. 2, p. 384. It seems unlikely that
British troops were any better behaved when they got out of control, though
accounts of the sack of Badajoz by the British Army on 6-7 April 1812 – one of the
worst atrocities of the Napoleonic Wars – tend to concentrate on looting, drunkenness and homicide.

22. Bray, *Homosexuality in Renaissance England*, pp. 81-114. This distinction
– see Bray esp. pp. 103-4 – between earlier perceptions of 'sodomites' as persons
who committed discrete acts of sodomy, without any assumption being made about
their general sexual orientation, and perceptions c. 1700 of 'mollies' as people who
had a sexual orientation that made them different from other men derives from

Mary McIntosh, 'The Homosexual Role', originally published in *Social Problems*, vol. 16 (1968), pp. 182-92 and reprinted in Kenneth Plummer, *The Making of the Modern Homosexual* (1981), pp. 30-44. It has become something of an orthodoxy among gay scholars but is difficult to reconcile with the prosecution of homosexual coteries on the continent in earlier periods.

23. *A Faithful Narrative of the Proceedings in the late Affair between the Rev. John Swinton and Mr George Baker, Both of Wadham College, Oxford ... To which is prefix'd a Particular Account of the Proceedings against Robert Thistlethwayte, Late Doctor of Divinity, and Warden of Wadham College, For a Sodomitical Attempt on Mr W. French, Commoner of the same College* (1739): quotations from p. 16 and p. 19. This pamphlet is most probably by George Baker himself.

24. Tobias Smollett, *The Advice* (1746), lines 95-6, 111-14.

25. William Mathews, ed., *The Diary of Dudley Ryder 1715-16* (1939), p. 143; *Select Trials, for Murders, Robberies, Rapes, Sodomy, Coining, Frauds ... From the Year 1720, to 1724, inclusive ... From the Year 1724 to 1732 inclusive* (2 vols, 1734-5), vol. 2, pp. 367-71 and Norton, *Mother Clap's Molly House*, p. 111.

26. Guido Ruggiero, 'Sexual Criminality in the Early Renaissance: Venice 1338-1358', *Journal of Social History*, vol. 8 (Summer 1975), pp. 18-37, at p. 23 and p. 35 n. 25; ibid., p. 23 and p. 35 n 26; Monter, 'Sodomie', *Annales*, vol. 29, p. 1026; Mary Elizabeth Perry, 'The "Nefarious Sin" in Early Modern Seville', in Kent Gerard and Gert Hekma, eds, *The Pursuit of Sodomy: Male Homosexuality in Renaissance and Enlightenment Europe* (New York 1989), pp. 67-89, at p. 67. Rafael Carrasco, *Inquisición y represión sexual en Valencia. Historia de los sodomi-tas (1565-1785)* (Barcelona 1990), p. 69, Table 1; Arend H. Huussen, 'Sodomy in the Dutch Republic during the Eighteenth Century', in *Eighteenth-Century Life*, special no. May 1985 entitled 'Unauthorised Sexual Behaviour during the Enlight-enment', pp. 169-78, at p. 175 – this collection was reprinted in 1988 as Robert P. Maccubbin, ed., *'Tis Nature's Fault: Unauthorised Sexuality During the Enlight-enment*; Michel Rey, 'Parisian Homosexuals Create a Lifestyle 1700-1750: the Police Archives', in the same *Eighteenth-Century Life* special no., pp. 179-91, at p. 187; Norton, *Mother Clap's Molly House*, pp. 68-9, 84-5. On the persecution of homosexuals in the Netherlands Norton, pp. 253-4, cites older material which indicates no less than sixty death sentences.

27. Perry ' "Nefarious Sin" in Early Modern Seville' in Gerard and Hekma, *Pursuit of Sodomy*, p. 75 and p. 87 n 28.

28. Alexander Robertson, *Poems on Various Subjects and Occasions* (Edin-burgh 1750), p. 83, and see also pp. 54-7, 'An Ode to K——— W———': both poems date from the 1690s: the question of William III's homosexuality is discussed in Stephen B. Baxter, *William III* (1966), pp. 349-52. A.E.H. Swaen, ed., *Sir John Vanbrugh* (1896), pp. 80, 81, 83.

29. *The Tryal and Conviction of Several reputed Sodomites, before the Right Honourable the Lord Mayor, and Recorder of London, at Guild-Hall, the 20th Day of October, 1707* (1707) broadsheet. See also *An Account of the Tryal, Examination and Conviction of Several Notorious Persons Call'd Sodomites* (1707) broadsheet. Norton, *Mother Clap's Molly House*, pp. 44-6 suggests the Societies had been behind the prosecution of Captain Edward Rigby of the Royal Navy for attempted sodomy as early as 1698.

30. *The Ordinary of Newgate his Account of the Behaviour, Confession, and Last Speech of George Skelthorp, that was Executed at Tyburn, on Wednesday the 23rd of March 1708/9* [i.e. 1709] broadsheet; Bray, *Homosexuality in Renaissance England*, pp. 82, 89-91, and cf. *The Three and Thirtieth Account of the Progress made in the Cities of London and Westminster and Places Adjacent, by the Societies*

for Promoting a Reformation of Manners printed with Richard Smalbroke, *A Sermon Preached to the Societies for a Reformation of Manners ... January 10th, 1727* (1728), p. 38.

It was surely no coincidence that the fullest report of the Castlehaven trial, *The Case of Sodomy in the Tryal of Mervin Lord Audley, Earl of Castlehaven*, was first printed 1708, with a second edition (produced by Edmund Curll) in 1710.

31. *London Journal*, 7 May 1726, p. 2a, and cf. *Hell upon Earth: or the Town in an Uproar* (1729), p. 43; [Holloway], *The Phoenix of Sodom, or the Vere Street Coterie: Being an Exhibition of the Gambols Practised by the Ancient Lechers of Sodom and Gomorrah, embellished and improved with the Modern Refinements in Sodomitical Practices by the Members of the Vere Street Coterie, of detestable Memory* (1813), p. 14; Public Record Office HO 79/1/66 Lord Hawkesbury to Lord Sydeney Ranger of Hyde Park and St James's Park, 8 Nov. 1808. For Moorfields as a homosexual resort see Norton, *Mother Clap's Molly House*, pp. 76-8.

32. Norton, *Mother Clap's Molly House*, pp. 35-43 makes a convincing case for *Love-letters* being genuine though G.S. Rousseau, *Perilous Enlightenment: pre- and post-modern discourses: sexual, historical* (Manchester 1991), pp. 139-71 treats them as fiction and dismisses the idea that Sunderland had anything to do with them; *A Ramble through London: containing Observations on Men and Things* (1738), pp. 12-13; Smollett, *The Advice*, p. 9, line 115 and n, cf. Smollett, *The Reproof. A Satire* (1747), lines 57-94 lampooning Cope's performance at Preston-pans; Alexander Pope, *The Dunciad* (1743), Book 1, line 349; W.S. Lewis, ed., *The Yale Edition of Horace Walpole's Correspondence* (48 vols, New Haven and Oxford 1937-83), vol. 9, p. 19, Walpole to George Montagu 13 July 1745; Tobias Smollett, *The Adventures of Roderick Random* (1979 Oxford edition), p. 310 (ch. 51) and see also pp. 197-9 (ch. 35).

33. Charles Churchill, *The Times: A Poem* (1764), lines 297-300 (Douglas Grant, ed., *The Poetical Works of Charles Churchill* (Oxford 1956), pp. 398-9); *Satan's Harvest Home*, p. 51: this passage is in a kind of appendix to the main text, with the title 'Reasons for the Growth of Sodomy, &c'; William Lithgow, *The Totall Discourse, of the Rare Adventueres, and painfull Peregrinations of long nineteene Yeares Travayles, from Scotland to the most Famous Kingdomes of Europe, Asia, and Affrica* (1632), p. 43; Armstrong, *Oeconomy of Love*, p. 42, lines 600-1; *Satan's Harvest Home*, p. 52; *The Prostitutes of Quality: or Adultery à-la-mode. Being authentic and genuine Memoirs of several Persons of the highest Quality* (1757), p. 179; Churchill, *The Times*, lines 293-6 (Grant edit. p. 398); Senelick, 'Mollies or Men of Mode', *Journal of the History of Sexuality*, vol. 1, pp. 60-6; Boyd Alexander, *England's Wealthiest Son* (1962), p. 107 foll.; H. Montgomery Hyde, *The Other Love: an Historical and Contemporary Survey of Homosexuality in Britain* (1970), pp. 73-4; Norton, *Mother Clap's Molly House*, pp. 226-30; Louis Crompton, *Byron and Greek Love: Homophobia in 19th-Century England* (1985), p. 46; H.S. Ashbee, *Index Librorum Prohibitorum: being Notes Bio-Biblio-Iconographical and Critical on Curious and Uncommon Books* (2 vols, privately printed 1877), vol. 2, pp. 340-1; Norton, *Mother Clap's Molly House*, pp. 212-14; R.G. Thorne, ed., *The History of Parliament: The House of Commons 1790-1820* (5 vols, 1986), vol. 3, pp. 71-2 *sub* Annesley, George.

34. Katharine C. Balderston, ed., *Thraliana: the Diary of Mrs Hester Lynch Thrale (Later Mrs Piozzi) 1776-1809* (Oxford 1951), p. 640, 27 June 1786; Norton, *Mother Clap's Molly House*, pp. 216-19; *The Case of the Rev. Thomas Jephson* [Cambridge 1823], p. 40; Francis Bamford, and Gerald, Duke of Wellington, eds, *The Journal of Mrs Arbuthnot* (2 vols, 1950), vol. 1, p. 183, 29 Aug. 1822; *Annual*

Register 1633, Chronicle p. 246; Henry Gunning, *Reminiscences of the University, Town, and County of Cambridge* (2 vols, 1854), vol. 2, pp. 340-3.

35. Carrasco, *Inquisición y represión sexual*, p. 120, Table 5; Public Record Office TS 11/506/1660 but cf. *Particulars of the Execution of Charles Clutton* [1824]; *Annual Register* 1806, Chronicle p. 438 – n.b. five others in this group turned King's evidence.

36. One of the British Library's copies of Holloway's *Phoenix of Sodom* – shelf mark Cup. 304, p. 12 – contains a number of contemporary press cuttings from which these details are taken, but cf. *Phoenix of Sodom*, pp. 12-13; ibid., pp. 10, 37, 40, and cf. *Genuine Narrative of all the Street Robberies Committed Since October Last by James Dalton and his accomplices* (1728), pp. 32-3, 39-40; Lytton Strachey and Roger Fulford, eds, *The Greville Memoirs* (8 vols, 1938), vol. 1, pp. 125-6, 30 July 1822.

John Newbolt Hepburn, the ensign who was hanged, does not appear to be in *The Army List*. From his age (forty-two, forty-six or forty-nine according to various accounts) he may have been a long-serving soldier recently promoted from the ranks, in which case he would have been of much the same social origins as his companions.

37. *Account of the Trial and Execution of William Arden, Esq., Benjamin Candler, and J. Doughty, for an Unnatural Crime* (1822) broadsheet, and *Annual Register* 1822, Chronicle p. 168.

38. Public Record Office MEPO 1/64/27.

39. Norton, *Mother Clap's Molly House*, pp. 199-211 – quotation is from *The Trial and Conviction of that Infamous Hypocrite John Church ... to which is added His Life ... etc.* [1817], p. 34.

40. Jean H. Hagstrum 'Gray's Sensibility' in James Downey and Ben Jones, eds, *Fearful Joy: Papers from the Thomas Gray Bicentenary Conference at Carleton University* (Montreal 1974), pp. 6-19 and Raymond Bentman, 'Thomas Gray and the Poetry of "Hopeless Love"', *Journal of the History of Sexuality*, vol. 3 (1922), pp. 203-22 and see also A.D. Harvey, *English Poetry in a Changing Society 1780-1825* (1980), pp. 30-1 for the excised stanzas from the 'Elegy'; Robert J. Corker 'Representing the "Unspeakable": William Godwin and the Politics of Homophobia', *Journal of the History of Sexuality*, vol. 1 (1990), pp. 85-101. For Somerset Maugham and the way his treatment of heterosexual passion seems to betray his private preferences see A.D. Harvey, 'The Homosexual as Novelist: the Case of Somerset Maugham', *London Magazine*, vol. 32 (1992), nos 5 & 6, pp. 67-79.

The oldest known copies of *Don Leon* belong to an edition issued in 1866 which was quickly withdrawn (as late as 1934 a reprinting was seized by the police), but 'I.W.' in *Notes and Queries*, series 1, vol. 7, p. 66 (January 1853) refers to an edition of what is clearly the identical poem 'printed abroad many years since'. The text has been attributed to Lord Byron and contains little he would not have known about, though the elaborate notes of the 1866 edition mostly refer to events of the 1830s, and some as late as 1857.

41. Crompton, *Byron and Greek Love*, pp. 19-21, 26-31, 39-53, 252-83, 383-6 and cf. Norton, *Mother Clap's Molly House*, p. 122; Roger Ingpen, ed., *Plato's Banquet* (privately printed 1931) including Shelley's introductory 'A Discourse on the Manners of the Antient Greeks Relative to the Subject of Love', pp. 13, 15, 16.

42. *Cowdroy's Manchester Gazette and Weekly Advertiser*, 23 Aug. 1806; *Annual Register* 1806, Chronicle p. 438; *The Whole Trial of Col. Rob. Passingham and John Edwards for a Conspiracy against George Townshend Forrester, Esq.* (1805), p. 13 – extorting money under threat of exposure as a homosexual became a statutory offence in 1826 by Geo IV c 19: various other case are discussed in Norton, *Mother Clap's Molly House*, pp. 135-44.

Some of the *unprinted* transcripts of sodomy trials are quite graphic: see e.g. Public Record Office Adm 1/5339, 22 April 1797 and HCA 1/61/395, 26 June 1807.

43. *The Trial of Richard Bransom, for an Attempt to commit Sodomy, on the Body of James Fassett, One of the Scholars belonging to God's-Gift-College, in Dulwich* (1760), pp. 24-5; *London Evening Post* 15 Feb. 1743; *Annual Register* 1763, p. 67; *Annual Register* 1780, p. 69, and see Peter Bartlett, 'Sodomites at the Pillory in Eighteenth-century London', *Social and Legal Studies*, vol. 6, pp. 553-72; press cuttings in British Library Cup 364 p. 12 – the quote is from a newspaper editorial.

44. John Bowles, *Thoughts on the Late General Election, as demonstrative of the Progress of Jacobinism* (1802), pp. 36-7, quoted in the approving review of this pamphlet in *Anti-Jacobin Review and Magazine*, vol. 13 (1802), p. 287; John Bowles, *Reflections on the Political and Moral State of Society at the Close of the Eighteenth Century* (1800), p. 172; John Bowles, *Remarks on Modern Female Manners as distinguished by Indifference to Character and Indecency of Dress; extracted from 'Reflections Political and Moral at the Conclusion of the War'* (1802), p. 7 – the passage about Germaine de Staël also appears in the fourth edition of Bowles' *Reflections* but not in previous editions.

The increase in prosecutions for forgery was of course related to the vast increase in the quantity of paper money circulating after 1797.

45. *Parliamentary Papers* 1899 CVIII pt. 1, pp. 27, 29; *Hansard: House of Lords*, vol. 46, col. 573, Earl of Desart – formerly Hon. Hamilton Cuffe – 15 Aug. 1921. The classic account of the mass-exodus following Wilde's conviction is in Frank Harris, *Oscar Wilde: His Life and Confessions* (2 vols, New York 1916), vol. 1, p. 250. See also Tom Cullen, *Maundy Gregory: Purveyor of Honours* (1974), pp. 35-6 for the alleged flight of associates of honours broker Maundy Gregory following his arrest in 1933. Such reports probably originate in dinner party anecdotes.

46. A.N. Gilbert, 'Buggery and the British Navy 1700-1861', *Journal of Social History*, vol. 10 (1976-7), pp. 72-98 and 'Social Deviance and Disaster during the Napoleonic Wars', *Albion*, vol. 9 (1977), pp. 98-113; John Foster, *Contributions ... to the Eclectic Review* (2 vols, 1844) vol. 2, pp. 114-15, first published Dec. 1810; William Barwick Hodge, 'On the Mortality arising from Naval Operations', *Journal of the Statistical Society*, vol. 18 (1855), pp. 201-21, at p. 213.

47. Some of the arguments in this paragraph are developed at more length in A.D. Harvey, *Britain in the Early Nineteenth Century* (1978), pp. 106-14 and A.D. Harvey, *Literature into History* (Basingstoke 1988), pp. 125-70.

The idea that attitudes to sexual behaviour were influenced by a moral panic ensuing from the French Revolution has been put forward by Lawrence Stone, *Road to Divorce: England 1530-1987* (1990), p. 278, citing as an authority Mary Douglas, *Purity and Danger: an Analysis of Concepts of Pollution and Taboo* (1966), an anthropological study showing how primitive communities attempt to impose order on a disorderly world by means of strict moral codes. The question really turns on whether or not the world was so very orderly before 1789.

48. *Satan's Harvest Home*, p. 54; Francis Bickley, ed., *The Diaries of Sylvester Douglas, Lord Glenbervie* (2 vols, 1928), vol. 1, pp. 4-6, 7 Dec. 1793; Joseph Richardson, French Laurence et al., *Political Miscellanies by the Authors of the Rolliad and Probationary Odes* (1787), pp. 21-3, eleven 'Epigrams on the Immaculate Boy'; Michael Elliman and Frederick Roll, *The Pink Plaque Guide to London* (1986), pp. 154-5 and frontispiece; [Holloway], *Phoenix of Sodom*, p. 44.

There may indeed have been something sexually unusual about Pitt. He and his brother, the second Earl of Chatham, had on their mother's side five male cousins. The seven men, who had between them four aristocratic titles to transmit to their descendants, managed between them to have two children, who between them had only one child. None of the younger brothers in the cousinage (i.e. none of those who had no titles to transmit) even married: but there is no evidence of any boyfriends either.

49. *W. Pitts geheime Lebensgeschichte ... aus dem Englischen des Hugh Greigh* (Hamburg 1801). The British Library's copy is the only one known to exist: apart from its subtitle there is no evidence of an English original and it was by no means unusual for squibs of this sort to be passed off as translations.

50. *The Whole of the proceedings in the Arches-Court between the Hon. Mrs Catherine Weld ... and Edward Weld Esquire, her husband* (1732) and Lawrence Stone, *Broken Lives: Separation and Divorce in England 1660-1857* (1993), pp. 131-5, referring to the Duchess of Beaufort's counter suit for nullity on the grounds of impotence following the Duke's initiation of legal proceedings against her lover in 1742. Another suit for nullity on the grounds of impotence, Rachel Dick *v.* the Rev. William Dick, was rejected in 1811. See also Pierre Darmon, *Le Tribunal de l'impuissance: virilité et défaillances conjugales dans l'ancienne France* (Paris 1979), pp. 301-2; Buchan, *Venus sine Concubitu,* p. 96.

51. Mock lyings-in are discussed by Norton, *Mother Clap's Molly House,* pp. 98-9. Norton's interpretation is different from the one given here, and is to be taken together with his claim – surely a very dubious one – that eighteenth-century homosexuals 'pursued their life styles with a bawdy insouciance, in marked contrast to the guilt-ridden behaviour of so many homosexuals from the 1860s through the 1950s' (p. 116).

7. Separating the Spheres

1. For the notion of separate spheres see Linda Colley, *Britons: Forging the Nation 1707-1837* (New Haven 1992), pp. 262-73 and Amanda Vickery, *The Gentleman's Daughter: Women's Lives in Georgian England* (New Haven 1998), pp. 292-4. The phrase was popularised by Brian Harrison, *Separate Spheres: the Opposition to Women's Suffrage in Britain,* published in 1978. For the argument that people in different social classes had different, but somehow equivalent, advantages see John Bowles, *Dialogues on the Rights of Britons* (1792), Second Dialogue, pp. 8-9, William Paley, *Reasons for Contentment, addressed to the Labouring Part of the British Public* (2nd edit. 1793), p. 12, [John Bowdler], *Reform or Ruin: Take your Choice* (1797), pp. 27-8. The quotation is from Charles Lucas, *The Infernal Quixote: A Tale of the Day* (4 vols, 1801), vol. 1, p. 169.

2. [T.J. Mathias], *The Shade of Alexander Pope on the Banks of the Thames* (1799), p. 49 n, quoted in *Gentleman's Magazine,* vol. 69 (1799), p. 682; [Richard Graves], *Senilities; or, Solitary Amusements: in Prose and Verse: with a Cursory Disquisition on the Future Condition of the Sexes* (1801), p. 197; Richard Polwhele, *The Unsex'd Females: a Poem* (1798), pp. 13-15, 25-8 and footnotes on pp. 9, 13, 28-9 for references to Mary Wollstonecraft, and p. 14 n 3 and pp. 20-1 n for references to Mary Hays.

3. John Bowles, *Remarks on Modern Female Manners, as Distinguished by Indifference to Character and Indecency of Dress* (1802), p. 13; ibid., p. 6; S.T., *Address to the Guardian Society* [1817], p. 10; Bowles, *Remarks,* p. 7; Robert Isaac Wilberforce and Samuel Wilberforce, *The Life of William Wilberforce* (5 vols, 1838), vol. 5, p. 264; S.T., *Address to the Guardian Society,* pp. 10-12.

4. [Charles Gildon], *The Post-boy rob'd of His Mail: or, the Pacquet Broke Open. Consisting of Five Hundred Letters, to Persons of several Qualities and Conditions. With Observations Upon each Letter* (1692), pp. 237-8; Edward Barry, *Essays, on* the *Following Subjects: Celibacy, Wedlock, Seduction, Pride ... Excess, Death* (Reading 1806), pp. 56-7; [Charlotte Palmer], *Letters on Several Subjects, from a Perceptress to her Pupils who have left School, addressed chiefly to Real Characters* (1797), p. 41; Adam Sibbit, *Thoughts on the Frequency of Divorces in Modern Times and on the Necessity of Legislative Exertion, to Prevent their Increasing Prevalence* (1800), p. 10; Tobias Smollett, *The Adventures of Roderick Random* (1979 Oxford edit.), p. 117 (ch. 22: the pernicious authors referred to are the Earl of Shaftesbury, 1671-1713, Matthew Tindal, 1657-1733, and Thomas Hobbes, 1588-1679); Sibbit, *Thoughts on the Frequency of Divorces*, p. 10; George Walker, *The Vagabond: a Novel* (2 vols, 1799), vol. 1, p. 174; Lucas, *The Infernal Quixote*, vol. 1, p. 135.

5. James Bacon, *The Libertine. A novel – In a Series of Letters* (1791), pp. vii-viii; Jane West, *A Tale of the Times* (4 vols, 1799), vol. 3, pp. 386-7.

6. S.T., *Address to the Guardian Society*, p. 56, and cf. Sydney Smith's remarks in *Edinburgh Review*, vol. 13 (1809), pp. 339-42; Donald Thomas, *A Long Time Burning: the History of Literary Censorship in England* (1969), pp. 77-8 for prosecution of Read, pp. 82-3 for prosecution of Curll; *Society for the Suppression of Vice* ['Plan for the Society: List of Members'] (1825), p. 10; *Parliamentary Papers* 1817 VII, pp. 480, 532, evidence of George Prichard, secretary of the Society for the Suppression of Vice, and cf. Thomas, *Long Time Burning*, pp. 189-96; Public Record Office TS 11/944/3434.

7. *Anti-Jacobin Review and Magazine*, vol. 13 (1802), p. 184; *Parliamentary Papers* 1817 VII, p. 479; ibid., p. 480.

Robert Isaac Wilberforce and Samuel Wilberforce, *The Life of William Wilberforce* (5 vols, 1838), vol. 1, p. 130 and, especially p. 132, where they print a letter of Wilberforce to William Hey, 29 May 1787, suggest that the royal proclamation was actually instigated by Wilberforce in order to launch a movement along the lines of the Societies for the Reformation of Manners, but this version of events seems doubtful.

8. *Parliamentary Papers* 1817 VII, pp. 479-80; ibid., p. 483.

9. J.L. Chirol, *An Enquiry into the Best System of Female Education; or, Boarding School and Home Education attentively considered* (1809), p. 111 n; ibid., pp. 120-1.

10. Henry Thomas Kitchener, *Letters on Marriage, on the Causes of Matrimonial Infidelity, and on the Reciprocal Relations of the Sexes* (2 vols, 1812), vol. 2, pp. 269-70; ibid., vol. 2, pp. 267-8, and cf. vol. 2, p. 74; Thomas Beddoes, *Hygeia: or Essays Moral and Medical on the Causes affecting the personal state of Our Middling and Affluent Classes* (3 vols, Bristol 1802-3), vol. 1, Essay Fourth, p. 55; Kitchener, *Letters on Marriage*, vol. 1, pp. 116-18.

The idea of keeping a grown woman in ignorance of the facts of life long after her adolescence is not as impracticable as a late-twentieth-century audience might think. One evening in 1878 Carey Thomas, a twenty-one-year-old graduate student at Johns Hopkins University, and two women friends raided her father's medical library: 'If passion and sensuality are sure factors I wanted to understand them.' After flipping through some of her father's medical books, 'I went to bed sick ... it seemed as if there was no such thing as ever believing in purity and holiness again, or ever getting my own mind pure again.' Marjorie Housepian Dobkin, ed., *The Making of a Feminist: the Early Journals and Letters of M. Carey Thomas* (Kent, Ohio, 1979), pp. 142-3, 7 April 1878. The tone of high-minded idealism in Carey Thomas' journal entry belongs to the final third of the nineteenth century – the interesting thing is the degree to which it *was* possible to keep even a highly-educated girl in ignorance of such matters.

11. *Parliamentary History*, vol. 28, col. 782, 10 May 1790; William Blackstone, *Commentary on the Laws of England* (4 vols, 1774), vol. 4, p. 204 (Book 4, ch. 13);

ibid., vol. 4, p. 93 (Book 4, ch. 6); *Gentleman's Magazine*, vol. 22 (1752), p. 189.

Killing one's father was not counted as petty treason, but Mary Blandy's crime was probably the most publicised sex-related murder of the eighteenth century. There are at least twenty different contemporary pamphlets, accounts of the trial, and other publications connected with this case – *Notes and Queries*, series 5, vol. 3, p. 119 says 26 – including a confession dictated to the ordinary (or as we would now say, chaplain) of Oxford Gaol, the Rev. John Swinton, formerly of Wadham College (see previous chapter) and a play, *The Female Parricide*. Mary Blandy had been induced to poison her father by her lover Captain Cranstoun.

12. *Notes and Queries*, series 1, vol. 2, pp. 50-1; *Gentleman's Magazine* (1786), pp. 524-5; *Notes and Queries*, series 1, vol. 2, p. 261, communication by Octogenarius, 21 Sept. 1850. See also E.J. Burford and Sandra Shulman, *Of Bridles and Burnings: the Punishment of Women* (New York 1992), pp. 40-7.

13. *Parliamentary History*, vol. 28, col. 782-83.

14. *Last Dying Words of Mary Saunders* etc. (1764) broadsheet; *Notes and Queries*, series 10, vol. 12, p. 35; *Notes and Queries*, series 1, vol. 3, p. 165, communication by Senex.

15. *Parliamentary Debates*, vol. 36, col. 932, 10 June 1817, quoting from the *Inverness Journal*. The private flogging of women in prison was abolished in 1820.

16. A.F.M. Willich, *Lectures on Diet and Regimen* (2nd edit. 1799), pp. 539-40 (cf. 1st edit. 1799, pp. 490-1); James Graham, *A Lecture on the Generation, Increase and Improvement of the Human Species* (1780), p. 25.

Flora Fraser, *Beloved Emma: the Life of Emma Lady Hamilton* (1986), pp. 8-9 says Emma Lyon could not have posed as Graham's Goddess of Health because he only opened his Temple of Health in 1781, when she was already living with Sir Harry Featherstonhaugh: but the tradition that she did so dates from the period, and the precise chronology of both James Graham's operations and Emma Lyon's is not always easy to settle.

Index

abortion, 5

Acts of Parliament, 57, 122, 125, 126, 152, 184 n 13, 189 n 15

Addison, Joseph, essayist and poet (1672-1719), 157

Adventures of a Rake, possibly by R. Lewis, 51

age at marriage, 4

Allen, Henry, Captain (executed 1797), 126

Alma-Tadema, Sir Lawrence, painter (1836-1912), 17

Ancaster, Peregrine Bertie, 3rd Duke of (1714-1778), 137

Annesley, George, *styled* Viscount Valentia, later 2nd Earl of Mountnorris (1770-1844), 137

Antoninus, St (Antonio Pierozzi) Archbishop of Florence (1389-1459), 112

Aquinas, St Thomas (1224-1274), 112

Aretin, Peter, the Celebrated Author, The Genuine and Remarkable Amours of, 13, 28, 44

Aretin Francais, 27-8, 173 n 20; *see also* plates 12, 16, 17, 25

Aretino, Pietro, miscellaneous writer (1492-1556), 26

Aristotle's Master-piece, 59-60, 168

Armstrong, John, MD, poet and physician (1709-79)
The Oeconomy of Love, 5, 8, 36, 120, 136

Ashbee, Henry Spencer, bibliographer (1834-1900), 52

Association for Preserving Liberty and Property against Republicans and Levellers, 146

Associations for the Prosecution of Felons, 146

Astruc, Jean, medical writer (1684-1766), 44-5, 176 n 8

Asylum for Female Orphans, 101, 102, 107, 109

Atherton, Right Rev. John, Bishop of Waterford and Lismore (1598-1640), 124

Aubrey, John, antiquary (1626-1697), 22

Auckland, William Eden, 1st Baron (1744-1814), 82, 151

Augustus the Strong *see* Friedrich August

Austen, Henry, brother of following (1771?-1850), 70

Austen, Jane, novelist (1775-1817), 31, 70, 163
Emma, 116, 163
Pride and Prejudice, 69, 85
Sense and Sensibility, 116

Aven, Edward, editor *c*. 1771, 120

Bacon, James, novelist *c*. 1791, 157

Bage, Robert, novelist (1728-1801)
Mount Henneth, 68
Barham Downs, 80

Baker, George, DA (*fl*. 1730), 127-8, 129, 130, 136

Baltimore, Frederick Calvert, 6th Baron (1732-71), 80

Barnard, Rev. Nicholas, Dean of Ardagh (1600?-1661), 124

Barrin, Jean, miscellaneous writer (1640?-1718), 112

Barry, Rev. Edward, DD, MD (1759-1822), 156-7

Barry, James Miranda, MD, military surgeon (1795-1865), 114-15

Bayntoun, Lady Mary (1754-84), 29

Beckford, William, miscellaneous writer (1759-1844), 137

Beddoes, Thomas, MD (1760-1808), 31, 117, 119, 121, 164

Bell, Andrew, engraver (1726-1809) *Anatomia Britannica*, 11

Benson, Arthur Christopher, miscellaneous writer (1862-1925) *Memoirs of Arthur Hamilton, BA*, 147

Bentham, Jeremy, philosophical writer (1748-1832), 143

Berkley, Theresa, keeper of a flagellation parlour c. 1793-1830, 36

Bessborough, Henrietta Ponsonby, Countess of (1761-1821), 57, 58

bestiality, 123

Bickerstaffe, Isaac, dramatist (1735?-1812), 136, 137, 141

Bidloo, Govard, anatomist (1649-1713) *Anatomia Humani Corporis*, 11; *see also* plates 2, 3

Bienville, J.D.T. de, medical writer c. 1771, 44-5

Blackstone, Sir William, judge (1723-80), 165

Blandy, Mary (executed 1752), 165, 196 n 11

Blunt, John (pseud. for S.W. Fores ?), 55, 56

Bocock, Elizabeth, alleged rape victim c. 1728, 76

Boileau, Jacques, French cleric (1635-1716), 13-14

Borel, Antoine, artist (1743-*post* 1810), 27

Borromeo, St Carlo, Archbishop of Milan (1538-84), 112

Boswell, James, biographer and diarist (1740-95), 2, 3, 89-90, 97

Botticelli, Sandro, painter (1445-1510) 'Birth of Venus', 13

Bourke, John, Private 5th Regiment of Foot c. 1805, 139

Bowes, Andrew Robinson (1747-1810), 82-3, 84

Brantôme, Pierre de Bourdeille, Seigneur de (1540-1614), 22

Bray, Alan, historian, 127, 130

Bridewell, London, 107

Bristol Penitentiary, 103, 106

Broderick, Isaac, school-teacher c. 1730, 129-30

Bronzino, Agnolo di Cosimo, *known as* Il (1503-72) 'Venus, Cupid, Folly and Time', 11

brothels, 36, 49, 52, 62, 90-1, 112

'Brown, William', female sailor c. 1815, 114

Buchan, Alex Peter, MD (1764-1824), 45, 117, 119, 121, 122

Burne-Jones, Sir Edward, painter (1833-98), 17

Butler, Lady Eleanor (1745?-1829), 113-14

Byron, George Gordon, 6th Baron Byron (1788-1824), 58

Caffin, John (executed 1817), 79

Cagnacci, Guido Canlassi, known as (1601-1681) 'The Death of Lucretia', 11

Cambridge Group for the Study of Population and Social Structure, 4-5

Campbell, Thomas, poet (1777-1844), 8

Cane, later Armistead, afterwards Fox, Elizabeth (1750?-1842), 91-2

Cannon, Thomas (*fl.* 1749), 125, 159

Caroline Matilda, Princess of Great Britain, Queen of Denmark (1751-1775), 4

Casanova de Seingalt, Giacomo, adventurer (1725-1798), 1

Castlehaven, Mervyn Tuchet, 2nd Earl of (1593?-1631), 123-4, 131

Castlereagh, Viscount *see* Stewart, Robert

Charles II, King of England (1630-1685), 34, 35, 183 n 3

Charlotte, Princess (1796-1817), 32

Charteris, Francis, Lieutenant-Colonel (1675-1732), 62

Chesterfield, Philip Stanhope, 4th Earl of (1694-1773), 154

Chesterfield, Philip Stanhope, 5th Earl of (1755-1815), 110

Chisholm, Rev. George, DD (d. 1825), 109

Christian VII, King of Denmark (1749-1808), 4

Church, Rev. John (1780?-*post* 1824), 140-1

Churchill, Charles, poet (1731-64)

The Times, 136, 141
City of London Truss Society, 102
Clark, Anna, historian, 81, 82
Claude Lorrain, painter (1600-1682), 25
Cleland, John, novelist (1709-1789)
   Fanny Hill aka *Memoirs of a Woman of Pleasure*, 1, 4, 13, 15, 23-4, 25, 37, 44, 51, 52, 111-12, 113, 118, 159
Clogher, Bishop of *see* Jocelyn, Right Rev., and Hon. Percy
Cogan, Rev. Thomas, MD (1736-1818), 21
Coleridge, Samuel Taylor, poet and critic (1772-1834), 8, 42
Collett, Mrs, keeper of a flagellation parlour *c.* 1825, 36
Colquhoun, Patrick, stipendiary magistrate (1745-1820), 70, 92-7, 108, 140
Conway, Hon. Henry, later Lord Henry (1746-1830), 82, 151
Cook, James, landlord of the Swan, Vere St. (*fl.* 1810), 139
Cooper, Sir Astley Paston, surgeon (1768-1841), 17
Cooper, William, 'The Hackney Monster' (*fl.* 1805), 116
Coote, Sir Eyre, General (1759-1823), 36-7
Cope, Sir John, Lieutenant-General (d. 1760), 135
Couper, Robert, MD (1750-1818), 42
Courtenay, Hon. William, later 3rd Viscount Courtenay and 28th Earl of Devon (1768-1835), 137
Cowley, Hannah, poet (1743-1809)
   Pitcairne Green, 61
Cowper, Emily, Countess, later Viscountess Palmerston (1787-1869), 58
Cowper, William, surgeon (1666-1709)
   The Anatomy of Humane Bodies, 11
Cranach, Lucas, the Elder, painter (1472-1553)
   'The Judgement of Paris', 21
crim. con. trials, 57, 150, 177-8 n 4
cross-dressers, female, 114-15
Cullen, William, MD, medical writer (1710-90), 44

Curll, Edmund, bookseller and publisher (1675-1747), 35, 159

Dallas, Robert Charles, miscellaneous writer (1754-1824), 158
Davies, Christian, female soldier (1667-1739), 114
Delacroix, Eugène, painter (1798-1863)
   'Liberty at the Barricades', 16-17
   'Martyrdom of St Agatha', 11
Del Piombo, Sebastiano, painter (1485?-1547)
D'Éon, Charles Geneviève Louis Auguste André Timothée, chevalier (1728-1810), 187 n 5
Des Rues, Claude Nicolas, French cleric *c.* 1726, 1
Devonshire, Georgiana Cavendish, Duchess of (1757-1806), 57
Devonshire, William Cavendish, 5th Duke of (1748-1811), 57
Dodd, Rev. William, miscellaneous writer (1729-1777), 95-8, 109-10
   The Sisters, 123
Don Leon, 141, 142, 192 n 40
Douglas, Sylvester, 1st Baron Glenbervie (1743-1823), 150
Downing, Rebecca (executed 1782), 166
Dryden, John, poet and dramatist (1631-1700), 118
Dye, Nancy, maid-servant, later courtesan, *c.* 1765, 82

Eldon, John Scott, 1st Baron (afterwards 1st Earl), judge, later Lord Chancellor (1751-1838), 59, 89
Eliot, George, novelist (1819-1880)
   Adam Bede, 70-1
Elliott, Robert, 'Gretna Green parson' (1784-*post* 1840), 58
Elluin, Franois, engraver (1745-1810), 27
Erskine, Thomas, 1st Baron, lawyer and politician (1750-1823), 59
Etty, William, painter (1787-1849), 16-19; *see also* plates 7, 8
Evangelical Movement, 104-5

Falloppio, Gabriello, anatomist (1523-1562), 3, 118

Fanny Hill see Cleland, John
Fell, Rev. John, DD (1625-1686), 27
Female Anti-slavery Associations, 156
Fielding, Henry, novelist (1707-1757), 47, 111
Findlater, James Ogilvy, 7th Earl of (1750-1811), 137
Fitzpatrick, Laurence (executed 1631), 124
Fivens, John, private 5th Regiment of Foot *c.* 1805, 139
Flemings, Thomas, alleged rapist *c.* 1817, 78
Foley, Lady Ann (*fl.* 1783), 28, 29
Folkestone, Viscount *see* Pleydell Bouverie, William
Foote, Samuel, actor and dramatist (1720-1777), 137, 141
Ford, Richard, stipendiary magistrate (1758-1806), 92
Fordyce, Rev. James, DD (1720-1795), 158
Foster, Lady Elizabeth, later Duchess of Devonshire (1760?-1824), 57
Foucault, Michel, historian (1926-1984), 7
Fountaine, Sir Andrew, collector (1676-1753), 134
Fox, Hon. Charles James, statesman (1749-1806), 91
Free, Rev. Edward Drax, DD (1765?-1843), 83-4
French, William, undergraduate at Wadham 1739, 127-8
French Revolution, 56, 81, 146-7, 149-50
French Revolutionary and Napoleonic Wars, 33, 56, 114, 148-9, 161
Friedrich August, Elector of Saxony, King Augustus II of Poland (1670-1733), 2, 170 n 1
Fund of Mercy, 102
Fuseli, Henry, painter (1741-1825), 16, 172 n 9 and 13; *see also* plate 9

Gardener, Sarah, alleged rape victim *c.* 1817, 78
Gay, Peter, historian (1923-), 6
Gentleman's Magazine, The, 30, 60, 64, 72, 154-5
George III, King of Great Britain (1738-1820), 4, 58, 92, 98, 137, 158

George, Prince Regent, later George IV (1762-1830), 32, 36, 58
Germain, Lord George, statesman (1716-1785), 137
Gibbon, Edward, historian (1737-1794), 86
Gilbert, A.N., historian, 148
Gilden, Charles, miscellaneous writer (1665-1724), 156
Giles, William, banker and miscellaneous writer (1744?-1825) *The Victim,* 73
Giorgone, Giorgio da Castelfranco, *known as* (1477?-1510), 13
Gisborne, Rev. Thomas (1758-1846), 158
Godolphin, George, later 8th Duke of Leeds (1802-1872), 58
Godwin, William, novelist and political theorist (1756-1836) *Caleb William,* 142
Goldsmith, Oliver, miscellaneous writer (1730-1774) *The Vicar of Wakefield,* 60, 70
Gordon, Rev. Lockhart, (*fl.* 1804), 53
Gordon, Loudoun, (*fl.* 1804), 53
Gordon, Thomas, miscellaneous writer (d. 1750), 134
Grafton, Augustus Henry Fitzroy, 3rd Duke of (1735-1811), 8
Graham, James, quack doctor (1745-1794), 120, 167-8
Graham, Sir Robert, judge (1744-1836), 144
Gray, Thomas, poet (1716-1771) 'Elegy', 142
Greer, Germaine, feminist (1939-), 85
Gretna Green, 58-9
Grey, Charles, afterwards 2nd Earl, statesman (1764-1845), 57
Grien, Hans Baldung, painter (1484?-1545) 'The Seven Ages of Woman', 12; *see also* plate 5
Grosvenor, Henrietta, Countess (1760?-1828), 98
Guardian Society for the Preservation of Public Morals, 96, 100, 102, 106, 107
'Gulliver, Lemuel', *The Pleasures and Felicity of Marriage,* 14

Guy's Hospital, 101

Hale, William, silk merchant *c.* 1809,
    70, 94, 107-8, 185 n 21
Hall-Stevenson, John, miscellaneous
    writer (1718-1785), 13, 14
Hamilton, Elizabeth, novelist
    (1758-1816)
    Memoirs of Modern Philosophers,
    158
Hamilton, George, writer on art (*fl.*
    1812-37)
    The Elements of Drawing, 20
Hamilton, William, painter
    (1751-1801), 16
Hamilton, Sir William, diplomat
    (1730-1803), 92
Hammet, Sir Benjamin, banker, MP
    for Taunton (1736?-1800), 164-5,
    166
Harris, Phoebe, execution of, in 1786,
    165-6
Hatfield, S., miscellaneous writer (*fl.*
    1802-16), 69
Hayes, Katherine (1690-1726), 165
Hays, Mary, novelist (1759?-1843), 155
Haywood, Eliza, novelist (1693?-1756)
    The British Recluse, 50
    Cleomelia, 51
    Idalia, 50-1
    Love in Excess, 46
Heber, Richard, MP, book collector
    (1773-1833), 138
Hessel, Phoebe, female soldier
    (1713?-1830), 82
History of the Human Heart, The, 23,
    173 n 14
Hitchen, Charles, under city marshal
    c. 1726, 133
Hitchen, Isaac (executed 1806), 139
Hodson, Rev. Septimus (1768-1833),
    102-3, 107, 109
Hogg, Alexander, publisher *c.* 1800,
    160-1
Hogg, Thomas, colonist at New Haven
    c. 1647, 123
Holcroft, Thomas, novelist and
    dramatist (1745-1809)
    Anna St Ives, 80
    Seduction, 65
Holloway, Robert, lawyer *c.* 1810
    Phoenix of Sodom, 133

homosexuality
    female, 111-18; prosecuted in
        European countries 112-13
    male, 122-53; prosecuted in
        European countries 130, 138-9
Horridge, Rev. George (*fl.* 1810), 109
Houdon, Jean-Antoine, sculptor
    (1741-1828)
    'Diana the Huntress', 16
Hunter, John, surgeon (1728-1793),
    120, 121

illegitimacy, 2, 4-5, 58, 92
impotence, 137, 151-2, 194 n 50
Inchbald, Elizabeth, novelist
    (1753-1821)
    Nature and Art, 60
Institution for Enabling Young
    Women who have left the
    Country to get places in London
    to return to their Families, so as
    to prevent them from Vicious
    Courses, 62

Jackson, William, miscellaneous
    writer and revolutionary
    (1737-1795), 137, 141
James I, King of England (1566-1625),
    34, 131
James II, King of England
    (1633-1701), 131-2, 183 n 3
Jephson, Thomas, Fellow of St John's
    College Cambridge (1785-1864),
    138
Jocelyn, Right Rev. and Hon. Percy;
    Bishop of Ferns and Leighlin,
    later Bishop of Clogher
    (1764-1843), 137-8, 140
Johnson, Samuel, miscellaneous
    writer (1709-1784), 14, 60, 71-2,
    157
Jones, Robert (*fl.* 1777), 124-5
Jordan, Dorothea, actress
    (1762-1816), 92

Keats, John, poet (1795-1821), 25
Kelly, Hugh, novelist and dramatist
    (1739-1777)
    Memoirs of a Magdalen, 63, 68, 89
Kenrick, William, miscellaneous
    writer (1725?-1779)
    Love in the Suds, 141

Kenyon, George, 2nd Baron (1776-1855), 104
Kenyon, Lloyd, 1st Baron, Lord Chief Justice (1732-1802), 150
Keppel, William, General (d. 1834), 58
'Kinsey Report' (i.e. *Sexual Behavior in the Human Male* by A.C. Kinsey, Wardell B. Pomeroy and Clyde E. Martin, 1948), 1
Kitchener, Henry Thomas (*fl.* 1812), 117, 121, 163-4
Kroeber, Alfred L., anthropologist (1876-1960), 33

Lackington, James, bookseller (1746-1815), 116-17
Ladies Physical Directory, The, 40-1, 175 n 4
La Madeleine reliefs, 12
Lamb, Lady Caroline, novelist (1785-1828), 58
Lawrence, Sir Thomas, painter (1769-1830), 16, 19
Lee, Prudence (executed 1652), 165
Lee, Rachel (1774?-1829), 53
Leeds, Duke of *see* Godolphin, George
Leicester, Earl of *see* Townshend, George, 3rd Marquess
Lely, Sir Peter, painter (1618-80) 'Nell Gwyn', 11; *see also* plate 4
Lemoine, Ann, publisher *c.* 1801, 115
Lennox, Charlotte, miscellaneous writer (1720-1804), 48
lesbianism *see* homosexuality
Le Vasseur, Thérèse (1721-1801), 2
Leveson, Lord Granville, later 1st Viscount Granville (1773-1846), 57, 58
Lewis, Matthew Gregory, novelist (1775-1818)
The Monk, 24, 52, 68, 79
Lock-Asylum, 102, 104
Lock-Hospital, Edinburgh, 96
Lock-Hospital, London, 96, 101, 102, 108
Lodge, David, novelist (1935-), 25
London Female Penitentiary, 102-5, 108
London Hospital, 101
London Society for Promoting Christianity among the Jews, 102

Lucas, Rev. Charles, novelist and poet (1764-1854)
The Infernal Quixote, 155, 157
Lyon, Emma, later Lady Hamilton (1765-1815), 92, 167, 196 n 16

Macaulay, Thomas Babington, essayist, historian and politican (1800-1859), 9
Mackenzie, Henry, novelist (1745-1831)
The Man of Feeling, 60
MacLaurin, John, lawyer (1734-96)
The Keekiad, 24
Magdalen Hospital, 83, 97, 101-4, 107, 109, 110
Rules and Regulations of, 103-4, 106, 107
Mandeville, Bernard, miscellaneous writer (1670-1733), 39, 98
Mary II, Queen of England (1662-1694), 98
Massey *alias* Miller *alias* Milwood, Oliver, suspected sodomite *c.* 1806, 140
masturbation, 118-22
Maugham, William Somerset, novelist (1874-1965), 142
Meibom, Johann Heinrich, medical writer (1590-1655), 35, 159
Melbourne, William Lamb, 2nd Viscount, statesman (1779-1848), 9, 58
menstruation, 4-6
Meredith, Sir William, 3rd Bart. (1725?-1790), 137
Middlesex Hospital, 101
Milton, John, poet (1608-1674)
Comus, 49
Moncreiff, John, poet (*fl.* 1748-67), 64
Montaigne, Michel de, essayist (1533-1592), 38, 40
Morton, Thomas, dramatist (1764?-1838)
Speed the Plough, 9
Moser, Joseph, stipendiary magistrate (1748-1819), 108
Mozart, Wolfgang Amadeus, composer (1756-1791)
Don Giovanni, 2
Murphy *alias* Bowman, Christian (executed 1789), 166

Navy, Royal, 126, 148-9

Newcastle, Henry Pelham-Clinton, 4th Duke of (1785-1851), 140

Nicolson, Nigel, miscellaneous writer (1917-)
Portrait of a Marriage, 1

Norton, Caroline (Hon. Mrs George Norton) (1808-1877), 58

nudity, 21-5

Nugent, Charles Edmund, Admiral of the Fleet (1759?-1844), 58

Nugent, Hon. Edmund (1731-1771), 58

Nugent, Sir George, Field Marshal (1757-1849), 58

Oliver, Helen *alias* John, cross-dresser *c.* 1822, 115

Onania, 118-19, 152, 168, 187 n 10

Onslow, Edward (1758-1829), 137

Opie, Amelia, novelist (1769-1853)
Adeline Mowbray, 80

Otway, Thomas, dramatist (1652-1685)
Venice Preserved, 85

paedophilia, instances of, 78-9, 108-9, 124, 129-30, 139, 189 n 15

Paisley, Joseph, 'Gretna Green parson' (1753-1810), 58

Pallavicino, Ferrante, miscellaneous writer (1615-44), 27, 43

Palmerston, Henry John Temple, 3rd Viscount, statesman (1784-1865), 58

Parsons, Eliza, novelist (d. 1811)
The Errors of Education, 64-5, 68

Parsons, James, MD, medical writer (1705-70), 113

Parsons, Nancy, later Viscountess Maynard (1735?-1814?), 8

Perceval, Hon. Spencer, statesman (1762-1812), 59, 160

Perkins, Jacob, inventor (1766-1849), 20

Peterborough, Charles Mordaunt, 5th Earl of (1758-1814), 28, 29

Petronius Arbiter (d. 66), 135

Piroli, Tommaso (1752-1824), 27

Pitt, Hon. William, statesman (1759-1806), 151-2, 193 n 48

Pleydell Bouverie, William, *styled* Viscount Folkestone (1779-1869), 104

Polwhele, Rev. Richard (1760-1838), 155

Ponsonby, Sarah (1745?-1831), 113-14

Pope, Alexander, poet (1688-1744)
The Dunciad, 134

Porter, Jane, novelist (1776-1850), 86

Poussin, Nicolas, painter (1549-1665), 25

Powell, Samuel, undergraduate at Queen's 1715, 129

Pratt, John (executed 1835), 125

Proclamation Society, 99, 149, 158, 160

prostitutes and prostitution, 3, 69-70, 89-110

Purcell, Henry, composer (1658?-1695)
Dido and Aeneas, 116

Queensberry, John Sholto Douglas, 9th Marquess of (1844-1900), 147

Raimondi, Marcantonio, engraver (*c.* 1480-*c.*1530), 26

Ralegh, Sir Walter, voyager and writer (1552?-1618), 22

Rambler, The, 60, 64, 71-2

rape, 75-88
law of, 77

Read, James, publisher *c.* 1708, 159

Reay, Martha, singer (d. 1779), 8, 58

Reformation of Manners, Societies for Promoting a *see* Societies for Promoting a Reformation of Manners

Refuge for the Destitute, 102

Relfe, Edward, 'sadler' at Lewes *c.* 1780, 61, 65, 86

Reynolds, Sir Joshua, painter (1723-1792), 16

Rhodiginus, Coelius, originally Ludovico Ricchieri, humanist (1469-1525), 38, 40

Richardson, Jane, anthropologist, 33

Richardson, Samuel, novelist (1689-1751), 46, 48
Clarissa, 14, 15, 46, 47, 50, 51, 67-8, 79, 80, 86
Pamela, 46, 47, 51, 80

Robertson, Alexander, 13th Baron of Struan (1670?-1749), 118

Robson, Rev. Edward (1758?-*post* 1820), 109

Romano, Giulio, Giulio Pippi, *known as*, painter (1499?-1546), 26, 27, 28

Rousseau, Jean Jacques, philosophical writer (1712-1778), 2, 60, 154

Russen, Rev. Benjamin (executed 1777), 108-9, 185 n 21

Ryder, Dudley, afterwards Attorney-General and Lord Chief Justice (1691-1756), 129

St George's Hospital, 101

Sánchez, Tomás, jesuit (1550-1610), 39

Sandwich, John Montagu, 4th Earl of (1718-1792), 8, 58, 109

Saunders, Mary (executed 1764), 166

seduction, 54-74
  defined, 54, 63
  law of, 61

Senefelder, Alois, inventor (1771-1834), 20

sexual positions, 25-9

Shadwell, Thomas, dramatist (1642?-1692)
  The Virtuoso, 35

Shakespeare, William, poet and dramatist (1564-1616)
  The Rape of Lucrece, 47
  Measure for Measure, 48-9

Shelley, Sir John, 4th Baronet (1692-1771), 135

Shelley, Mary, novelist (1797-1851)
  Frankenstein, 142

Shelley, Percy Bysshe, poet (1793-1822), 143-4

Simeon, Rev. Charles (1759-1836), 104

Sinibaldi, Giovanni Benedetto, medical writer (1594-1658), 13, 26, 38

Skelthorp, George (executed 1709), 133

Smith, John (executed 1835), 125

Smollett, Tobias, novelist (1721-1771), 136
  The Advice, 128-9, 134
  The Adventures of Roderick Random, 135, 157

Snell, Hannah, female soldier (1723-1792), 114

Societies for Promoting a Reformation of Manners, 90, 99, 101, 132-3

Society for Carrying Into Effect His Majesty's Proclamation against Vice and Immorality *see* Proclamation Society

Society for Promoting the Civilisation and Improvement of the North American Indians, 102

Society for Superseding the Necessity of Climbing Boys, 102

Society for the Suppression of Vice, 90, 91, 99, 109, 146, 149, 158-62

Society of Friends of Foreigners in Distress, 102

Sparshott, John (executed 1835), 125

Staël, Germaine de, miscellaneous writer (1766-1817), 146

Steele, Sir Richard, essayist (1672-1729), 15

Stevenson, Dorothy, maid-servant *c.* 1789, 82

Stewart, Harriet Arundel (1800?-1852), 58

Stewart, Robert, *styled* Viscount Castlereagh, later 2nd Marquess of Londonderry, statesman (1770-1822), 138

Stone, Lawrence, historian (1919-), 2-3

Strathmore, Mary, Countess of (1749-1800), 4, 5, 82

Struensee, Johann Friedrich *Graf*, statesman (1737-1772), 4

Sturgis, Howard, novelist (1855-1920)
  Tim, 147

Sunderland, Charles Spencer, 4th Earl of, statesman (1674?-1722), 134

Swift, Very Rev. Jonathan, Dean of St Patrick's (1667-1745), 84

Swinton, Rev. John (1703-1777), 127-8, 129, 136, 196 n 11

Talbot, Mary Anne, female soldier and sailor (1778-1808), 114

Taylor, Thomas, philosophical writer (1758-1835), 155

Thistlethwayte, Rev. Robert, DD (1691?-1743), 127-8, 129

Thomas, Rev. John (*fl.* 1809), 108

Thornton, William, Lieutenant-General, MP for New Woodstock (1763-1841), 167

Tissot, Samuel Auguste André David,

medical writer (1728-1797), 119, 121, 122, 188 n 11

Titian (Tiziano Vecellio), painter (1488-1576), 13
'Venus and the Organ Player', 21-2, 172 n 13

Tolstoy, Lev Nikolayevich *Graf* (1828-1910)
Resurrection, 60

Tomlins, Sir Thomas Edlyne, legal writer (1762-1841)
Law-Dictionary, 76-7

Toscanini, Walter, book collector, 27, 28

Townshend, George, 3rd Marquess (styled Lord Chartley 1784-1807, Earl of Leicester 1807-11) (1778-1855), 137

Tucker, Henry St George, East Indian Co. official (1771-1851), 77-8

Turner, Joseph, Mallord William, painter (1775-1851), 19

Tylney, John, 2nd Earl (1712-1784), 137

Tylney Long, later Pole Tylney Long Wellesley, Catherine (1789-1825), 92

Valentia, Lord *see* Annesley, George, *styled* Viscount Valentia

Vanbrugh, Sir John, dramatist and architect (1664-1726)
The Relapse, 132, 146

venereal disease, 2, 3, 93, 101, 102, 183 n 4

Venette, Nicolas, medical writer (1633-1698), 26, 28, 38-9, 40, 41, 52

Venn, Rev. John (1759-1813), 104

Venus in the Cloister, 13, 112, 159

'Venus of Willendorf', 12

Vere Street, 139-40, 144-5

Vice, Society for the Suppression of *see* Society for the Suppression of Vice

Waite, Elizabeth, maid-servant *c.* 1789, 82-3

Waldeck, Jean-Frédéric-Maximilien *comte* de (1766-1875), 28

Walker, George, bookseller and novelist (1772-1847)
The Vagabond, 70, 155

Wallace, Rev. Robert (1697-1771), 41-2, 118

Watson, Joshua, High Church leader (1771-1855), 104

Wellesley, Richard Colley, 1st Marquess, statesman (1760-1842), 8

West, Jane, novelist (1758-1852), 157-8

Westmorland, John Fane, 10th Earl of, statesman (1759-1841), 58

Wilberforce, William, Evangelical leader (1759-1833), 104, 156, 195 n 7

Wilde, Oscar Fingal O'Flahertie Wills, dramatist (1854-1900), 147-8

Wilkes, John, politician (1727-1797), 50

William III, King of England (1650-1702), 131-2

William IV, King of Great Britain and Ireland (1765-1837), 58, 92

Williams, Rhynwick, woman-stabber *c.* 1790, 81

Williams, Sarah, mistress of Francis Charteris, 62

Wilmot, Edward Sloane, MD (*fl.* 1775), 44

Wilson, Edward 'Beau' (d. 1694), 134

Wilson, Harriette, courtesan (1789-1846), 4, 72

Windham, William, statesman (1750-1810), 56

Wolcot, John MD ('Peter Pindar') satirist (1738-1809), 89-90

Wollstonecraft, Mary, pioneer feminist (1759-1797), 60, 66, 98, 117, 154-5, 168-9

Woodward, Rev. Robert (*fl.* 1816), 78

Wordsworth, William, poet (1770-1750), 67

York, HRH Frederick, Duke of, Prince of Great Britain and Ireland (1763-1827), 104